CHATHAM DOCKYARD

CHATHAM DOCKYARD

THE RISE AND FALL OF A
MILITARY INDUSTRIAL COMPLEX

PHILIP MACDOUGALL

Ocelot, the last Royal Navy submarine to be built at Chatham, is one of three important warships currently open to public boarding in the historic enclave of the dockyard that is now managed by the Chatham Dockyard Historic Trust.

Frontispiece: Achilles, laid down in the No.2 Dock at Chatham in August 1861. *Achilles* represented the start of a new era for Chatham as she was the first iron-built battleship to be built in any government yard. The ship is seen in 1864 undergoing completion prior to her commissioning into the Channel Squadron.

First published 2012

The History Press
The Mill, Brimscombe Port
Stroud, Gloucestershire, GL5 2QG
www.thehistorypress.co.uk

British Library Cataloguing in Publication Data.
A catalogue record for this book is available from the British Library.

ISBN 978 0 7524 6212 7

Typesetting and origination by The History Press
Printed in Great Britain

CONTENTS

INTRODUCTION

In acquiring this book it might initially be wondered whether it is simply a reissue of my earlier history of the dockyard that was published in two editions during the 1980s. Of this it needs to be made absolutely clear; this book is a completely new history of the massive industrial complex that was Chatham dockyard. Of that earlier book, this has been out of print for nearly twenty years. While there has always been considerable interest in having the book reprinted, my own continued interest in the dockyard has resulted in the unearthing of considerable new material. It would therefore be unfortunate if the opportunity were not taken to include this new research, so making this book complementary to the earlier book rather than a simple update.

So, how are the two books different? First and foremost, the earlier book directed an equal amount of attention to all periods of the dockyard's history and did not attempt a more detailed study of any particular period. In this new history, attention is directed to the later years. It is here to which much of the new research undertaken has been directed, so permitting a better understanding of how Chatham dockyard was affected by the Industrial Revolution and, in turn, greatly contributed to the bringing about of a number of essential improvements in technology and workforce management.

Chatham dockyard, from its creation in the latter years of the sixteenth century, through to its final closure in 1984, was a military industrial complex of some considerable significance. At times it was employing the largest number of civilian workers to be found in any single industrial enterprise in Britain, with numbers employed during the late seventeenth century averaging 900 and going on to reach a massive 2,000 artisans and labourers by the early nineteenth century. While Portsmouth has often been regarded as the largest and most important of the home yards, this is only correct for certain periods of history. From its inception and continuing into the first decades of the eighteenth century, Chatham was not only the most important of the royal dockyards but came close to being the largest and most energetic naval dockyard in the world. In effect, it was only the state-owned Ottoman yard of Constantinople and the declining yard of Venice that were of a size that overshadowed the repair and building capacity of the yard at Chatham.

Much of the new material that has been used to inform this book has come from the National Maritime Museum (NMM), the National Archives (TNA), the Royal Naval Museum (RNM) and the Scottish Records Office (SRO). This has allowed for more careful focusing on the mid-eighteenth century through to the late nineteenth century. In addition, and to make up for an earlier shortage of material relating to the dockyard during the final decades prior to its closure, more attention has also been given to this period. While the earlier book looked at these final years through a series of interviews that I conducted with some of those who were employed in the yard, a considerable amount of new material has now emerged. This has been used to provide a more useful glimpse of a dockyard workforce that had been promised much by successive governments but was ultimately sacrificed.

Philip MacDougall (Dr)

1

THE EARLY YEARS

The founding date of Chatham dockyard lies somewhere between the years 1567 and 1572; as to the precise year, much depends on what significant event might be regarded as of sufficient importance to constitute the founding of such an important future military-industrial complex. Was it the initial planning, undertaken around 1567, or would it be the work that begun during the following year on both clearing the site and preparing the foundations? Alternatively, it could be the completion of the first usable facility or the later raising of the flag of St George that announced the site to be that of a working naval ship repair facility.

Of one thing that is clear, the frequent suggestion of a much earlier date for the founding of the dockyard, and one that roots back to the early sixteenth century, is most certainly incorrect. Such a suggestion refers to a very different event. Instead of the formation of the dockyard, it is the period in which the river Medway was being developed as a naval supply base and safe anchorage. This in itself is important, the Medway at that time being utilised by an increasing number of royal ships that were using the river as a winter home. During the early part of his reign, Henry VIII (1509–47), having established a fairly sizeable navy, determined upon bringing an increasing number of these ships into the Medway, knowing that they would be safe from all but the most severe winter storms. Eventually it was decided to turn this into a more permanent arrangement when, in 1547, a building for the storage of maritime equipment was hired at a cost of 13s 4d per year, this located alongside 'Jillyngham Water'.[1] Over the years, a whole host of writers have put forward dates between 1510 and 1547 as marking the founding of the dockyard, confusing the concept of a naval base, albeit one having limited maintenance facilities, with that of a purpose-built dockyard.[2]

From 1547, the annual statement of accounts, as presented to the Exchequer, shows the continued payment of rents, with the amounts steadily rising as the demand for storehouses increased. By the year 1561, the cost to the Exchequer had more than quadrupled:

> Also paide by the said Accomptants for the rents and hyer of Storehouses for the storage of part of the said provisions viz. at Deptford Strand 105s. Jillingham 60s 5d.[3]

Unfortunately, nothing is said of the more precise location of these buildings. Certainly it would be wrong to jump to the conclusion that the storehouses were all located close to the river at 'Jillingham'. The subsequent construction of the dockyard at Chatham combined with the use of Chatham Reach, rather than Gillingham Reach, as the favoured stretch for the mooring of ships, would suggest many of these storehouses lay within the parish of Chatham. Perhaps only the first rented storehouse was located in 'Jillingham', with the name subsequently used as shorthand for all Medway storehouses, irrespective of where they were located. A recent archaeological dig has certainly revealed evidence of an early Tudor storehouse located below St Mary's church, where the subsequent Elizabethan dockyard was built.

The increasing value placed upon the Medway as a naval anchorage is amply demonstrated by two sets of orders from 1550. In June the Lord High Admiral was informed:

> That the Kinges shipps shulde be harborowed in Jillingham Water, saving those that be at Portsmouth, to remaigne there till the yere be further spent, for avoiding of all inconveniences, and that all masters of shippes, gonnes and pursers be discharged except a convenient nombre, till the danger of the yere be past, and afterwards ordered as it hath been accustomed in time of peace.[4]

Admittedly, in having brought warships to the Medway, the government did not simply leave them neglected or untended. A small crew of ship keepers would have remained on board to assist in preparing the vessels for the following season. Items of ageing equipment would have been renewed while rotting timbers were cut out and replaced. From the storehouses, those responsible for the upkeep of these vessels would have been able to draw such necessities as rope, pulley blocks, ships' timbers and sail cloth. Such tasks must certainly have been undertaken upon ships brought into the Medway prior to 1547, but it is only in that year that accurate surviving financial records begin to provide absolute evidence. In that year, it is clearly stated that £4,167 was expended on maintaining and preparing ships in the Medway, this in addition to the hiring of a storehouse and a separate reference to the employment of a victualler and clerk.[5]

It is possible to acquire an even more definitive picture of what was happening at the Medway anchorage. The wording of a Privy Council instruction of 1550 makes it clear that ships arriving in the Medway should be 'caulked and grounded'.[6] The first of these two tasks, caulking, referred to the need to ensure that the timbers of each ship were completely watertight, especially those that formed the underside of the hull. To achieve this, caulkers would be employed on driving fresh oakum (once the old oakum had been removed) into the seams between the planks.[7] Normally, this task was associated with the general cleaning down of the outer hull for the purpose of retaining overall sailing efficiency, the process of cleaning being known as graving. In any period at sea, timber-hulled warships collect large amounts of seaweed, barnacles and other accretions that will generally hamper their seagoing qualities. The removal of these through graving could only be achieved by grounding the vessel. As undertaken in the Medway, the process of grounding, also known as careening, was carried out through heaving the vessel down on to a soft mud embankment so that the underside of the hull was revealed. The various accretions would then be burned off (known as breaming) with the hull caulked and then given a coating of tar that would help seal it from water incursion. After one side had been so treated, the vessel was floated off on the tide, turned round and the process repeated on the opposite side.[8]

An additional aspect of 'Jillingham Water' as a supply base was that of the acquisition of a separate storehouse at Rochester, this to supply ships with victuals rather than on-board equipment. Again, this was a considerable undertaking, with over £6,000 being expended upon replenishing ships from the Rochester storehouse between 1550 and 1552.[9] Once again there is no certainty as to the exact location of this storehouse but given that a subsequent victualling yard was also established in Rochester, close to where both Chatham and Rochester interlink, it does not seem unreasonable that this was also the site of the Tudor victualling storehouse.

Despite the increasing use of the Medway as a naval base, the available facilities could only be adapted to routine repairs and maintenance. Anything more demanding would have to be undertaken at an alternative location that possessed additional specialised equipment: in other words, a purpose-built dockyard. At Woolwich and Deptford, both established much earlier in the century, such facilities most certainly existed. At Woolwich, for instance, which dates to the year 1513, a yard had been established that contained a dry dock, numerous workshops and a considerable range of storehouses. As for Deptford, also established in 1513 this was adapted to the fitting out of ships through having a basin that admitted ships into an enclosed area of water that was unaffected by the rise and fall of the tide. This basin could also be usefully employed for the careening of ships, as it had the addition of capstans that could be used for the controlled heaving of a ship over to one side and allow those employed in the yard to clean the now-

Breaming. In this illustration a ship has been heeled over and the pitch on the underside of the hull is being burnt off. It was a common practice on the mud banks of the Medway prior to the establishment of a dockyard at Chatham sometime around 1570.

The site of the Tudor dockyard constructed *c.*1570. Later occupied by the Ordnance Wharf, it lay immediately below St Mary's parish church.

exposed hull.[10] In addition, the yards at Deptford and Woolwich were also engaged in constructing new ships, and had additional facilities, such as building slips, to permit the undertaking of this task. Overall, while £30,300 was spent upon ship repair and building work at Deptford between 1548 and 1551, this same period saw the much smaller sum of £6,600 being spent at 'Jillyngham'.

Among the earliest features to be added to the dockyard at Chatham was that of a mast pond 'for the better preserving' of mast timbers and which appears to have been completed in the year 1570.[11] This was a specialised facility and was to be of sufficient size as to allow a total of seventy-seven mast timbers to be held in storage fully immersed in water. Converted from fir trees grown in northern Europe, it was necessary that these timbers were kept underwater so as to ensure that they did not dry out and so become unusable when taken on board a ship. In addition to the building of a mast pond, a mast house would also have been necessary, this needed by the mast makers who would have been employed in the cutting and shaping of the mast timbers prior to their transfer to the pond. However, the permanent staff at Chatham was still small, consisting of a clerk, purveyor and rat catcher. In addition and temporarily brought to the anchorage in that year, were sixty shipwrights and caulkers from Deptford, these employed on the twenty or so ships moored there during the winter period.[12]

A further feature of the year 1570 was the acquisition of Hill House for use by those responsible for both administering the new yard and work carried out upon ships moored in the Medway. The house was a large and recently built property that fronted the modern-day Dock Road, overlooking the site of the new yard. Owned by the Dean and Chapter of Rochester, who also owned much of the land that had also been purchased for the new dockyard, it was stipulated that the 'Officers of the Marine Causes' should use Hill House to 'mete and confere together of the weightie affairs of the said office'.[13] The house, later renamed Queen's House, was to remain in the possession of the Admiralty until its demolition in the late eighteenth century. For virtually the entirety of that period, Hill House was under lease to the Admiralty rather than being under direct ownership.[14]

During 1571 further land was rented from the Dean and Chapter, this time used for construction of a forge or anchor smithery, with a number of new storehouses also built. Confirming the entire site as a working naval dockyard and site of an important industrial military complex was the purchase of a flag bearing the cross of St George. Hoisted each morning, it summoned to work the 120 shipwrights who were at that time employed upon the repair and maintenance of the royal fleet.

As for the already existing population in the village of Chatham, the increasing use of the area by the Navy was beginning to bring considerable financial benefits. Previously dependent on farming the fields that surrounded the village or from fishing the Medway, a number of alternative opportunities now existed. For one thing, a new merchant class came into being, either employing local villagers or emerging from among the villagers themselves. For the most part, they would have been small-time traders, supplying the needs of the skilled workers of the yard and seamen on board the ships. Other villagers would have found direct employment within the dockyard. For the most part, this would have been the young and able bodied. Although none would have possessed shipbuilding skills, they could certainly have undertaken various unskilled tasks associated with running a dockyard. The least ambitious could enter as labourers, while others might seek employment as teamsters (driving cart horses in shifting large objects) or sawyers.

Other landmarks in the early history of the yard quickly followed. On 25 March 1572, Matthew Baker (1530–1613), the royal Master Shipwright, was appointed to the yard, while in September of the following year Queen Elizabeth (on the throne from 1558–1603) undertook an official visit. Baker, who was the leading English shipbuilder of his age, had turned the practice of designing ships into a science. Whereas earlier shipwrights had relied upon line of sight and rule of thumb to achieve their end product, Baker planned out his future ships through geometrical calculations. In doing so he also adopted draught plans from which curved patterns or moulds could be cut and then used for the accurate shaping of timbers that were used to build his ships. However, Baker would not have been employed exclusively at Chatham, as most of his shipbuilding work was concentrated on Deptford. Instead, he must have journeyed frequently between the two yards, encouraged to give his advice on the layout and necessary facilities for the new yard being constructed at Chatham. For this, Baker was ideally suited, having already visited a number of foreign dockyards including the grand naval arsenal at Venice.

Under the supervision of Baker, other buildings were soon being added to the yard, including sawpits, further workshops and storehouses, while the whole area was fenced with a hedge in 1579.[15] Of further significance was the addition of a wharf and crane in 1580. The purpose of the wharf was to offload heavy items such as ordnance and unused stores prior to a vessel undergoing repair. The crane, which was capable of carrying loads of up to 3 tons, would have had a treadmill drive located inside a protective house structure and from which a swing jib projected. The unloading wharf itself was some 378ft in length and 40ft wide. It is recorded that construction of the wharf was undertaken at a cost of 5s per foot.[16]

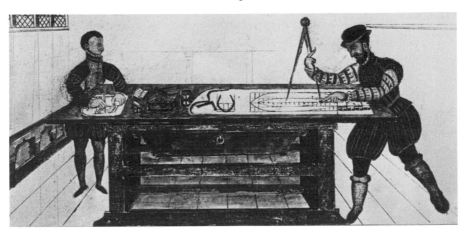

The drawing office of a Tudor shipwright with a young apprentice writing down a series of figures as they are read off by the master. The 'sweeps' were usually of this size, being used for acquiring the shape of lengthwise curves. It is not impossible that the shipwright is Matthew Baker, the man usually accredited with designing the *Sunne*, Chatham's first launched warship. (Science Museum)

Giving an early specialism to Chatham and foreshadowing its later important role in carrying out long-term repair work on the most important ships of the Navy, was the construction of a dry dock in 1581. This was very directed in its use, designed only for the accommodation of galleys. At the time, most commonly associated with the Mediterranean, galleys were shallow drafted, lightweight vessels that were propelled by oars. As such, they were not best suited to northern waters, being unable to withstand the pounding of heavy seas. Nevertheless, such ships were not unknown in the waters of northern Europe, being free of a dependency on the wind and able to easily outmanoeuvre an enemy warship that, through being only sail powered, might well have found itself becalmed. As regards the Navy of Queen Elizabeth, the number of galleys employed, during any one period of time, never exceeded five. Some were built in England while others had been captured in battle. The first galley to be brought into the new dry dock at Chatham was *Eleanor*. Described by contemporaries as large, *Eleanor*, later renamed *Bonavolia*, had a total crew of 300, and was originally captured from the French during the 1560s. It was, perhaps, for this reason, that one role allocated to *Eleanor* while at Chatham, was the entertainment of foreign dignitaries whom the Queen wished to impress. Other than this, the main duties on which the royal galleys were employed under Elizabeth was that of towing dismasted vessels, while *Eleanor* was also responsible for undertaking a survey of the Thames in 1588.

The graving dock at Chatham, which was designed to accommodate galleys, would have been very different in appearance from those built at a later date. For one thing, it would have been much shallower in depth, the dock not needing to accommodate the larger, deep-draughted sailing ships that were to totally dominate the yard in later years. Furthermore, the galley dock may not even have had any special flooring, the dock being just a trench cut into a mud embankment. As for the entrance to the dock, this would also have been of earth and laboriously broken up and then repaired every time a ship moved in or out of dock. Although this was the normal entrance design for such docks at the time, the system clearly had its drawbacks. Thus, about a year after the galley dock first came into use, it was fitted with a pair of floodgates.

With Baker involved in the planning of this major new dockyard at Chatham, he finally decided that the role of the yard could be extended into the realms of ship-building. Nothing too dramatic as it happens, with the first vessel to be constructed at Chatham, *Sunne*, a pinnace of only forty tons in weight. Designed to operate in advance of the fleet, her role was to warn of approaching danger. In service during the Armada campaign of 1588, she was present at the final and decisive Battle of Gravelines. Any contemporary mariner, even one with only the most rudimentary knowledge of ship design, would instantly have recognised *Sunne* as one of Matthew Baker's products. Apart from anything else, she looked like a warship, being designed for speed through her sleek lines and low forecastle with approximately five guns on her deck.

While specific mention has been made of the two royal dockyards of Deptford and Woolwich, nothing so far has been said of Portsmouth as a naval dockyard. This might seem surprising, given that Portsmouth was not only the first permanent naval dockyard to be established in Britain, but is usually regarded as the largest and most important of such establishments. However, during the first century of Chatham dockyard's existence, Portsmouth was relatively insignificant. Having been established during the reign of Henry VII, Portsmouth had seen the construction of a dry dock (be it of a similar primitive design to that of the galley dock at Chatham) together with other shipbuilding and repair facilities. Yet, and primarily as a result of developments in the Medway and Thames, the yard at Portsmouth was little used. Not that it was abandoned; a small number of ships were retained at Portsmouth for the defence of the south coast, with these vessels maintained by a small workforce that continued to be employed at the dockyard.

In future years, a clear love-hate relationship would emerge between those who either worked in or favoured the yard at Chatham and those similarly connected with Portsmouth. An early contributor to this debate was Admiral Sir William Monson, an experienced naval officer and writer of a series of tracts that debated the form in which the Navy of the early seventeenth century should develop. Monson was absolutely convinced that Chatham had a number of advantages over Portsmouth:

> Chatham is so safe and secure a port for the ships to ride in that his Majesty's may better ride with a hawser at Chatham than with a cable at Portsmouth.

To this, he added:

> The water at Chatham flows sufficiently every spring tide to grave the greatest ships. And it is a doubt whether it can be made to heighten so much at Portsmouth as to do the like.
>   No wind or weather can endanger the coming home of an anchor in Chatham, and the rival affords sufficient space for every ship to ride without annoying one

another. As to the contrary, a storm, with a wind from the north-east to the south-south-east, will stretch the cables in Portsmouth; and if any of their anchors come home they cannot avoid boarding one another, to their exceeding great damage and danger, the channel being so narrow.

To finally drive the point home, Monson concluded:

> In comparison betwixt Chatham and Portsmouth, Chatham is the best and safest place, and I wish that our whole navy may be kept at Chatham and not make any continual residence but there only, considering the former reasons.[17]

While Portsmouth was being sidelined, the yard at Deptford was viewed very differently. Of limited value as a naval base, it having an inadequate harbour, Deptford nevertheless possessed a highly valued dockyard. Since its creation, this yard had taken on the building of the nation's largest warships, with its proximity to London serving as a further advantage, allowing administrators in London to easily oversee the progress of work at this yard. For this reason, at a time when thought was being given to the funding of new and extensive repair and refit facilities, Deptford was considered a prime candidate. Alternatively, this new facility could be built at Chatham. Either way, wherever this new facility was located, it would establish the chosen yard as the nation's premier naval industrial complex.

The debate over the siting of the new repair facility reached its peak in 1611 when an important government enquiry was underway. One argument advanced for it not being built at Chatham was a concern that the Medway was subject to increased silting that would, at some point in the future, seriously reduce its overall depth. This, as it happens, was to be proved correct, with the yard at Chatham, during the eighteenth century, finding itself seriously threatened by rapid shoaling that made it difficult for larger ships to reach the dockyard.[18] For this reason, it is interesting to note that such concerns existed some 200 years earlier. As to the cause, accusatory fingers at that time were being pointed at both the use of chalk in 'fitting up the piles' of Rochester Bridge and to colonies of mussels newly arriving in the Medway. As regards the former, it seems that large quantities of chalk were being used to support the stanchions of the bridge, with much of this chalk subsequently washed into the Medway and supposedly heightening the overall depth of the river. Even more fanciful, was the suggestion that naval warships now moored in the river were bringing large numbers of mussels that 'bred upon the [outer hulls of those] ships'. In turn, these mussels would be regularly removed through the process of graving and 'bed in the river' and 'make such banks as will stay the current and fill it up'.[19] Ultimately, both arguments were rejected, it being suggested that the river, as a result of the following evidence, was actually gaining in depth:

> The Navy Royal, which before the Queen's time [Elizabeth I] consisted of only small ships, could not in former time come up above Gillingham, three pulls below Chatham. But being in her reign doubled in number and greater ships they ride now between Upnor and Rochester Bridge.[20]

As to why this should be, the reasons, so it was suggested, were twofold:

> 1.   The inning of the Marshes above the Bridge has strengthened the Channel and so forced the tide to go quicker [and] ground the River deeper … and this appears in trial betwixt Chatham and the opposite north shore [where] none might in memory have gone a foot over at a low water tide, whereas now [it is] twelve foot at the north shore.
> 2.   By continual riding of the [naval war] ships the cables do continually move up and down and by so beating the ground loosen the silt and wear the Channel deeper.[21]

However, the two factors that won the argument and ultimately brought the new facility to Chatham were those of economy and the ease with which ships could be brought to Chatham when compared with Deptford. On the latter point, it was estimated that in the additional time it took for a ship to be transported to Deptford and back 'a ship with small defects may be repaired' and to be returned to sea, if sent to Chatham.[22] As for the financial savings, it was considered these could be brought about in two ways. First, it was estimated by making greater use of Chatham, a large number of artisans could be permanently housed there, rather than being sent on a temporary basis and having to be given the inducement of a lodging allowance on top of the normal wage. Inevitably, this made Chatham a popular place to work, since those employed here were considerably more affluent than those employed at Deptford where no such allowances were paid. In 1611, for instance, the Christmas quarter witnessed a total of 259 shipwrights, caulkers and other artisans employed at Chatham and receiving lodging allowance.[23] The second financial economy was that Chatham, due to the availability of nearby land, was unrestricted in the extent to which it could be enlarged, and might completely replace the yard at Deptford. This was certainly a possibility that was seriously canvassed, it being suggested that the facilities at Deptford might, at an estimated sum of £5,000, be sold 'to Merchants for a Dock Site'.[24] Ultimately, however, Deptford was retained, but it is clear that Chatham was seen as a potential replacement yard, the facilities it eventually gained being considerably beyond those of the initial plan that had not gone much beyond the building of a single dry dock, unloading wharf with additional storehouses and workshops.

With the decision taken to build the new facility at Chatham, careful thought had to be given as to where exactly it should be located. As it stood, the existing yard was too constrained, having insufficient space for the new dry dock and wharf. To overcome this problem, it was decided that considerable additional land would need to be taken in, with 71 acres acquired from three separate landowners: Robert Jackson, the Dean and Chapter of Rochester and the Manor of West Court. Conveniently situated immediately to the north of the original Tudor yard, it forms the bulk of the land that is held by the present-day Chatham Historic Dockyard Trust, while the original area of the yard was to be eventually transferred to the Ordnance Board and converted into a gun wharf.

On the newly acquired site, construction work appears to have begun sometime around 1616, with initial building efforts directed to the new dry dock, wharf and the planned storehouses, together with a brick wall to secure the site. All were to be completed in 1619,

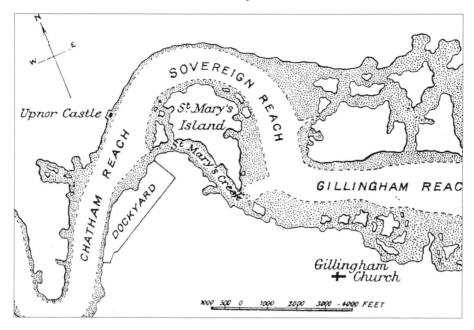

During the early seventeenth century, a completely new yard was established at Chatham, this located to the north of the original yard and closer to Upnor Castle. As this map shows, it lay alongside Chatham Reach and well inside the parish of Chatham.

the original combined estimate for construction standing at £4,000. However, the project was to see at least a doubling in cost, it having been decided that if Deptford dockyard was to be replaced, the yard at Chatham should be given an even greater range of facilities. Ultimately, these were to include a new mast pond, sail loft, ropery, residences for officers and a double dock, all of which was completed by 1624. Each of these, in its own right, was a massive undertaking; the ropery, for example, was eventually responsible for the manufacture of most of the rope and cable required by the ships of the Royal Navy. However, the decision to close Deptford was at that time deferred, it being felt that the facilities there were still of value. Perhaps, indeed, this explains the sudden curtailment placed upon the expansion of Chatham, with the decision to build an expensive wet dock or basin (to replace the already existing one at Deptford) being cancelled. As a result, Deptford was to remain, for a great many years, the only royal dockyard with such a facility.

The expansion of Chatham necessitated a considerable increase in the numbers employed at the yard, with the combined force of artisans and labourers reaching some 800 by about 1660. Within the nearby village of Chatham, which by now should more correctly be referred to as a town, considerable pressure was placed on existing accommodation and bringing about a considerable demand for new housing. From having once been a typical farming village, Chatham was rapidly becoming a crowded, unhealthy metropolis that had little in the way of carefully planned or delicately beautiful buildings. Instead, it was the recipient of hastily built and densely packed houses for the working classes, with the more affluent choosing to live beyond the perimeters of this newly developing township.

Among those who aided the construction of housing suitable for the artisans of the yard was Phineas Pett, a senior officer of the yard, and one of the leading shipbuilders of the day. He was also someone who never missed a trick when it came to the accumulation of money. Within the dockyard itself, and while serving as Master Shipwright, he found himself charged, on two occasions, with major scams that involved the misuse and sale of considerable amounts of government property.[25] As for his involvement in the housing scheme, Pett, in a classic case of insider dealing, made his first land purchase in 1616, aware that the government was about to push forward on its scheme to expand the dockyard and so increase the numbers employed there. In his autobiography he noted, 'The 8th day of April [1616] I bought a piece of ground of Christopher Collier, lying in a placed called the Brook in Chatham, for which I paid him £35 ready moneys'.[26] Just four weeks later he made a further acquisition, 'The 13th day of May, I bought the rest of the land at the Brook, of John Griffin and Robert Griffin, brothers, and a lease of their sister, belonging to the College of Rochester'.[27] Before many months had passed, and like a highly skilled player of the board game Monopoly, he soon ensured that these once-vacant sites were now packed with tiny houses that were designed to inflate his own personal income.

Phineas Pett, a slippery character with a super-charged ability to avoid recrimination and punishment, was appointed to the post of resident Commissioner at Chatham in 1630. Indeed, he was the very first to hold such office, it being a newly created post that had not yet been adopted in any other yard. This now made Pett entirely responsible for coordinating the general workings of the yard as well as providing him with a position on the Navy Board, the body in London that was charged with administering all matters connected with the civilian side of the Navy. Given his propensity for lining his own pocket, Pett was now in a unique position. In striding around the yard, he would identify various items of naval property and condemn portions of it as 'decayed property'. In the resulting sale, for the dockyard regularly disposed of such materials in this way, Pett appears to have retained some of the sale money for himself. Eventually this did come to the attention of other officers on the Navy Board, resulting in his temporary removal from office in February 1634. But Pett had influential friends, not least of which was the reigning monarch, Charles I (on the throne 1625–49). Only a week later, having been informed of the situation, he had Pett quickly reinstated with a full pardon. Pett, unharmed by such charges, remained resident Commissioner until 1647 when he happily handed the office, together with his position on the Navy Board, over to his son Peter, an equally skilled shipbuilder and embezzler of government money.

Another name to conjure with is that of Samuel Pepys who, during the mid-seventeenth century, became a frequent visitor to Chatham dockyard. Although most famed for his diary writings that spanned the period 1660–69 he was, like the two Petts, a member of the Navy Board, with Pepys holding the post of Clerk of the Acts. In modern-day speak, this can most closely be translated as secretary, although it should be added that he also had full voting rights on the Board. As such, he did not just handle the paperwork relating to matters connected with the civilian administration of the Navy but could both regulate and advise on a wide range of associated matters. Furthermore, when visiting the dockyard at Chatham, his status automatically meant that he was accommodated in Hill House, a building that Pepys, in a diary entry for 8 April 1661, describes as 'a pretty pleasant house'. In coming to Chatham, Pepys was charged with inspecting the efficiency of the yard and to head off any emerging problems. On a number of occasions, and through his diary, Pepys expressed concern at the way Peter Pett was carrying out his duties as Commissioner. In July 1663 he confided:

> … being myself much dissatisfied, and more than I thought I would have been, with Commissioner Pett, being by what I saw since I came hither, convinced that he is not able to exercise that command in the yard over the officers that he ought to do.

And, again, in August 1663:

> Troubled to see how backward Commissioner Pett is to tell any faults of the officers and to see nothing in better condition here for his being here than they are in any other yards where there is [no Commissioner appointed].

Pepys' first significant visit to the dockyard was made in April 1661, when he was required to supervise the auctioning of a number of items of ageing dockyard property. Was it a visit designed specifically to keep an eye on how Pett was handling matters, given the various accusations that had been made against his father? Certainly Pepys made a point of viewing 'all the storehouses and old goods that are this day to be sold'.

Pepys was also present at Sheerness in August 1665 for the planning of a second dockyard to be sited on the Medway:

> … and thence to Sheerness, where we walked up and down, laying out the ground to be taken in for a yard to lay provisions for cleaning and repairing ships; and a most proper place it was for that purpose.[28]

In time, the dockyard at Sheerness was to take on a subsidiary role to that of Chatham, concentrating on the refitting of smaller vessels, especially frigates. For much of its existence, the yard at Sheerness was also under the authority of the Commissioner at Chatham, rather than the yard having its own Commissioner.

These, as it happens, were serious times, the country going through a succession of trials and tribulations. In the Civil War that had resulted in the beheading of Charles I, the dockyard at Chatham had been relatively little affected, having quickly fallen into the hands of parliament. However, following the Restoration of 1660, the country had entered into a string of wars with the Dutch, these primarily fought at sea. The position of Chatham, located close to the east coast, was of paramount significance, so the dockyard was called upon to undertake the bulk of repair and maintenance work on an increasing number of ships on active service in the North Sea and Channel. However, the Treasury was hard put to support the war, choosing to make economies that were, given the importance of the work being carried out at Chatham, quite suicidal. It was simply decided to delay paying the workforce their regular wages, with not a penny made available for months on end. In November 1665, Pett was reporting that the men were on the verge of mutiny and there was absolutely no way of disciplining them. Most of the men at Chatham were under-employed, for the lack of money also meant a lack of stores. In November all the workmen in the yard laid down their tools and attended a mass meeting in which they demanded their wages. Further trouble was only averted when a number of the leaders were put into the dockyard stocks before being transferred to prison. With something like £18,000 owing in wages to the men at Chatham, this was hardly a suitable long-term solution and there were a number of incidents in which the men stopped working completely.

Worst still, in 1667, the river Medway was subjected to a direct raid carried out by a Dutch squadron of warships. The object was the destruction of both naval warships moored in the river and the dockyard at Chatham. Over a period of four days, the Dutch gradually inched along the Medway, destroying both government facilities and naval warships as they progressed. Having entered the Medway on 10 June, the Dutch squadron had reached as far as Upnor by the morning of 13 June. A number of ships had either been destroyed or captured with the destruction of the dockyard look-ing inevitable. However, the Dutch, under the command of Vice-Admiral Willem van Ghent, were concerned that an English fleet might well be in the vicinity and could possibly trap them within the river. To avoid this fate, which was not even a develop-ing possibility, van Ghent chose to withdraw, leaving the yard at Chatham to build and repair for another day.

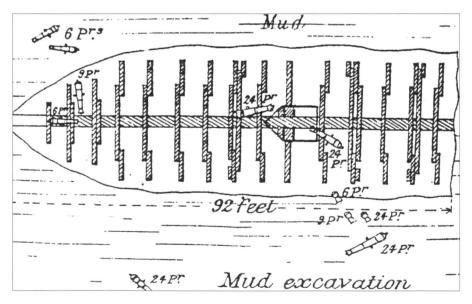

In 1667 the dockyard at Chatham was the ultimate goal of a Dutch squadron that raided the Medway. At the time a number of ships moored in the Medway were sunk, with evidence of one such sunken vessel revealed during the nineteenth century when work was being undertaken on an extension of the yard. Although the remains were not retained, this drawing was made of the find. (TNA Works 41/114)

Upnor Castle, which lies opposite the dockyard at Chatham, played an important part in the defence of the yard at the time of the Dutch raid.

Once again, Peter Pett was viewed with suspicion, described by Pepys as 'in a very fearful stink for fear of the Dutch, and desires help for God and the King and the kingdom's sake'.[29] A further witness to the Dutch raid, Thomas Wilson, the Navy victualler, together with his assistant, Mr Gordon, provided members of the Navy Board with a first-hand account of the progress of the Dutch squadron. Somewhere off Gillingham they had seen 'three ships burnt, they lying all dry, and boats going from men-of-war to fire them'.[30]

The unwillingness of the government to pay yard workers their hard-earned wages did not help the situation within the dockyard. In choosing to reject government promises of future payment they chose to withdraw their services during the period of crisis with most seeming to take the view that, if the government would not pay them, then there was no reason why they should risk their lives. According to the Duke of Albemarle, who commanded the English fleet in the Medway, 'I found scarce twelve of eight hundred men which were then in the King's pay, in His Majesty's yard, and these so distracted with fear that I could have little or no service from them'.[31]

Once the Dutch retreated the yardmen began to return, but even then they were reluctant to work without wages. To encourage them they were offered a shilling a day extra. According to William Brouncker, a Navy Commissioner, this failed to enthuse them:

> But all this stops not the mouths of the yard, who have two quarters [six months' pay] due to them, and say they deserted not the service but for mere want of bread, not being able to live without their pay. We are fain to give them good words, but doubt whether that will persuade them to stand in the day of trial.[32]

The stringent economies and lack of available money to be spent on the dockyard at Chatham were eventually terminated in 1684 when Charles II (1660–85) sanctioned a programme of expenditure that was designed to reverse the sad state into which both the Royal Navy and its support facilities had fallen. For Chatham, plans began to be put in hand for a further extensive enlargement when additional land was acquired, this in two separate purchases, one from the Manor of West Court and the other from the Dean and Chapter of

Rochester. The object was to create sufficient room for two new dry docks built of timber together with a possible enclosed basin that could be used for the more efficient refitting and graving of ships. In the event, only the two dry docks were to be built, these both having a length of 200ft (61m), under very different arrangements. While the workforce of the dockyard constructed one themselves in an attempt to reduce overall costs, the other was built under contract by a certain John Rogers. His tender was for a total payment of £5,310 with estimated time for construction being approximately sixteen months from the signing of the contract. Under James II (1685–88) further improvements to the yard saw the addition of a large brick storehouse situated in the ropery together with ten mast houses. While another round of improvements would undoubtedly have been made if James had remained on the throne, he was usurped after a short reign by the Duke of Orange, who claimed the throne as William III (1689–1702). Equally naval minded, the new King continued to sanction money being spent on Chatham, agreeing to the construction of a second mast pond and a further mast house. Additional stores were also built together with a smithery, painters' shop and two substantial houses to be occupied by the yard surgeon and his assistant. Finally, with all this new work deemed complete, the original wall of the yard was extended, ensuring that the new mast pond and other facilities were fully secure from the attentions of uninvited visitors.

These important improvements that took place during the latter part of the seventeenth century naturally increased the capacity of Chatham dockyard. Not only that, but it also allowed Chatham to retain its premier position among the royal dockyards. Whereas the other four long-established dockyards, those of Portsmouth, Woolwich, Deptford and Sheerness, could only muster five dry docks between them, Chatham could boast four. Furthermore, Chatham had the addition of a ropeyard with Woolwich the only other yard with such a facility. Finally, through the recent addition of a range of new storehouses and workshops, Chatham was given a further edge over the other naval yards.

Unfortunately for Chatham, however, its supremacy over the other yards was not to remain unchallenged. The new century was to bring a great number of wars, of which France was invariably the enemy. Battlegrounds changed, with the Atlantic and, eventually, the Mediterranean being the future theatres of war. Chatham, in this changing environment, was somewhat ill-placed when compared with the other royal dockyards. Portsmouth began to expand and, within a few years, was able to boast a greater workforce than that of Chatham. Plymouth, an entirely new dockyard, also grew rapidly. Established in 1691, it had, by 1703, a workforce just under half that employed at Chatham. By the middle of the century this had expanded so that it was about equal to that of Chatham.

Not that Chatham ceased to have an important role to perform. Increasingly it was seen as a dockyard more suited to constructing the nation's warships and less suited to fitting out fleets during times of mobilisation. The result was that many of the nation's greatest warships – including *Victory* – were to be built there. In doing so, the dockyard at Chatham had lost one role, but was to take on a new and equally important role. As such, it is to this important warship building and heavy repair work to which the rest of this book is devoted, this initial chapter serving only as an introduction to a yard that was to become pre-eminent in its role as the nation's most important warship building yard.

2

IN THE FOOTSTEPS OF
BLAISE OLLIVIER

On Monday 2 May 1737 Blaise Ollivier, Master Shipwright at Brest, the French government's most important naval dockyard, passed without restriction into the dockyard at Chatham. Carefully concealing his identity, although his heavy accent and limited knowledge of English clearly marked him out as a foreigner, he was on a very special mission and one that had been sanctioned at the very highest level. His task: that of securing information on working methods used at Chatham and how this compared with those used in the French yards. In other words, Ollivier was a spy, and one who was to report directly to Jean Frédéric, Comte de Maurepas, Secretary of State for the Marine.

That Ollivier was so easily permitted to enter this major military industrial complex might, in this day and age, raise a few eyebrows. After all, Ollivier came from a country with which Britain was frequently at odds, a war breaking out between the two countries only eight years after his infiltration of the dockyard. Yet it was not unusual at that time. Rather than keeping shipbuilding technology a secret, it was often openly shared. The more talented shipwrights sometimes took employment in the yards of other nations, either because they wished to gain a greater range of experiences or had been headhunted and offered a much higher level of remuneration. Certainly, it is known that shipwrights from the British yards had at various times worked in the state yards of Spain, Holland, Russia and Denmark.[1]

In turn, the British yards, during earlier periods of their existence, had employed naval shipwrights trained in the arsenal at Venice. Perhaps the best example of this openness to foreign visitors was that of William III giving the Tsar of Russia, Peter the Great (1672–1725), full access to the yard at Deptford. Here, Peter spent a considerable period of time talking to the master builders and making copious notes on both shipbuilding techniques and dockyard procedures. Furthermore, 'whenever he came into contact with someone he believed could be useful to him, he tried to lure him into service'.[2] As a result, some sixty specialists returned with the Tsar to Russia, these including shipwrights, mast makers, anchor smiths and joiners, all of whom served at the newly created Admiralteiskie Verfi Shipyard in St Petersburg, advising on the facilities and layout necessary for the creation of this yard before going on to lead in the design and construction of a number of large battleships.[3]

Given that it was not so unusual for foreign nationals to be given access to a British naval dockyard, this is not the reason for attention being directed towards Ollivier. Instead, it is because of the copious notes that he took, which were turned into a full report that was subsequently submitted to Maurepas. In arriving at Chatham, he cast his professional eye over the activities of the yard, commenting not only upon the unusual and different but also everyday common practice – the type of activities that are difficult for historians to fathom out because nobody sees the point in noting down such occurrences. Furthermore, as the Master Shipwright at Brest, charged with the construction of some of the largest warships being built for a rapidly expanding French Navy, he makes the occasional comparison, indicating whether he considered French or British practice to be superior.[4]

On first entering the dockyard at Chatham, Ollivier would have passed under the pedestrian arch of the Main Gate, the same structure that still does duty as the main gateway for those approaching the yard from the town of Chatham. At that time, however, this three-storey brick structure was the only point of entry; all other gates date from the nineteenth century. Completed in 1720, and now known as the Main Gate, its two raised wings at that time provided accommodation for the yard porter and Boatswain of the Yard. Here, Ollivier would have been required to present his letter of authority. Already provided by the Navy Board, this permitted him entry not only into Chatham but all of the other royal dockyards of Deptford, Woolwich and Portsmouth.

Once inside the yard, Ollivier would have followed a well-worn dirt track, the dockyard not at that time having been paved, which took him in the general direction of the Master Shipwright's office. This was a single-storey wooden building that stood close to the South Dock and provided a convenient location for the Master Shipwright to

Blaise Ollivier would have entered the yard at Chatham through the Main Gate, built in 1720. A three-storey brick building, it was designed to resemble the gateway of a contemporary fortress and housed the yard porter and boatswain.

observe progress on the repair and building of ships. For purposes of administration, Ollivier had now entered the jurisdiction of the Extraordinary, the part of the yard managed entirely by the Master Shipwright, one of the principal officers of the yard. This area concentrated entirely on the building, repair and maintenance of warships. In addition, there were two other administratively separate areas also headed by principal officers: the ropery, under the charge of the Clerk of the Rope House; and the moorings of the river Medway, known as the Ordinary, and under the authority of the Master Attendant. While the Commissioner of the dockyard coordinated and had a watching brief over all areas of the dockyard, his actual authority was fairly limited and frequently he had to defer to the authority of his principal officers.

Remaining with Ollivier in the Extraordinary, he would certainly have taken an early glimpse at the various dry docks and beginning, most probably with the South Dock. This had begun life in the early seventeenth century as the Double Dock but had been converted in 1703 to a single dock, achieved through the process of reducing its length while also giving it greater width. Experience had demonstrated that the value of a double dock, whereby two vessels, end to end, could be taken into the same dock, was limited. Apart from anything else, it meant that the vessel at the far end of the dock, often a ship under construction, was trapped in position, and could only be moved when work had been completed on the vessel nearest to the dock entrance. Furthermore, with the growth in size of vessels, the dock itself had been generally too narrow, hence the need to increase its width. According to Ollivier, who carefully measured the size of all of the yard docks, the South Dock, at that time, had length of just over 186ft (56.8m) and a width of 68ft 3in (20.8m). [All measurements given by Ollivier were given in French feet, but converted into imperial and metric for purposes of this publication.] Nearby was the North Dock, this having begun life as the original single dock that had been constructed in the early seventeenth century. It also had undergone numerous alterations and now mirrored the South Dock in the dimensions given by Ollivier. A further pair of dry docks, these being the ones built in 1686, stood approximately 400ft (121.9m) to the north and, despite now being over forty years old, were known as the First and Second New Docks. These were fundamentally unaltered since their time of construction, although one of them had been substantially repaired during the previous year, the total cost being £7,000. Ollivier in measuring them, found them both to be of 160ft (48.8m) in length with a width of 64ft (19.5m).[5]

To reach the Master Shipwright's office, the pathway followed by Ollivier had first skirted around the ropery, a collection of buildings on his left side, while to the right was the resident Commissioner's House and garden together with the officers' residences. While most of the buildings belonging to the ropery dated back to the early seventeenth century, the various residential buildings in the yard were of much more recent construction. Regarding the Commissioner's House, this had been completed in 1704 at an approximate cost of £912. Still in existence, and now known as Medway House, it is a spacious three-storey residence with additional attic and basement. Constructed of brick, it was built at the behest of George St Lo, Commissioner of the yard between 1703–14. On first taking office at Chatham, St Lo had indicated his disappointment at the small size of the residence built during the early part of the previous century and forcibly made it clear that it was not suitable for a Commissioner charged with the most important yard in the country. Some twenty years later, a terrace of houses allowed to the officers of the yard, some twelve in number, was also constructed following the demolition of a set of houses dating, once again, to the early seventeenth century. As with the Commissioner's House, they are still a feature of the modern-day yard with their combined construction cost amounting to £4,000.[6]

Intriguingly, Ollivier makes reference to a fifth dry dock and one that was 'empty or in poor repair'. As it happens, there was no fifth dock at Chatham, with Ollivier either erroneously transcribing his own notes or misunderstanding what he was being told. The latter is quite likely, given that Ollivier had such a limited understanding of the English language. For whatever reason, Ollivier is clearly confused by the presence of an abandoned building slip, one of the earliest in the yard, and situated between the North and South Docks. In Ollivier's own words, it was 'empty and in poor repair'. At the time it was in the process of being filled in, with a replacement slip having already been constructed. It was probably the fact of it being partially filled with soil and standing so close to two of the existing docks that led to Ollivier making such a basic error. As to the reason for its abandonment, this related to the recent increase in width that had been given to the North and South Docks, the workmen employed now finding the available workspace far too limited for their needs and so requiring the removal of that particular building slip.[7]

On reaching the Master Shipwright's office, Ollivier would have made contact with John Ward, the Master Shipwright at Chatham. Whether this was on the first morning of Ollivier's arrival or later in the week is not verified. However, one thing is clear, Ollivier received considerable assistance, Ward happily showing his French visitor the drawings of a seventy-gun ship then under construction in the yard while also revealing a series of modifications that were being introduced to newly built British warships. In fact, Ollivier was even in position to measure off the principle dimensions of this new seventy-gun warship, the future *Elizabeth*, together with 'many notes concerning [her] lines'.[8] However, it also becomes clear from this meeting with Ward that Ollivier had not admitted to his true background or level of technical expertise, declaring in the account he presented to Maurepas that, 'I could not without compromising myself extend my curiosity further.'

In stepping out of the Master Shipwright's office, it seems not unreasonable to assume that Ollivier's attention would, once again, have been absorbed by the dry docks and slipways that lined the central river frontage of the dockyard. His interest in the dry docks was considerable, with Ollivier going to great lengths to describe both their design and usage, accompanying his notes with a number of detailed drawings. All four of the docks were of timber construction at this time, with the floor of each laid with a covering of oak planking. Along the sides of the dock, which had an upward slope of approximately seventy degrees, were two stepped platforms, or altars, that were used both to support shores that supported the vessel and to allow artisans ready access to the upper hull of the vessel upon which they were working. The docks themselves were reliant upon gravity drainage, meaning that when a ship was brought into a dock on an appropri-

An important facet of the dockyard at Chatham was that of the river, used for the mooring of warships out of commission and for the carrying out of repair and refit work on vessels that had either been dry docked or did not need to be docked. At one time, therefore, Chatham Reach, seen here in this photo, would have had a number of vessels moored and under the authority of the yard.

ate tide, water could flow out with the receding tide. To assist in this drainage, each of the docks had an approximate declivity of about three degrees. However, a further and lesser-known feature of each dock was that of the floor having a gradual rise towards the centre. The purpose of this was to better accommodate incoming vessels that had, through service at sea, witnessed the hogging of the keel. Caused by the action of waves, it was where the keel had been forced out of true, with the two ends lying lower than the middle. On commenting upon this, Ollivier indicated that 'without this precaution the ship would take up her original shape on settling in the dock, and would then lose it again suddenly on leaving the dock, and would thereby be exposed to leaking'.[9]

As for the use to which these docks were put, this was more wide ranging than in the French dockyards. Whereas the use in France was directed entirely to the repairing of ships, in Chatham it was also common to briefly dock a vessel for graving. At one time, of course, this had been carried out on the mud banks on the river Medway while it is also possible that in the early Tudor yard there might also have been a specialised careening wharf. However, with the construction of two docks during the early seventeenth century and a further pair of docks some sixty years later, it would no longer have been necessary to have a separate wharf for hauling vessels over for the purpose of careening. Ollivier was especially favourable to the practice carried out at Chatham, considering it to be less costly, more expeditious and likely to place vessels under less strain. He noted, for instance, that in graving vessels while still afloat, it not only necessitated the construction of a specialised wharf but also the retention of a number of 'boats, barges and ballast lighters' to support those engaged in the work of cleaning down the hull. All of these could be dispensed with if dry docks were used for graving. Ollivier's recommendation, therefore, was that French yards should generally increase the number of docks they possessed, as this 'would be paid back in but a few years through the savings which we would achieve'.[10]

Ollivier was particularly fortunate in having arrived on 2 May, as he was able to witness the ninety-gun *Union* being brought into dock. Undertaken on a high tide, the vessel was brought round from her moorings in the river some 30 minutes before the full height of tide had been reached. Assembled around the dock were some 100 labourers and shipwrights, their task to provide muscle power, hauling upon the cables that would gently bring the vessel through the entrance and line her up with the centre of the dock. As the tide had flowed out, and now only requiring sixty shipwrights, timber shores were placed in position for the purpose of securing the ship once the water had fully drained from the dock. Depending on the precise nature of work to being undertaken, the vessel might have to be brought to rest on blocks, but if no work was required upon the keel, the ship would settle directly on the timber-lined floor or working platform.[11]

Once the dock had drained, it was then necessary for the dock gates to be lifted into position. The process was fairly complex as the gates were formed of three separate timber panels, the two side panels held fast against the dock and a third positioned in the middle. All were manoeuvred into position by use of blocks and tackle, with the panels secured to each other and the side of the dock through the use of iron straps. Once the gates were closed, timber shores were wedged against them, these to provide additional support.[12]

In turning his attention to the building slips, Ollivier correctly noted the existence of two, the South Slip and the New Slip, with the latter having only been recently completed. Both were fully employed at the time, with the frame of a future seventy-gun vessel, the already mentioned *Elizabeth*, standing on the South Slip. Of the forwardness of this vessel, Ollivier noted that she was 'planked from the keel to the planksheer' while both her decks were finished. At the time of his visit, the workmen of the yard were 'installing the beams of the forecastle and quarterdeck and working on the apartments of the hold'. On the New Slip, and the first vessel to be laid on this slip, labourers were readying it for construction of a fifty-gun vessel, the future *Guernsey*. Among the tasks being undertaken was the 'lofting up of some of her full size frames'.[13]

Over on the north side of the yard was an area set aside for the storing and making of masts. Its most obvious feature was the mast pond that had been dug out and formed from an existing creek during the 1690s. Used to immerse finished mast sticks under a covering of seawater, it had been constructed with thirty-two brick arches that kept the sticks permanently submerged. The total cost of constructing the pond, including the excavation work, two pairs of gates, wharfing slips and the arches had been £3,180. Celia Fiennes, an English traveller who had visited the yard in 1697, described it in the following manner:

> … there was in one place a sort of arches like a bridge of brick-work, they told me the use of it was to let in the water there and so they put the masts into season.[14]

Ollivier himself says nothing of the use of the mast pond but does refer to the mast houses, of which there were twelve at this time, explaining that this was where the mast makers 'work their masts'.[15] During his spying mission on the yard, Ollivier observed the making of the main mast for *Royal Sovereign*, a 100-gun first rate that was undergoing repairs in one of the larger dry docks. This was a major undertaking as the mast, comprising lower, top and topgallant sections, had a total height of 114ft (34.7m). In all, twenty fir sticks would be required, with the lower mast section being 'made up of two trees joined by a scarph [join] 32ft [9.75m] long' and joined with 'plain coaks' or tenon joints. On the outside, the two mast sticks upon being joined together were shaped into the form of an octagon and to 'each of these eight faces a side tree [was] fayed' and fastened with 'nail and iron bolts, which pass right through the mast, and which are clenched over roves'.[16]

Immediately to the east of the docks and slips, and occupying much of the central part of the yard, was a vast area set aside for the storage of timber. According to Ollivier, most of this was 'East country plank, or from New England'. He also noted that timbers were often marked, this demonstrating their country of origin. Whilst Ollivier may have been correct with regard to his observation as to the origin of the timbers he was looking at, he made nothing of the importance of oak grown in the two counties of Kent and Sussex. Generally, this was considered by the Navy Board to be without rival and was specifically reserved for the frames that formed the hull of any large and important warship. The reference to the timber being marked is worth exploring a little further as this was a device to more effectively manage and account for all timbers in the yard. It is unlikely, despite Ollivier's claim, that the markings indicated a country of origin. A series of old ship timbers that were used in the construction of the wheelwright's shop, a structure added to the dockyard in 1790, had markings that seem to indicate only the dockyard that first received the timber together with the year and a reference number. In later years, these markings were to carry even more information but never, so it would seem, its originating country.

In giving his attention to this area of timber storage, Ollivier must have been surprised by the methods used to store this huge shipbuilding resource: it simply being 'piled one timber on another'. Quite simply, with the cut marks difficult to see amidst those disorganised piles, there was no way of easily extracting a particular timber, identifying its age or determining whether it had been adequately seasoned. Furthermore, through lack of adequate ventilation, timbers would often begin to rot while in storage and then be introduced into ships under construction or repair. Possibly this helps explain why ships constructed during the eighteenth century had such a short service life, with Clive Wilkinson, in a recent study, indicating that ships of the line would only see twelve to sixteen years of service. Furthermore, Wilkinson suggests that the problem peaked during the 1730s, coinciding with Ollivier's spying mission, and was due to an added environmental factor, with strong westerly airflows creating a long series of mild winters. Consequently, timber cut during these years contained greater levels of sap and required even longer periods of seasoning. Given, as demonstrated, that no extended and effective period of seasoning was allowed, Wilkinson notes that ships-of-the-line built during this period had an even shorter period of longevity, estimated as less than nine years on average.[17]

One experiment undertaken at Chatham was that of immersing in salt water certain of the shipbuilding timbers. Ollivier indicates that this was being undertaken in a large pond 320ft (97.5m) square. Only one feature of the yard fits this description, that of a

A common feature of many of the earlier buildings in the dockyard at Chatham is the introduction of reused ships' timber, such as seen here in the mast house at Chatham that dates to the mid-eighteenth century.

second mast pond that had been added to the yard in 1702 and which stood at the far north of the yard.[18] Into this, Ollivier adds, various timbers, mostly those destined to form the frames of a vessel under construction, were totally submerged for about six months. The effect was to help wash out some of the remaining sap, so making the wood harder and more durable. In turn, timber treated in this fashion also had a tendency to attract moisture and would, therefore be more prone to wet rot. At Chatham, it was not an experiment deemed to have been successful, with Ollivier noting that from the original six months, the length of time for immersion had eventually been reduced to three months and, at the time of his visit to Chatham, it was no more than 'one or two weeks' with many frame timbers no longer immersed in this way. However, the scheme was not totally abandoned. While the timber pond was converted back to use as a mast pond shortly after Ollivier's visit to Chatham, a further and much smaller pond, known as the pickling pond, was created for the immersion of oak timbers. Situated at the centre of the yard, amidst the area set aside for the storage of timber, it measured 210ft (64m) by 90ft (27.4m) and was fitted with a ramp that enabled these heavy timbers to be more easily hauled out when their period in soak had been completed.[19]

While in the timber storage area, Ollivier's attention was drawn to a steam kiln that was used for the curving of planks that were to be fitted to both the bow of a ship and the rounded areas toward the stern. In these areas, straight timbers would be inappropriate. As far as the French yards were concerned, timbers were cut to shape using templates. However, this was both time-consuming and costly in the amount of timber used, making Ollivier determined to encourage the introduction of kilns into the French yards. As used at Chatham, seasoned planks were first soaked in fresh water and then placed inside a box that was heated from a coal-fired boiler. Each plank remained in the kiln 'for about an hour and a quarter for every inch of thickness'. Once removed, the plank was easily curved to the correct shape and then held in position by a series of stakes. Once cooled, the planks were then taken to the ship under construction for fitting. At that time Chatham had but one steam kiln, this sited just to the north of the two new docks.

A sail loft, a brick building constructed in 1723 which had replaced an earlier building on the same site, stood adjacent to the east wall of the yard, about 370ft (112.8m) forward of the gate. As with a number of buildings and structures that Ollivier would have seen, the sail loft still exists. The sewing and cutting of new sails would have been undertaken on the upper floor, an area completely unencumbered by structural supports. On the lower floor, sails were stored:

> … in such a manner that they leave a space [of just over] three feet wide all round the walls of the loft' while 'between the walls and sails [was] a curtain, to which [were] made fast a series of brails which [allowed] it to be raised when they wish to air the loft'.[20]

Something that Ollivier does not mention, but is an interesting feature of the sail loft, is that some of the ground-floor pillars had been formed out of the ribs of old warships. This was a common practice in the dockyards, with every effort made to reuse timbers from ships that were no longer sea-going and had been brought into dry dock for dismantling. Any reusable timbers might either be used on another ship under construction or, if not up to this standard, used elsewhere in the dockyard. The name and date of the ship from which the timbers were taken is unknown, but would certainly have been one that had originally been built during the previous century. Immediately between the sail loft and the east wall was the sail field used to dry sails taken off vessels when they were brought into dry dock for repair. Of this area, Ollivier noted:

> Next to the sail loft is a very great courtyard in which several sheers are set into the earth, 52ft to 62ft [16–19m] high, each braced by four shores, and at the head of these sheers are set up tackles with which the sails can be hoisted up when it is desired to dry them.[21]

A further building involved in manufacturing important items of shipboard equipment was the smith's shop, eventually to be known in the royal dockyards as a smithery. Sited close to the First New Dock it was a substantial, well-ventilated brick building of 130ft (39.6m) in length and 60ft (18.3m) wide. Immediately adjoining was a coal yard and an iron house, the latter being where the uncorked wrought iron was stored. Within the smithery were approximately twenty fires that were most commonly used in the manufacture of anchors, although other items were also produced in the smithery. Ollivier, for instance, when he entered the Chatham smiths' shop, noted that among work being undertaken was the 'forging of the mooring chains' that he indicated were used 'for securing the cables of ships' moored in the Medway. Providing further information, he went on to say:

> The links of these chains are twice as long as those that we [in France] employ, and are made of iron bar, which is about 0.2in [4.5mm] thicker. I was told they used to

make them taller and less fat, and they showed me some that were proportioned like the links of our chains, but they have changed this usage, since the links being fatter are also stronger and are slower to be consumed by rust.[22]

Dominating the north end of the yard and adjacent to the Anchor Wharf was the ropery. It was very different to the present-day ropery as overseen by the Chatham Dockyard Historic Trust, as the one seen by Ollivier consisted of timber buildings mostly constructed during the previous century. While the French spy says little about the design of these buildings, he does make the point that 'there were two roperies'. What he means by this is that there were two adjacent buildings engaged in the process of rope manufacture, one more correctly referred to as the spinning house and the other the ropewalk. In addition, and unmentioned by Ollivier, were the hemp and tarring houses together with several specialised storehouses. Clearly, this was not an area in which Ollivier had a great deal of knowledge, as otherwise he would have dwelt considerably upon the mode of production and how it differed from the manufacture of rope for French warships. As for the use of these various buildings, bales of raw hemp, the basic material required for the manufacture of rope, was stored in the hemp house and removed when required. Initially, the hemp had to be combed, or unknotted, with this undertaken in the hatchelling house, the tangled hemp pulled across a board that was set with sharp pointed iron nails and known as a hatchel. The next stage was to transfer the combed hemp to the spinning house where spinners would twist portions of the hemp fibre over a hook on a manually turned spin-

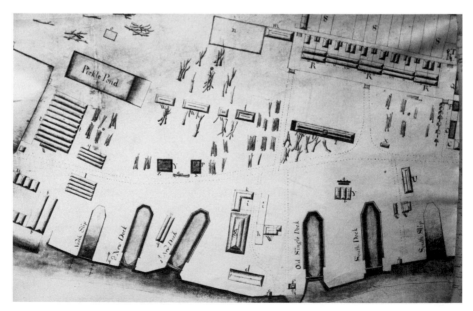

Ollivier was particularly interested in the mid-section of the dockyard where the various docks and slips were located. In this plan of 1746, drawn just nine years after his visit to Chatham, a clear impression emerges of the yard at that time, with measurements taken from this plan agreeing with those recorded by Ollivier at the time of his visit.

ning frame. As the frame turned, the spinner would slowly walk backwards, allowing yarn to be formed under the guidance of his left hand. At the same time, from a bundle of hemp thrown over his shoulder, and using his right hand, further hemp would be added to allow the yarn to lengthen out. The next stage was that of tarring the yarn, carried out in the tarring house, with the yarn pulled through a large kettle containing heated tar.

The tarred yarn, having been allowed to dry and wound on to bobbins, was transferred to the ropewalk. This was a massively long building, 1,155ft (352m) in length.[23] Here was undertaken the final two stages of the rope manufacturing process, that of combining the individual yarns into strands and then the strands into rope. The first process was achieved through the mounting of the bobbins at one end of the floor and attaching the yarn ends to a rotating hook mounted on a wheel frame. The wheel frame, manually powered and mounted on wheels, travelled the length of the laying floor, drawing out yarn from the bobbins and twisting the strands together. Each strand, to prevent theft, had the government mark inserted in coloured worsted through the whole length of the strand, the mark at Chatham being yellow. The final stage, that of 'laying' or closing the great ropes, necessitated the strands being laid out along the length of the ropewalk floor, one end of the strands connected to hooks that could be rotated on a fixed point, while the remaining ends were attached to a wheel frame, in the case of small rope, or a larger jack wheel. To both separate the strands, and keep them at a constant height, trestles were placed at intervals between the jack wheel and back frame, removed in turn as the jack wheel moved forward. The hooks, both at the fixed point and on the jack wheel were then turned by manual labour, this twisting the frames to form rope with the jack wheel drawn along the laying floor.

Four basic types of rope were produced on the laying house floor and these were known as cable, hawser, towline and warp. Each was of a different dimension with each performing a specific task on board a man-of-war. Cable, the heaviest, was composed of nine strands laid first into three ropes and then into one large rope. Used to secure the anchors, its circumference varied from a maximum of 20in down to 9in. A 20in cable weighed 7,772lbs and contained 1,943 threads of rope yarn. A 9in cable, on the other hand, was of 1,572lbs and contained 393 threads of rope. According to William Falconer, who wrote his maritime dictionary while employed in the Ordinary at Chatham:

> All cables ought to be one hundred and twenty fathoms in length; for which purpose the thread or yarn must be one hundred and eighty fathoms; in as much as they are diminished one third in length by twisting.[24]

The method of manufacture for the other three basic types of rope was different, as they were all hawser laid rather than cable laid. This meant that instead of each being of nine strands, as with cable, they were of three strands, with the number of yarns in each strand differing according to the size of rope required. Warp was the smallest, being used to remove a ship from one place to another while in port, road or river; towline was the next smallest and was generally used to remove a ship from one part of a harbour to another by means of anchors or capstans; hawser was smaller than a cable but larger than a towline, and most frequently used for swaying up topmasts.

A particularly impressive feature of the dockyard was the numerous storehouses, with the largest, 340ft in length, situated on the Anchor Wharf and within the area of the ropery. In addition, and immediately north of the Old Single Dock was a further storehouse of substance, this erected between 1723–24. Three storeys in height and of brick construction, its primary use was that of housing materials that were immediately required in the shipbuilding and repair process. In addition, the ground floor of this building sheltered several sawpits, while in the roofing was a loft used for the laying down of the full-scale plans of ships under construction and known as a mould loft. A centrally positioned clock tower, a useful addition in an age where pocket watches were rare and wristwatches unknown, was centrally positioned on the roof of this building, allowing it to become known in later years as 'the Clock Tower Building'.

One who was clearly impressed with the various storehouses that were to be found in the dockyard and, as it happens, in the adjoining gun wharf was Daniel Defoe. He paid a visit to Chatham sometime around 1720 and gave particular attention to these buildings, referring to them as like 'the ships themselves' being 'surprisingly large, and in their several kinds, beautiful'. As for what kinds of stores they had been built to accommodate, Defoe goes on to explain that they contained:

> … the sails, the rigging, the ammunition, guns, great and small shot, small arms, swords, cutlasses, half pikes, with all the other furniture belonging to ships that ride at their moorings in the river Medway. These take up one part of the place, where the furniture of every ship lies in particular warehouses by themselves and may be taken out on the most hasty occasion without confusion, fire excepted. The powder is generally carried away to particular magazines to avoid disaster. Besides these, there are storehouses for laying up the furniture and stores for ships; but which are not appropriated, or do not belong (as is expressed by the officers) to any particular ship; but lie ready to be delivered out for the furnishing of other ships to be built, or for repairing and supplying the ships already there, as occasion may require.[25]

Ollivier, himself, although impressed, did not feel the storehouses at Chatham compared favourably with those in the dockyards of France, considering them to be less commodious. Perhaps he was disappointed by their overall height, with each floor being only about 10ft above the other. Ollivier enquired as to the reason for their lack of height and was informed that 'there was no reason for any great height in the storeys of a storehouse, it is but wasted space unless it be filled up completely'. He was further told that 'if it is desired to fill it up then much time is required to stow and remove the stores which can be placed there'.[26]

Ollivier also drew attention to differences in practice in the system of storage used at Chatham compared with that in the French dockyards. Whereas in France a ship coming into the dockyard would have all its stores taken off and stored in one place, this was not so at Chatham. Instead, all of the stores of one type were kept together and taken to individual storage areas 'with labels on which they write the name of the ship to which they belong'. Ollivier considered this to be wasteful of time, but was informed that if the French method was adopted 'it would require a greater number of Storekeepers to watch over the stores, since it is their practice here to look after them continuously, to inspect them, to replace those that are spoiled, and to maintain them all in good state as long as possible.'[27] Specifically, he was asked to consider the advantage of keeping ships' blocks all under the same roof, irrespective of the vessel they came from:

> A block maker, for example, is in charge of the block store; he has under his eye all of the blocks of all of the ships, and thus he is able to look after them better and with less expense than if they were dispersed among different storehouses; and likewise for all other stores.[28]

Unfortunately Ollivier only gives limited attention to the Ordinary, which was geographically centred on the river. Here were the moorings that were set aside for ships laid up when out of commission. Placed under the authority of the Master Attendant, the principal officer of the Ordinary, were the various ship keepers who had been placed on board each of the vessels held in the Ordinary, together with the sail makers and riggers, those whose work brought them in closest contact with the moored vessels. As each vessel entered the Ordinary, a process most commonly witnessed at the end of a period of hostility, it would have its masts, sails, rigging and guns removed. The ship keepers, who would normally already have been part of the ship's crew, being attached to a vessel for the life of that vessel, were the gunner, boatswain, carpenter, purser and cook. Each had a specific duty and was supposed to ensure that the vessel remained in a watertight condition and ready for a return to service in the event of mobilisation.

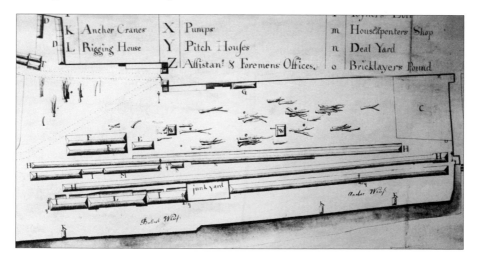

Detail of a plan of the yard that dates to the time of Blaise Ollivier's visit. The buildings to be seen are mainly those of the ropery that had been built in the previous century. Of particular note is that of a separate spinning and laying floor, these later to be combined into one building. Note the rather haphazard storage of timbers, a point noted by Ollivier in the account that he later wrote.

At this time, the Ordinary at Chatham had somewhere in the region of fifty moorings, each vessel positioned according to her draft and depth of water available.[29] Referring to the cables used in the mooring of these vessels, Ollivier indicates that each vessel was:

> … moored with but a single cable [and] made fast to an iron mooring chain lying on the bottom; they also have a stream anchor at the ship's side or hanging from the cathead ready to let go should the mooring cable fail.[30]

A mooring, at this time, to expand on Ollivier's remarks, consisted of two anchors, fixed on opposite sides of the river, with a chain extending between them. In the middle of the chain was a long square link, its lower end terminating in a swivel attached to a bridle. From this bridle stretched a rope cable that was drawn into the moored ship by way of its mooring point.

It has already been noted that the Medway was subject to increased shoaling, but it is not a point mentioned by Ollivier. During the sixteenth century, when the Medway was first used for the harbouring of ships, the entire Tudor Navy could be located in this single river. However, as ships increased in size, the Medway proved a less attractive proposition. A map of 1685 shows eight first and second rates moored in the river, together with fifty third rates. Moving forward to 1774, a subsequent map of the river indicated sufficient depth for only three first and second rates and five third rates. Partly, the problem was that of silting, but an additional factor was an increase in the size of warships and the depth of water they required. In the 1680s, most first rates moored in the Medway would not have exceeded 1,600 tons but by the time of Ollivier's mission, the larger ships usually weighed in at 1,800 tons or more.

An examination of the Ordinary, together with some of the ships held at moorings in the river, marked the completion of Ollivier's espionage mission to Chatham. Already he had visited the yards at Deptford and Woolwich and while at Chatham, possibly on Thursday 4 May, he also visited the yard at Sheerness. Finally, and before returning to London, he visited the yard at Portsmouth. As for the rapidly expanding yard at Plymouth, this he was unable to fit into his itinerary. His final task before leaving England was that of carefully writing up his notes ready for these to be handed over to Maurepas upon his return to France.

It was not, however, until January 1738 that Ollivier was finally able to return to Brest, where he was returned to his old office of Master Shipwright. As well as spying on the dockyards in England, he had also been given the task of supplying a similar report on the dockyards of the Dutch Navy, requiring him to spend several months in the Netherlands. Doubtless Ollivier would have been destined for great things if it had not been for his contracting tuberculosis, resulting in his premature death on 20 October 1746. However, during those final nine years of his working career, he was responsible for overseeing the design of several significant warships, while also ensuring that the dockyard at Brest was given additional dry docks, this resulting from his observations at Chatham and his view of their usefulness in the graving of ships.

3

THE VIEW FROM THE
COMMISSIONER'S HOUSE

The resident Commissioner may well have been regarded as the most senior officer of the yard, but his authority was fundamentally limited to that of receiving and passing on instructions from the Navy Board. Nevertheless, his residence was an exceedingly fine building and was completed in 1704. This is an early plan produced for the house and it is interesting to compare this with the house as actually built.

In any modern-day industrial enterprise there will exist one clear and indisputable manager: a person from whose office a variety of orders, guidance notes and day-to-day directions emanate. In addition, through the appointment of both a managing director and various sub-managers, a clear line of authority will be apparent and areas of individual responsibility firmly established. For the dockyard at Chatham, from the

The Commissioner's House (now known as Medway House) as it appears today. Constructed
at the behest of George St Lo, who was resident Commissioner from 1703–14, its most
outstanding feature is that of a magnificent ceiling painted at the head of the main staircase
and which depicts Neptune crowning Mars. Supposedly it was originally painted for the
great cabin of *Royal Sovereign* and transferred at a time when this vessel had been brought into
Chatham either for a rebuild in 1728 or when she was broken up in 1768.

time of its inception through to the early years of the nineteenth century, this was not
how things were arranged. Instead, the applied management system was confused,
directionless and top heavy. Furthermore, it was impossible for anyone to be held
entirely accountable for shortcomings in areas of dockyard output, as often there were
two named managers responsible for undertaking similar duties.

As to why this should be, and to offer a partial defence, this relates to the uniqueness of what was being achieved at this time. Nowhere else in the world, other than
the royal dockyards, was there any single industrial enterprise employing such a large
workforce. Between them, the six royal dockyards were employing, by the end of the
eighteenth century, over 10,000 labourers and artisans, with only the fighting forces
able to boast a number that was greater in total. In their efforts to direct and control
this massive workforce, the various managers of the dockyards were pioneers, working
to achieve something that no other business enterprise had ever been called upon to
undertake; as such, they developed both new systems of management and a methodology for measuring and improving efficiency. For achieving what they did, they should
be lauded. Mistakes made were prolific, with lessons often appearing unlearned.
Eventually however, albeit over a long period of time, reforms were introduced and
past failings obviated. Finally, by the end of the nineteenth century, the dockyards had
established an approach to management that was eventually borrowed and effectively
used in a great many other expanding industrial enterprises.

Standing at the pinnacle of naval administration and charged with overseeing all matters relating to the Navy (including the dockyards) was the Board of Admiralty. At one time, the duties of the Board had been performed by an individual holding the title of Lord High Admiral or directly by the Crown. The Duke of York had himself been appointed Lord High Admiral for life, a post he continued to hold upon succeeding to the throne as James II. However, from 1689 onwards, and with a few brief interludes, the Board had become a permanent feature of naval administration. Consisting of a First Lord and six subordinates, the Board of Admiralty regularly met at the Admiralty offices situated on the west side of Whitehall. As an organised body, the Board of Admiralty had overall responsibility for the preparation and disposition of fleets, being additionally concerned with the supply and manning of warships, together with the appointment and promotion of particular officers. Some of these powers however, were indirectly exercised, particularly with regard to the dockyards.

It was the Navy Board that oversaw the dockyards on behalf of the Admiralty, having to submit regular reports to the superior Board. A body of long standing, the Navy Board actually predated the Board of Admiralty, having been originally established during the reign of Henry VIII. As to the precise responsibilities of the Navy Board, these were, from time to time, laid down in written form, with the Instructions of 1662 of particular significance. James, Duke of York, had promulgated these when he had held the office of Lord High Admiral, and listed twenty duties for which the principal officers and Commissioners of the Navy Board were responsible. These confirmed the Navy Board's overall responsibility for the material condition of the fleet, the building, fitting out and repairing of ships, the administration and maintenance of the dockyards, the purchase of naval stores and the appointment and dismissal of dockyard workers.

Originally, the London offices of the Navy Board were in Seething Lane, with a move to larger offices in Somerset House completed in 1789. As with the Admiralty, the Navy Board held regular meetings, usually for purposes of making policy, approving expenditure and justifying their actions to the Admiralty. Central to the workings of the Navy Board were the principal officers who, according to the Instructions of 1662, actually comprised the Navy Board. Although each was an expert in their own right and appointed because of past accumulated experience, none had overall control of a particular area, the Board adopting a consensus approach to decisions taken, so undermining the possibility of any one single officer being held accountable for any actions taken. This was in contrast to the Admiralty, where the First Lord could, and frequently did, overrule his colleagues. The senior officer of the Navy Board was the Comptroller, commanded by the Instructions of 1662 'to lead his fellow officers as well as comptrol their actions', a phrase that fell far short of giving him absolute authority. Always drawn from among the ranks of senior naval captains, this provided him with a degree of status that helped him in the upholding of the terms of his office.

Of particular significance for the dockyards was the office of Surveyor, generally considered to be second in seniority to the Comptroller. Given responsibility for the design, construction and maintenance of ships, anything presented still required the approval of

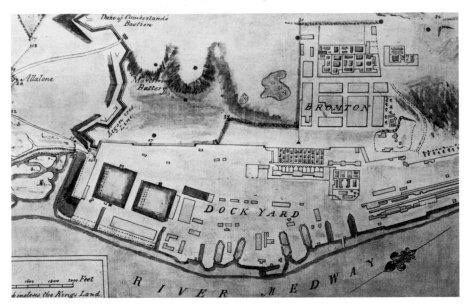

A general plan of the dockyard as it appeared in 1756. The north side of the yard is dominated by the two mast ponds while the ropery is still characterised by separated spinning and laying floors. Immediately outside the dockyard wall is the rapidly developing hamlet of Brompton, this providing housing, due to its close proximity, to a number of those who worked in the yard. Some of the finer houses of the period are still in evidence at Brompton.

the entire Board. Always appointed from among the senior shipwright officers within the royal dockyards, it was from Chatham that Sir Robert Seppings, generally reckoned to be one of the most successful holders of this post, was appointed. It was from the office of the Surveyor that the sheer draught or plans of any new vessel originated, being dispatched to Chatham or an alternate building yard. Any new class of vessel first had to be approved by the Surveyor, while the design or alteration to any vessel might well be the product of the Surveyor himself. Apart from responsibility for ships, the Surveyor also concerned himself with the raw materials needed for a successful construction and repair programme, together with the design of buildings and the overall layout of a yard. An obvious weakness of this system was that a trained shipwright would need to be able to direct himself in this diverse range of skills. Further to this, by always being appointed from among those already employed within the royal dockyards, it meant that the appointee rarely had an appreciation of advances made within some of the commercial building yards and which could be applied to the naval dockyards.

Other members of the Navy Board who had a particularly close connection with the dockyards were the Controller of Storekeepers' Accounts, the Extra Commissioners appointed to the Board, and the Clerk of the Acts. The first of these, the Controller of Storekeepers' Accounts, had most of his attention directed to the overseeing of stores supplied to the dockyards, ensuring their quality and proper distribution. It was to his office that the Storekeepers of each dockyard were supposed to submit their regular accounts. As to the Extra Commissioners, whose numbers varied according to the demands placed on the Navy Board at any point in time, they had no precise duties, being there to support the other officers of the Board. As such, they might be involved with either the Storekeeper or Surveyor and were occasionally called upon to visit the dockyards and report on particular issues or problems that had emerged or were under consideration. Finally, the Clerk of the Acts was, as much as anything, a secretarial post, with all instructions from the Navy Board passing through his office. During the seventeenth century, when one such post holder included Samuel Pepys, this post had carried with it principal officer status. Over time the post underwent changes, including occasional suppression, with the holder of the office becoming a servant of the Board rather than a voting member. In recognition of the changed status, the office holder, who supervised all of the clerks of the Navy Office, eventually acquired the title of Secretary.

Between the Navy Board and Admiralty there existed an occasional strained relationship that would contribute to an overall hindering of managerial efficiency. Consequently, the system of having two Boards overseeing the affairs of the Navy was sometimes presented as one of the failings of the system. Quite the opposite, however, it was a very real strength, the Admiralty not being the obvious body to handle the intricacy of matters associated with ship construction, maintenance and repair. Instead, the Board of Admiralty needed to give attention to strategy and direction without being sidelined by background detail.

In reality, the problem was that of the inferior Board having acquired too much authority, able to ignore and challenge the superior Board. Underpinning this ability to reject Admiralty requirements was the simple fact of the appointed officers of the Navy Board being secure for life with removal, even by an irate Board of Admiralty, quite impossible.

With the Admiralty unable to remove those who had been given the task of overseeing the dockyards, individual personality differences became a feature of the more serious clashes that occurred between the two Boards. In addition, and also helping discourage full cooperation, was that of those composing the two Boards having both differing backgrounds and objectives they wished to meet. Frequently, Navy Board members had been involved in administration for decades, while those in the Admiralty had a more recent association with the fighting side of the Navy. In the words of Mahan, writing in 1908:

Samuel Pepys. A regular visitor to the dockyard during the late seventeenth century, he was a senior member of the Navy Board, holding the office of Clerk of the Acts.

The military man having to do the fighting, considers that the chief necessity; the administrators equally naturally tends to think the smooth running of the machine the most admirable quality.[1]

That this proved very much the case with members of the Navy Board is partly shown by their apparent stubbornness concerning Admiralty requirements for an increase in the size of warships during the time of the War of Austrian Succession (1740–48). For the Admiralty, such an increase in size was the means to acquire greater fighting efficiency; for the Navy Board it was a matter of simple inconvenience. Apart from anything else, each dockyard would have to hold in store additional sets of equipment, while dry docks would have to be increased in size. Mahan, once again, says of the naval administrator, that he:

> Tends to over value the orderly routine and observance of the system by which it receives information, transmits orders, checks expenditure, files returns, and, in general, keeps with the service the touch of paper; in short the organization which has created for facilitating its own labours.[2]

Even the fighting man, once caught up in administration, can also succumb to some of the attached dangers, as seems to have happened with Sir Andrew Hamond, Comptroller of the Navy Board in 1801. Although a former 'dashing' commander of the seventy-four-gun *Roebuck*, he seriously clashed with the Board of Admiralty and, in particular, its first Lord, John Jervis, Earl of St Vincent. John Markham, a close companion of St Vincent, but one who had also served under Hamond, commented upon how the latter had seemingly switched his loyalty:

> As the representative of the Navy Board, he soon quarrelled with Lord St Vincent, and this representative of routine and circumlocution equally disliked the proceedings of the junior lords. With a character deteriorated, and judgement warped and dwarfed by years passed in public office, the jobbing old Comptroller was a very different man compared with the dashing captain of the *Roebuck*.[3]

In an attempt to bring pressure to bear on the Navy Board, the Admiralty would occasionally resort to the use of official inspections, known as visitations, with the First Lord or his secretary writing up the findings. During these visitations the First Lord, accompanied by members of the Navy Board, would inspect each yard. In theory, these inspections were supposed to be conducted annually, but in reality they were very infrequent. One particular visitation, carried out in 1749 and falling hard on the heels of a previous visitation held a mere sixty-three years earlier, concentrated on the failings of the various officers of the yards. Numerous shortcomings were uncovered, these including the employment of too many aged workers, allowing of underage apprentices, failing to properly oversee repair and building works and deliberate fraud. One issue remarked on was that of Storekeepers and the irregularity with which they were submitting their accounts to the Navy Board:

The general neglect of the storekeepers in not transmitting their accounts to your office [the Navy Board], surprised us, and requires immediate redress; and we cannot help observing that you should have represented this failure in the execution of their duty to us, that we might have removed those who had been most negligent, which we are now determined to do unless they immediately transmit their accounts to you that are in arrears.[4]

At Chatham, members of the visitation enquired as to when the Storekeeper had last submitted his accounts and were informed that they 'were three years and a half in arrears'.[5]

Under the Earl of Sandwich, who held the post of First Lord from 1771–82, a more systematic series of visitations were undertaken, with these also giving attention to the work of the officers. It seems that the Storekeepers, despite the observations of 1749, were still no better at presenting their accounts, with Sandwich requiring that Standing Order 569 should be circulated, this to the Storekeeper at Chatham together with those at the other yards. The standing order referred to the earlier visitation and reminded the Storekeepers that they were still not submitting their quarterly accounts:

These are to direct and require you to complete your accounts, abstracts and balances to 31 December last … and to continue sending them at the expiration of each quarter.

Sandwich was to note that the shipwright officers, both at Chatham and the other yards, operated as if they were independent of the Navy Board and often countermanded the instructions of that Board:

Esteeming themselves better judges and being solicitous to be considered among the men as their advocates and patrons against the Navy Board; hence they have ever exercised a power of granting many undue indulgences, particularly taking in, and continuing many unfit persons under pretext of charity, or for other reasons. They also misemploy many of the men, excusing their favourites from the most laborious work, conniving at the negligence and indolence of the people [workforce] in general, in order to make themselves popular among them.[6]

Of one particular officer at Chatham it was noted:

It does not appear that the chaplain of this yard has done any duty for several years past, though he receives his pay and four pence from the ordinary and had two of the guard ships.[7]

The visitations led by Sandwich also gave attention to the supply and storage of timber. It seems that the methods adopted for storing this vital and expensive commodity had changed little since Ollivier's spying mission some thirty years earlier. In May 1771, Sandwich and the other members of the Board of Visitation, while at Chatham:

Took a view of the timber, plank and thick stuff in the yard, observing all the plank to be laid on the flat and in high piles which is the worst method for seasoning and preserving it; that great party of the rough timber is laid in 2 and 3 tiers high; although there are many vacant spaces in the yard.[8]

As a direct result proposals were made for a number of seasoning sheds, designed with interior racks and louvred gables, which admitted a free circulation of air while keeping out the rain. The Navy Board, however, failed to cooperate; pointing out that insufficient space within the yards precluded the erection of such new structures. Sandwich, though, was able to counter this argument, pointing out the most obvious locations. At Chatham, the original seasoning shed was to have been 500ft in length, but eventually consisted of four smaller sheds, the largest of which measured 100ft. A map of the dockyard dated 1772 indicates three to have been completed by this particular date, with only the site of a fourth marked out.[9] The final shed was to be completed in 1774:

The foundation of the new seasoning shed, which completes the proportion of sheds, that are deemed sufficient for use of this yard, is now just finished, and the whole building will be erected, and filled in [during] the course of this summer.[10]

Despite these new sheds, the older method of storing timber was by no means abandoned. A point noted during the 1773 visitation to Chatham:

As we have observed that the seasoning sheds are in great forwardness, and some of them completed and fit for the reception of thick stuff, planks and knees we are very sorry to find that several parcels still lye abroad exposed to the weather, we direct you to cause the whole to be collected and put into the sheds as far as they are now and may hereafter be ready to receive them.[11]

In addition to the timber seasoning sheds, a series of standing orders was also issued in order to ensure the better use of timbers. One, in particular, also affected the storage of timber, with it being declared that two thirds of the timber should, in future, be stored in a sawn state, while knees should be shaped as soon as they arrived in the yard.[12]

The resident Commissioner was often caught in the crossfire between the two Boards. Appointed by the Navy Board, and also a member of that same Board, it was from this body that all his instructions and orders were supposed to emanate. Yet this did not prevent him receiving direct correspondence from the superior Board of Admiralty, this either seeking information or making suggestions as to a course of action to be followed. Adding to his difficulties was that of not undergoing any induction procedure upon first being appointed, with only a set of standing orders and the past correspondence of his predecessor to guide him.

It was this vagueness as to the duties of a newly appointed Commissioner that prompted Francis Hartwell, appointed to Chatham as Commissioner in April 1799, to communicate the following to his colleagues at the Navy Board:

> Never having received any particular instructions for my guidance as resident Commissioner of the Navy, I have endeavoured in every case, to conduct myself according to the records of my predecessors.[13]

Frequently the Admiralty urged the Navy Board to draw up more specific instructions, but nothing appears to have been done until June 1801. At that time a series of draft instructions were prepared, which were eventually distributed to each yard Commissioner and subsequently published as part of a more general report into the operation of the dockyards.[14]

One thing of which a Commissioner was certainly aware was his general lack of authority within the dockyard. He was unable to issue any instructions without the authority of the Navy Board, having to seek permission for even the most mundane matters. Thus agreeing to a local contract, the entering of additional workers, and even the docking and undocking of ships all had to be approved by the London office. Not surprisingly, it led to an immense degree of correspondence, with this sample letter, written by Charles Proby, Commissioner at Chatham from 1771 until 1799, indicative of just how little authority he actually possessed:

> Gentlemen – I have received your warrant to this yard to carry out the scheme of works for the present month as proposed; two warrants and a letter to supply a main and foretop to the *Arrogant*, to dispense with the absence of the *Meleager* for three months and not to send the new canvas and kersey therein mentioned to Sheerness, with a warrant to the latter to receive a main and foretop from Chatham for the *Arrogant*.[15]

In fact, the major function of the Commissioner was that of keeping the Navy Board informed of all events occurring within the dockyard, this through a regular stream of letters to the Navy Office that contained information as to the progress of vessels repairing or under construction, notice of petitions submitted and reference to incidents such as theft of stores, reported grievances or local fires, when a dockyard engine might have been in attendance. According to the codified instructions of 1801:

> He [the Commissioner] is to make his constant residence in the dockyard in order to his always being in readiness to receive and see executed all orders from the Admiralty and Commissioners of the navy relating to the service of the navy and not to absent himself from the post without permission first had to that purpose in writing from the Admiralty.[16]

The officers' offices. Now known as the Admiral's Office and constructed in 1795, this was the building set aside for the various administrators of the yard with rooms also being used by the various clerks attached to each of the principal officers.

If the Commissioner had authority in any one area, this was with regard to his supervision of the workmen within the yard, where he had the right to appoint, discharge and chastise labourers and artisans. However, with respect to the officers, this same level of authority simply did not exist. Instead, his only recourse with an officer was that of issuing a severe reprimand. To this, however, should be added the right of a Commissioner to recommend any officer for promotion and this, in itself, might encourage a greater level of efficiency among those beneath the rank of Commissioner.

Despite his seeming lack of authority, the Commissioner was well rewarded. Apart from anything else, he was accommodated, at no cost to himself, in the attractive three-storey house that stood slightly back from the main working area of the yard, but close enough for him to observe the general comings and goings of the yard in general. Helping to secure his privacy within the yard was that of it having an extensive walled garden. As to his overall income, a parliamentary enquiry found that Commissioner Proby, in the year 1784, received the grand sum of £624. The bulk of this was an annual salary of £500 with the rest coming from various allowances and permitted expenses. In addition, all coal and candles consumed by his family were funded by the Navy Office as also were any alterations and repairs to the house.

As to how successful a Commissioner was in the carrying out of his duties, confused as they were, this often depended on the character of the man. Charles Proby showed himself to be reasonably enlightened in that he allowed £50 annually to the poor of Chatham and made numerous other charitable donations, while also attempting both to understand the workforce and not cocoon himself within that grand dockyard house. When meting out punishments to those caught in acts of theft Proby did not always seek out the harshest form of punishment, while he would also help diffuse tension during a dockyard dispute. His successor, Francis Hartwell, was much more elitist, removing himself from undue closeness to those of lower status. Within a few months of his arrival in Chatham in 1799, he requested a small railing outside the Commissioner's House, this to prevent artisans from assembling too close. As regards the parish church, he made one further request:

The seat in the gallery of Chatham church appropriated to the use of the resident Commissioner and fitted up at the expense of the government, being extremely exposed to the opposite side, I am to request you will authorise me to give orders to the purveyors of this yard to purchase a rod and curtain to be put up in front of the seat, the estimate of which is about eleven pounds.[17]

In general, the workforce had a great deal of respect for the Commissioner. It was normal, upon the retirement or departure of this superior officer of the yard, for those employed in the yard to offer some sort of farewell gesture. Even the elitist Hartwell, who remained at the yard for a mere twenty-two months, being appointed to the Navy Board in January 1801, was the subject of one such gesture. On 16 January, the *Kentish Chronicle* reported:

The officers and workmen were ranged from his house to the yard gates on both sides of the way, the young men took the horses from his carriage and insisted on drawing it, which they did through the gates, half way along the dock lane, and would have drawn it to Rochester, but he treated they would not.

As to the real centre of power within the dockyard, this was in the hands of the principal officers, of whom there were five: Master Shipwright, Master Attendant, Storekeeper, Clerk of the Cheque and Clerk of the Survey. However, to this group might be added the Clerk of the Ropeyard, a post that was sometimes viewed as being of principal officer status. As with the Commissioner, the respective duties of these officers were not written down, each new appointee having to review the work of his predecessor to discover the true nature of the duties they were to perform. One thing that was straightforward was their relationship with the Commissioner, receiving from him their instructions from the Navy Board. For this purpose, each officer attended a regular morning meeting with the Commissioner, during which the newly arrived orders and warrants from London would be distributed. This was a useful occasion as it was also followed by a discussion as to the best methods of coordinating any work that involved more than one department. For the Commissioner, it permitted him to be fully informed of the activities of the principal officers allowing him to report more accurately to the Navy Board on all matters relating to the work that they had instructed to be carried out in the dockyard.

Of the five principal officers, the Master Shipwright was undoubtedly the most important. Not only was he responsible for overall supervision of the shipwrights but also all those other trades connected with the repair and building of ships and which included caulkers, sawyers and house carpenters. Additionally, the general running of the yard was his responsibility and for this purpose both labourers and scavelmen were placed under his charge. Specifically, the Master Shipwright took responsibility for overseeing the building, repair and refitting of all ships together with the surveying of any newly arrived vessels. Launchings, dockings and undockings also fell within the Master Shipwright's area of authority, with the codified instructions of 1806 calling upon the Master Shipwright as follows:

You are to be constant in your personal attendance at the launching, undocking, grounding, and graving of all ships, and diligently apply yourself to the execution and dispatch
of all works carrying on in your department, whether in building or repairing of ships.[18]

Sitting less comfortably on the shoulders of the Master Shipwright was the responsibility for all work performed in connection with the repair, replacement and
construction of new buildings within the yard. Patently unsuited for such a task, the
Master Shipwright had absolutely no training in these duties. Indeed, this situation had
sometimes brought considerable financial loss to the Navy Board, Master Shipwrights
often overestimating costs. However, it also explains why a number of the buildings
of the dockyard have internal support structures that would appear more at home on
a warship than in a dockside work area, with the wheelwright's shop in the dockyard at Chatham employing deck beams to support the roof. To remove the Master
Shipwright from this particular task, in 1777 the Admiralty, on the recommendation of
the Navy Board, appointed John Marquand, a civil engineer, to supervise all naval civil
building contracts. Although he was to hold office only until 1786, Marquand would
have been involved with the design of the still extant Anchor Wharf Storehouse at
Chatham, while another task given to him was that of overseeing all work connected
with construction of the Marine Barracks built alongside Dock Road and immediately adjoining the dockyard. In May 1777 the Admiralty reported:

Judging that nothing is more likely to contribute to the well performance of the
building intended for Marine Barracks at Chatham, than the appointing a person
properly qualified to superintend and oversee the carrying on of the said work, and
to give his constant attendance thereat.[19]

However, the idea of separating the office of Surveyor from that of designing and
constructing civil buildings within the dockyard was not totally abandoned. In 1796,
the Admiralty established the post of Inspector General, with Samuel Bentham, the
appointed holder of the office, heading the briefly existent department of Navy
Works. Bentham's instructions from the Admiralty were mainly guided by a desire to
see increased use of steam machinery being brought into the yards. While the arrangement had much to commend it, the fact of it being an Admiralty imposition meant
that it was greeted by considerable Navy Board resistance. Only upon the department
being transferred to the Navy Board, with Bentham joining the Navy Board as Civil
Architect and Engineer, did cohesion begin to be established. Undoubtedly, though,
Bentham was still tainted by his earlier associations with the Admiralty, resulting in
an early abolition of his post and the appointment of Edward Holl as Surveyor of
Buildings, although without a seat on the actual Board. Both Bentham and Holl are
significant in the progression of building works at Chatham, with Bentham initiating
work on a revolutionary saw mill and Holl responsible for overseeing its completion,
while providing designs for both the chapel and Admiral's Office.

Returning to the post of Master Shipwright, promotion to this office was, theoretically, open to all shipwrights employed in the dockyard. In reality however, only shipwrights whose apprenticeship had been served under an existing Master Shipwright were likely to reach such an exalted position. Indeed, such a situation was akin to a type of eighteenth-century class barrier. Master Shipwrights tended to be selective in their choice of apprentices while they also expected to be paid a lump sum in the form of a fee, usually given by parents, which was in the area of twenty guineas. All of this effectively prevented long-range social mobility occurring through the dockyard promotion structure. Even given this, it would not be possible to acquire the rank of Master Shipwright at Chatham without having gained considerable experience in other yards, Master Shipwrights tending to have held office in several other yards before arriving at Chatham. In the case of Israel Pownall, who held the office from 1775–79, he had previously been an Assistant Master Shipwright at Chatham before going on to serve as Master Shipwright at Sheerness (1755), Woolwich (1755–62) and Plymouth (1762–75) prior to his return to Chatham.

Working in close cooperation with the Master Shipwright was the Master Attendant. He was the principal officer responsible for all vessels held in the Ordinary and had under his authority the sail makers and riggers of the dockyard. Another aspect of his work was that of maintaining all buoys and mooring points together with appointing the pilots who were responsible for moving vessels between the yard and the entrance of the Medway. It was essential that the Master Attendant and Master Shipwright worked in close cooperation, for they really shared two halves of the same job. While the Master Attendant maintained the vessels in the Ordinary and retained a gang of shipwrights for this very purpose, he also had to allow shipwright officers on board those ships to carry out exhaustive surveys. Additionally, when it was necessary to dock a vessel, both the Master Shipwright and the Master Attendant had to agree upon dates and times so that the officers under the Master Attendant might bring the vessel to the dock, with those workmen under the Master Shipwright actually bringing her through the dock gates. Instructions issued to the Master Attendant stated:

> You are to attend to the docking, grounding, and graving of all ships, by day or night, and you are to take charge of them whilst transporting from and to their moorings, whether for docking or any other purpose, causing the proper officers and people of the ordinary, with the riggers if necessary, to give their attendance on all such occasions.[20]

Also, if a ship was refitting, it was necessary for the Master Shipwright and the Master Attendant to cooperate, with the latter instructed that:

> When a ship is bringing forward to commission, you are to apply to the Master Shipwright, in order to obtain the probable time when she may be completed; and you are carefully to keep pace with him in providing and fitting the rigging stores, agreeably to the Establishment.[21]

The remaining principal officers of the dockyard all headed clerical departments, taking responsibility for a wide range of administrative matters. None had any technical expertise, being appointed from among the senior clerks employed in either the Navy Board or Admiralty. Most senior was the Clerk of the Cheque, the officer charged specifically with keeping the yard pay and muster books:

> All artificers, and workmen of every description employed in the yard are to be mustered by you or your clerks, every time they come into the yard to work, and also upon their leaving it at night.[22]

It was from the muster books that pay could be assessed, with the Clerk of the Cheque's office carrying out the necessary calculations.

As for the Storekeeper and Clerk of the Survey, both were responsible for the distribution and safekeeping of stores: the Storekeeper only for items used within the area of the dockyard and the Clerk of the Survey for those destined for ships either in the Ordinary or being prepared for service. Neither was to release stores without a note signed by the respective officers under whom requisitioned material was to be used, and both were to accept returned unused items. Since the Instructions of 1662 the Storekeeper, in particular, was charged with the protection of all stores from such 'waste as decay, stealth and embezzlement'.

Finally, the Clerk of the Rope House was technically not a principal officer but was often considered as such. In common with the principal officers he reported directly to the Commissioner, having a regular meeting that was separate from the other officers. Given entire responsibility for all matters associated with rope making, his domain, the ropeyard, was completely separate from the rest of the yard, with the Clerk of the Ropeyard also responsible for his own accounts, the mustering of the ropeyard workforce and all materials used by the rope makers.

As a group the principal officers, including the Clerk of the Rope House, were clearly set apart from the rest of the dockyard. Other than the Commissioner, they received higher salaries than anyone else in the yard, together with free accommodation. It was for them that a number of terraced houses were built, these close to the outer wall of the dockyard and near the Commissioner's own house. As for salaries, these were all established in 1696 with each receiving £200 annually but with additional fees also allowed. The Master Shipwright, for instance, claimed a fee when taking on new apprentices and a premium on the appointment of a new clerk to his office. Also, as regards clerks, of whom the Master Shipwright at Chatham was allowed five, he was entitled to half of their received income. Finally, he received from the Navy Board a customary present upon the launching of each new ship, this in the form of a piece of plate 'or money in lieu of' and varying according to the size of the vessel. In all, therefore, during the year 1784, the Master Shipwright at Chatham, Nicholas Phillips, received the total sum of £508. Other principal officers also received total yearly incomes well in excess of their actual salaries. In 1801 all

The timber seasoning sheds that were constructed, by order of the Earl of Sandwich, during the 1770s and which still exist in the dockyard.

fees and gratuities were abolished, but the principal officers at that time received a considerable salary increase as compensation.

It has already been noted that the dockyard at Chatham had an overwhelming surplus of managers. Among the principal officers there was clearly room for a reduction; as has been shown, the Storekeeper and Clerk of the Survey had posts that were identical in nature, differing only as to whether the stores issued were destined for the dockyard or the Ordinary. In addition, the Clerk of the Ropeyard had duties that could easily be absorbed elsewhere, with both the Storekeeper and Master Shipwright well suited to dividing his tasks between them. However, in terms of the number of inferior officers (the name given to all managers in the dockyard below that of the Commissioner and principal officers), many of them undertook tasks that were fairly minor in nature. The number of tasks did not necessarily require the immensity of numbers actually carrying them out. Over time, and adding to the confusion as to who did what, more officers were introduced, with other levels of officer removed. As such, a detailed examination of each and every officer post would become tedious. To avoid this, a more brief reference will be given to that huge pool of personnel that existed at the inferior officer level.

It was the Master Shipwright's Department that had the greatest reserve of inferior officers, these consisting of, in order of seniority: two Assistant Master Shipwrights, a master of each trade, four foremen of shipwrights and numerous quartermen. Of these, the need for two assistants would appear a necessity, given the huge range of tasks performed by the Master Shipwright. Primarily, their duties were those of disseminating the instructions given to the Master Shipwright and taking a more supervisory role across the yard. As a reflection of their importance, each was allowed a terraced house in the dockyard and an annual salary of £100 with this increased to £360 in 1801. Over time, an Assistant Master Shipwright might expect promotion to the rank of Master Shipwright, but only after having served in a number of other yards for purpose of gaining experience. Rarely, however, did this experience encompass working in private yards, which only tended to be visited when such a yard was building a vessel for the Royal Navy and the work needed to be inspected.

The masters of each trade varied considerably in status. The Master Caulker, because of being charged with a large number of workers, was of similar status to the Assistant Master Shipwrights, receiving an identical salary and accommodation in the dockyard. At the other extreme however, there were some masters whose trade had such a small number employed within the yard, that their continuance on a salary not far short of that received by an Assistant Master Shipwright appeared somewhat disingenuous. Moving down the chain of command, the foremen of shipwrights were responsible for directly supervising the day-to-day activities of the shipwrights, with two serving afloat (the Ordinary) and two within the dockyard (the Extraordinary). Finally, the quartermen were each responsible for supervising a gang of twenty shipwrights, and were paid at a rate that was nearly always double the amount received by those they oversaw.

Of course, this list far from exhausts the number of inferior officers employed in the dockyard at Chatham during the eighteenth and early nineteenth centuries. Still remaining with the Master Shipwright's Department, there was the Boatswain of the Yard who was responsible for supervising the scavelmen and labourers. Receiving an annual salary of £80 he was given accommodation in one wing of the Main Gate, to ensure his availability for night time dockings. In addition there were measurers. They were responsible for measuring off work performed by the artisans of the yard who were not paid by the day, but by the amount of work achieved; this was known in the yards as task work. Moving away from the Master Shipwright's Department, inferior officers under the Master Attendant also included a number of trade masters, specifically the Master Rigger and Master Sailmaker. Under the Clerk of the Ropeyard there was but one master artisan, the Master Ropemaker. As for the Storekeeper and the Clerk of the Survey, inferior officers in their respective departments included cabin keepers and senior clerks. While cabin keepers were responsible for overseeing the distribution and safe keeping of stores, the senior clerk in each department oversaw the work of a small number of junior clerks. Finally, a senior clerk of inferior officer status also ran the Clerk of the Cheque's office.

This huge range of officers naturally became subject to criticism, particularly during the 1830s when the whole subject of dockyard expenditure was being minutely examined. Radical politicians in particular found no end of support when directing themselves to the need for dockyard reform, with the writers of the radical *Black Book* making the point in the following terms:

The expenditure in the Royal Dockyards and Arsenals is most lavish in storekeepers, clerks, chaplains, surgeons, measurers, master-attendant, master-shipwright and
others, many of whom are apparently kept up for mutual superintendence, and
forming a gradation of offices and multiplication of expense wholly unnecessary.
Not a single trade is carried on without a master; there is a master smith, bricklayer,
sailmaker, rigger, ropemakers, painter and others.[23]

Attempts at improving the system during the eighteenth century were fairly minimal. Although the Admiralty, the sole customer of the dockyard product, could
identify problems, it was unable to bring sufficient pressure to bear upon the Navy
Board to bring about any real improvements. Admittedly, through the enforcement
of an occasional visitation led by the First Lord, a few reforms were achieved, with
the Navy Board also initiating important amendments to the system. Upon the
appointment of the Earl of St Vincent to the Admiralty in 1801, matters very much
came to a head. An entrenched Navy Board, which at that time was pitched against
an Admiralty determined to bring about changes that it wished to dictate, created a
crisis situation in which the Admiralty, through the withholding of finance, forced
a series of stringent economies. Ultimately, this did more damage than good, with
Mahan, a leading naval theorist, commenting that 'when war broke out again, the
material of the navy in ships and stores was so deteriorated and exhausted as to
impair dangerously the efficiency of the fleets.'[24]

So contentious was the issue of dockyard management reform that it became the
major factor in the fall of the Whig government, under which St Vincent had served.
Some thirty years later, when the Whigs were returned to power with a secure
majority in parliament, they turned themselves on the Navy Board, determined
to take revenge for that earlier rebuke. On that occasion, the Whigs overstepped
the mark; by abolishing the Navy Board and introducing a series of far-reaching
changes, they inflicted a good deal of damage upon the efficient management of
the yards. But, in so doing, they further highlighted aspects of management that had
both worked and not worked in the past, allowing a more gradual series of reforms,
these dating to the late nineteenth century, that were to produce a coherent and
more workable system that sparkled in its efficiency and ability to achieve everything that was required and expected.

4

SHIPWRIGHTS, SCAVELMEN AND LABOURERS

Throughout the eighteenth century the numbers employed at Chatham dockyard, together with the numerous support facilities that included both the Ordnance Wharf and the victualling yard at Rochester, steadily increased. Most significant, of course, was the dockyard, which, at the beginning of the century, was employing a workforce of approximately 1,000. Admittedly, during the period of peace that followed the War of Spanish Succession (1702–14) the size of the workforce declined, having fallen to around 700 by the year 1718. After that it steadily began to rise again, and at the height of the Seven Years War (1756–63) the dockyard was employing a workforce in excess of 1,700. In 1770, a peacetime year, this figure had fallen back to 1,378 but within ten years, with the War of American Independence (1776–83) drawing to a close, it had once again exceeded a figure of 1,600. By 1800, the final year of the century and with the French Revolutionary War (1793–1802) still underway, over 2,000 were employed in the dockyard.[1]

In looking more closely at those numbers, three distinct groups of workers can be identified: artisans, skilled labourers and the unskilled. Not that those who made up the workforce recognised such a division, individually recognising themselves in terms of trade and labouring groups. As such, complicated hierarchies emerged, only broken during periods of intense wage demands in which the need for cooperation became paramount. Thus a shipwright had very little communication with members of other non-artisan groups. Invariably shipwrights apprenticed their own sons into the same trade, lived in a similar area of town and mixed socially only with other shipwrights. Overall, they considered themselves just a little superior to all other members of the workforce. Similarly, the unskilled labourers, who invariably emanated from a poorer part of town, frequented different hostelries and lived in areas made up from those of similar standing, also viewed themselves as distinct.

Shipwrights, through their immensity of skills, were at the very heart of the yard, with approximately 40 per cent of the yard workforce normally composed of those who made up this trade. Among tasks they undertook were those of assembling the frame of any vessel under construction, the laying of planks, interpreting the sheer draught, cutting templates and preparing the slipway. Throughout, of course, a good deal of lifting work was undertaken, but labourers who were attached to each shipwright gang moved many of the heavier timbers. Despite having undertaken an apprenticeship that lasted seven years, few shipwrights were anything more than artists – guided by 'rule of thumb' over qualities of exactness. For them, if it looked right, then it was right. Additionally, few shipwrights were literate, a point noted in several official reports.[2]

The basic work unit for the shipwright was the gang. At Chatham, this consisted of twenty men, plus apprentices, who were chosen through an annual shoal that was at one time held on Lady Day but moved to the end of the year in 1771. A shoal allowed each gang to be formed through a system by which the inferior officer charged with each gang, the quarterman, alternately chose those they most favoured to be part of the gang they oversaw. A good description of 'shoaling' was contained in a Navy Board warrant that was sent to each yard in March 1730. In referring to 'servants', the instructions were using this term for apprentices, while the 'double men' were those who had the dual skill of being both a shipwright and caulker. According to the issued warrant, the quartermen were to choose their respective gangs with:

> … the eldest quartermen making the first choice, beginning with the double men
> of one man with his servant, and then the next quarterman according to his senior-
> ity till each quarterman has chosen a man and a servant, and so continue until the
> double men and their servants are all chose, and then to begin again by the choice of
> a single shipwright and to go on until their gangs are complete.

As for the rationale behind the use of shoaling, the warrant explained that it was 'for the better keeping of the shipwrights to their duty'. It was stated that, by removing the pretence that the workmen in one gang were 'not so good as those in other gangs' it would prevent quartermen using this as an excuse for his gang not working as well as another.[3]

Caulkers were considered next in order of seniority, receiving the same basic daily wage as a shipwright. Ensuring any vessel brought into dry dock was watertight, old rope that had been untwisted and separated by oakum boys was rolled in the palm of the hand and applied to the seams of the hull with the help of a caulking iron. Once pushed beneath the surface, the seam was filled or 'payed up' with pitch. Not that the task of a caulker started at this point, in the case of vessels that required re-caulking, the old caulking had first to be removed by means of a 'rake' or 'hoe', an iron instrument of about 12in and shaped rather like a foreshortened 'S'. As with a shipwright, the very safety of a ship depended upon the skills of the caulker, for just the right amount of oakum had always to be used – too little and the vessel would leak; too much and the seams would spring.

Another of the highly skilled maritime trades was that of the sail maker. Working in and around the sail loft, sail makers were responsible for the manufacture of sails and other canvas items used on board ships. Basic equipment consisted of a bench, stretching hooks, a twine spool, sail stabbers, needles, seam rubbers and a fid. All work was carried out by hand, with much of the sail-making process conducted by the sail maker seated at his bench. The first stage however, was for a full size sail to be drawn onto the floor of the loft with the corners of the sail marked with a sail pricker driven into the floor. Sailcloth could then be placed over and above this outline, subsequently being cut to the right size and shape. Additional material was also allowed, so that adequate tabling or a hem might be included. Once cut, the sail would again be pegged to the floor and seam rubbers would be used to create sharp folds for the hem. Later, fids would be introduced for the purpose of opening up various holes for boltropes and similar.

Apart from the manufacturing of sails, the Chatham sail makers were also called upon to survey ships held in the Ordinary, repair the sails of returning warships and produce such canvas items of furniture as dodgers and cots which were requisite items on board a sailing man-of-war. Perhaps August 1778 represents a typical period for the Chatham sail makers. In that month, the Navy Board was informed of the exact work being undertaken by each of the thirty-two sail makers then employed. The largest number, sixteen, were employed upon making new sail suits, with nine of this number working on a mainsail for *Wasp*, an eight-gun sloop. A further eleven sail makers were engaged in the repair of a topsail and staysail, three in surveying the twenty-eight-gun *Shark* and two in making canvas furnishings for the cutter *Wells*.

One of the least pleasant of the working environments was the smithery, frequently engaged in the manufacture of anchors. Here, the heat was often unbearable with the smiths themselves allowed eight pints of strong beer each day for the purpose of quenching an undoubted thirst. The No.1 Smithery was constructed from 1806–08 and has recently been refurbished to house an important new exhibition that includes the chance to glimpse some of the original forges once used in this building.

Particularly demanding in terms of the physical effort required was the trade of anchor smith, this through the need to wield huge hammers and being in close proximity to an unbearably hot forge. During the summer months the large anchor fires had to be abandoned, as few smiths were capable of withstanding the intense heat being emitted. Work for the anchor smith consisted of making the various parts of an anchor, namely a shank, two arms and a ring with their flukes. Additionally they forged bolts and one or two of the non-specialist metal items used in ship construction. As for the anchor, once the separate parts had been forged these would be welded round the stock – two pieces of oak bolted together and secured by four iron hoops. Largest of the anchors, and these sometimes weighed as much as five tons, were the giant sheet anchors. Additionally though, the Chatham anchor smiths were responsible for the bower anchors and the much smaller kedge and grappling irons.

Probably no artisan worked as hard as the anchor smiths, expected to arrive in the yard before the main body of workers to get the fires started. From then on, they spent the entire day in a most unhealthy atmosphere. For this reason, it was difficult to augment their numbers, with apprentices hard to acquire. As a result, many of the anchor smiths who were employed in the yard were found as a result of newspaper advertisements and came from as far afield as Birmingham, Suffolk and the Isle of Wight.[4] Seemingly typical of such anchor smiths was Israel Durnford. According to the 1779 description book of artificers he first entered the yard in November 1779, having served a blacksmith apprenticeship in Dorsetshire. At that time aged twenty-seven, it can be assumed that he had worked elsewhere prior to taking up his dockyard post. He was to remain at the dockyard until his death in January 1806.[5]

Three other artisan trades, those of bricklayer, house carpenter and joiner, were employed in the yard but were engaged in maintaining the fabric of the yard itself. House carpenters and joiners were frequently employed in the repair of timber docks, while all three tradesmen would be used in repairing and maintaining buildings within the yard.[6] Between 1783 and 1790, for instance, a number of additional bricklayers were recruited for new building work to the ropery.[7] On other occasions, bricklayers, house carpenters and joiners were brought into the shipbuilding programme itself. Brick makers, for instance, were responsible for paving the galley as protection against fire, while house carpenters and joiners were used in the repair of storerooms on board warships.[8] As with many other artisans, these tradesmen were frequently trained within the yard. In November 1772, the thirty-nine joiners at Chatham included four apprentices, the sixty-three house carpenters had three apprentices and the thirteen bricklayers had three apprentices.[9]

Another group of artisans were the wheelwrights, plumbers and block makers. All were employed in particularly small numbers with the allowed complement at Chatham standing at two wheelwrights, one plumber and two block makers. None of these had apprentices at the time of the November 1772 report.[10] Wheelwrights and plumbers, of course, were not specifically maritime trades, with the former retained for the purpose of maintaining carts in and around the yard, while plumbers undertook work on pipes

Various workshops around the yard once specialised in various tasks associated with the building and repair of sailing ships. At the northward end of the yard, and still extant, are a wheelwrights' shop (dating to the end of the eighteenth century) and a range of mast houses (1753–56).

and fittings associated with water supply to some of the building and manufacturing areas. Blockmakers, on the other hand, were responsible for repairing pulley blocks used on board sailing ships, the blocks all manufactured by the Southampton firm of Taylor. Blocks were relatively easily repaired, the only required equipment being a bench, a lathe and several smaller tools such as a maul, gauge and burr.

One other artisan should be mentioned at this point: the dockyard brazier. While much of the brass used within the dockyard was manufactured under contract, its upkeep was the task of a permanently employed brazier. Apart from dealing with most of the decorative brass work, much of it restricted to the houses of the senior offices, this individual had also to maintain the dockyard lamps. At night he lit each of the lanterns while replenishing wicks and oil. One particularly long-serving holder of this post was Daniel Wilkins who was appointed in September 1781. Serving his apprenticeship in the town of Chatham, he was recorded as being a freeman of the borough of Maidstone.[11]

Two final groups of artisans were the riggers and spinners. Despite neither having a recognised apprenticeship system within the dockyard, proficiency instead being gained through seven years of employment, both trades deserve to be seen as of artisan status. Indeed, the Description Book of Chatham Artificers actually includes a reference to riggers but fails to include spinners. This in itself is surprising. Both trades required an equal amount of skill, with the rigger having to know a great deal about sails, ropes and seamanship, being responsible for the positioning of both the running and standing rigging of warships held in the Ordinary. The spinners, on the other hand, had to have considerable 'feel' for any ropes being manufactured, always introducing the right amount of hemp, yarn or strand. Moreover, should either fail to perform his task properly then an entire warship could meet with a disastrous end.

Spinners, who were employed within the area of the ropeyard, were responsible for spinning newly hatchelled hemp into yarn while eventually laying strands into rope. As for the skills required, these are best illustrated by reference to *A Universal Dictionary of the Marine*, an eighteenth-century work written by William Falconer while serving on *Glory*, a thirty-two-gun frigate laid up in the Medway. He describes the manufacture of cables – the heaviest of four types of rope produced at Chatham:

> A cable ought to be neither too [sic] twisted too much nor too little; as in the former state it will be extremely stiff and difficult to manage; and in the latter, it will be considerably diminished in its strength.

Falconer also goes on to indicate how important it was that spinners were fully cognisant with the tasks they had to perform: 'Many good ships have been lost only on account of a deficiency in this important article.'[12]

Turning to the second distinct group employed within the dockyard, that of the skilled labourers, these were the sawyers, scavelmen and teamsters. Between them, they undertook a series of specialist jobs that required only a minimal amount of training. As such, no apprenticeship or artisan status was attached, but each would be rewarded with a higher rate of pay and an increase in status over and above that of the ordinary labourer. Skills attached to these jobs were acquired over time, with entrants initially supervised by a more experienced worker.

Of the three semi-skilled tasks, that of sawyer seems to be the least desirable. Working as one of a pair, they spent their entire day sawing the huge timbers and planks required within the dockyard. Throughout the day, their centre of activity would be based around one of the many saw pits spread across the yard, with one man standing within the pit and the other above. Paid at first by the day and latterly by the amount of timber sawn, the work was nearly as gruelling as that of the anchor smith. Of the pair, the top man was paid the most, as he was the one responsible for directing the two-man saw and keeping it sharpened.

Scavelmen, usually drawn from among the ranks of the ordinary labourers, had acquired certain skills that helped them become more proficient in the running of the yard. They were the workers responsible for keeping the yard clean, opening and closing the docks, operating the pumps, digging out and cleaning the drains and removing ballast from ships about to enter dry dock.[13]

Finally, the teamsters, who worked as a pair, were responsible for looking after the heavy draught horses used for shifting the largest of timbers around the yard. Their tasks included care of the horses, maintenance of livery and controlling the horses while at work. Stables for these horses were located close to the offices' terrace.

Within the dockyard, approximately 20 per cent of the workforce was unskilled. Of these, most were labourers, although a few carried out more specific tasks such as hatchelling and pitch heating. Additionally, employment also existed for a number of boys who were engaged in the picking of oakum and the turning of the spinning and laying wheels in the rope yard. Of the ordinary labourers, primarily they were employed to collect requisite items from the stores, carry messages and support the shipwrights in the moving of timbers. However, storehouse labourers helped with specific stock within each storehouse, while the main occupation of those within the ropery was that of tarring the ropes and supplying the various needs of the spinners. Also within the Rope House were the hatchellers, who were responsible for hatchelling hemp fibres. Finally, pitch heaters worked alongside the caulkers, ensuring that there was a sufficient amount of heated pitch so that newly caulked hulls could be sealed.

Not surprisingly, levels of remuneration varied considerably between these various work groups, but other work-related factors, such as the length of the dockyard day, were identical. With respect to pay, two different rates existed: a day rate and payment by results. The former, which had been used to remunerate workers since Tudor times, was set at a less than generous level, especially when compared with those of similar trades employed outside of the naval dockyards, and remained virtually unchanged throughout the entire eighteenth century. As for payment by results, this was first introduced into the royal dockyards in 1758, but at that time restricted only to labourers and scavelmen. Known either as 'task work' or 'job work', according to whether it was new construction or repair work, it was not initially allowed to the skilled trades as there was a fear that it would encourage skimping. Only in 1775 was it finally allowed to virtually all classes of workers, with shipwrights at that time refusing to accept this method of payment for a further six years.[14] In addition to pay, whether at the day or piece rate, many workers were also entitled to the perquisite of 'chips'. This was the right to take from the yard small cuts of timber, that were of no further use in the shipbuilding and repair process, such bundles to compose of timber of no more than 3ft in length and to be carried out of the gate under the arm. It was generally recognised that these bundles were financially useful, often sold for 6d or more to town traders.[15] Alternatively, instead of the allowance of chips, the smiths were allowed to remove their moulds from the yard.

The basic day pay, which for shipwrights and caulkers stood at 2s 1d but fell to 1s 1d for labourers, was paid for the completion of a full 12-hour working day (6 a.m. to 6 p.m. in summer but less in winter) that included a 90-minute lunch break. In all, six days in every week were worked, with Sunday counted as a non-working day and Saturdays finishing an hour early. Periods of overtime were also permitted, these coming in 1½-hour and 5-hour units, the former being known as 'tydes' and the latter 'days'. The working of overtime was most frequent in the summer, with the dockyard authorities fully utilising the longer daylight hours. During emergencies, however, even winter evenings would be worked, with artisans and labourers employed by candlelight. As for holidays, these were, more or less, non-existent. Since 1715 only four had been allowed, these being the King's Birthday, Coronation Day, 5 November and Oak Apple Day (29 May). On such days, the workforce was employed until noon but received a full day's pay. At Chatham, but not all yards, it had become customary for the entire workforce to be offered a further day's holiday upon the launching of a ship.

The methods by which piece rates operated varied considerably between each group of worker. In most cases it was according to the size and type of product. This was particularly the case with mast making, boat building and sawyers, the range of finished items being limited. For other groups of workers, payments were more complicated. Scavelmen were frequently paid for amounts of ballast removed or lengths of drainage cut while spinners were paid so much for the length of yarn, strand or finished rope that was completed. Caulkers, where new work was known as 'stint' rather than task, had portions of work variously estimated, a recognition also existing that certain parts of a warship were more difficult to caulk. Most complicated however, was the working of piece rates when worked by shipwrights, vessels divided into twenty-five separate units, known as articles, with completion of an article leading to the

The tools of the caulking trade. Caulkers, of whom there were often nearly 100 employed in the yard, were responsible for ensuring the watertightness of a ship by driving quantities of oakum (old rope twisted and pulled apart) into the seams of planks in the ship's deck or side to prevent the entrance of water. Most important in the carrying out of this task was the mallet and various caulking chisels, all of which are to be seen in this picture.

payment of a fixed sum. Once completed, all work performed by 'task' or 'job' was assessed for payment by measurers, inferior officers specifically created upon the introduction of work by output rather than by the day. Piece rates represented a very real increase in wage levels but at no point completely displaced the use of day pay, with the latter continuing at an unchanged rate until the following century.

The one group of workers rarely paid piece rates were the anchor smiths. The Navy Board were more than aware of the exigencies of their work and did not expect smiths, when engaged in the manufacture of heavy anchors, to be paid by result. To compensate, the smiths were allowed an increase in their day rates, hammermen being allowed 12s per week when working on the twenty-hundredweight hammers.

Helping offset the relatively low wage that was paid to the dockyard worker, with piece rates also failing to bring about parity with those employed outside the yards, was that of continuous employment, job security and the availability of a pension following thirty years of continuous service. [16] Furthermore, the dockyard also provided workers with sick pay and access to the dockyard surgery. Outside of the dockyards, most employment was neither guaranteed nor permanent. While this might not matter to a young and able worker who was prepared to travel, this was a clear disadvantage to a family man or one who was ageing. The latter, in particular, found it especially difficult to secure alternative work should they become unemployed. In the royal dockyards, while there were lay-offs, these were comparatively rare. Indeed, the Navy Board preferred not to dismiss highly skilled artisans, for it was not always possible to re-employ them at short notice. The result was that Chatham dockyard, during peacetime years, was oversubscribed in the artisan trades, but to the Navy Board this was a preferable situation to lack of numbers at a time of rapid mobilisation. Most at risk were the unskilled. Ordinary labourers, for instance, were only employed for short periods, perhaps in the autumn, for unloading the ships that were bringing hemp for the ropery.

Within each of these work groups there was a clear sense of group consciousness, with its strength varying in direct proportion to the level of skill possessed by each group. Thus the shipwrights, the most skilled of the dockyard workers, showed a very high degree of group loyalty while the unskilled labourers formed a group in name only. Rope makers, smiths and sail makers were among other workers with a developed sense of individual work group consciousness, although none of these approached the shipwrights.

Helping ferment this consciousness was the interaction that occurred within the membership of those trades. This resulted from both living and working in a confined space, together with the traditions and culture of the group itself. The past successes of the group, the stories of which were passed from one generation to the next, showed the ability of groups to achieve sought-after goals, reinforcing intra-group loyalties. Even more important, however, was participation in a particular struggle, for a successful outcome would keep individual members permanently committed.

It was the eighteenth century industrial dispute which can most probably account for this strengthening of interpersonal group relationships. These disputes also created a strong group consciousness among the numerous artisan groups but, most noticeably, that of the shipwrights. Most of these disputes concerned various trade groups, with each, in turn, threatening to withdraw their labour knowing that a skill, in short supply, would make the Navy Board anxious to appease. Engaged as they were in the working of a military industrial complex, such pressure was most often brought during a wartime situation, when the chance of artisan success was greatly increased. The unskilled labourer, on the other hand, bereft of such skills, had no such bargaining position and rarely disputed with the Navy Board. Having, therefore, no tradition of group success, the dockyard labourer had only an insignificantly developed group consciousness.

For the shipwrights in particular, a distinct group consciousness was not simply restricted to the dockyard at Chatham. For them, there was an extended consciousness that encompassed those with this same skill and employed in the other five naval dockyards, this displaying itself in mutual support and frequent cooperation, both during industrial disputes and in other more general areas. These links were initially facilitated by the movement of shipwrights between yards, but formalised by frequent letters and messages circulated between the several shipwright groups. Even more interesting, however, was that this highly developed brand of group consciousness was not restricted to the royal dockyards but if necessary, might extend to supporting and receiving the support of those shipwrights employed within the private yards. In March 1795, for instance, the shipwrights at Chatham submitted a petition to the Navy Board requesting that an instruction to allow house carpenters to undertake work, normally performed by shipwrights, on board ships in the Ordinary be rescinded. In a show of support, the shipwrights of the Thames-side yards submitted their own petition to the Admiralty that supported the Chatham shipwrights.

Among the various artisan groups, there were also clearly established patterns of behaviour that were essential, both for the survival of the group and ensuring it could achieve prized goals. As such, the majority of group members accepted the need to conform, feeling it to be essential, if they, themselves, were to be adopted by that particular group. Failure to conform, and not all dockyard workers were totally integrated, would lead to the introduction of sanctions designed to correct any deviant pattern of behaviour. The most usual sanction, especially if a strike was in progress, was the use of violence, both actual and threatened. On occasions, for his own safety, the Navy Board might have to move a non-striking artisan to an alternative yard, to prevent his continued victimisation. Methods used by artisan groups to prevent a decline in support during a period of strike included mass demonstrations and frequent meeting of group members at selected hostelries. During the dispute over the matter of house carpenters being allowed to work 'afloat', the shipwrights would assemble early in the morning on Star Field and march, 'in a regular body', to the dockyard gate. This both maintained solidarity and strengthened the resolve of those considering a return to work. Star Field was chosen for assembly, as it was adjacent to the Star Inn on Chatham Hill, where the leaders of the strike, together with a good number of shipwrights, were usually to be found.

However, something else was also occurring among the workforce at Chatham during the eighteenth century: the creation of a much more extended group consciousness and one that was to eventually absorb all workers, irrespective of the skill they possessed. Perhaps the earliest sign of this took place in 1783, as a result of a Navy Board decision to impose more stringent rules on the carrying of 'chips' out of the yard. Whereas the ruling was that such bundles should be carried under the arm, the majority of those entitled to this perquisite were taking larger amounts by carrying bundles over the shoulder. Given that the enforcement of this rule affected all the timber working trades, and not just the shipwrights, it resulted in a degree of inter-trade consultation. However, at no point was leadership placed in the hands of any group other than the shipwrights, with the most important of these petitions, submitted by the shipwrights, suggesting a compromise solution, of artisans being allowed 'three pence a day in lieu of chips'.[17] Despite the unity fostered on this occasion, the workforce was unsuccessful in their wish to carry chips over the arm, this a result of the dispute taking place during a time of peace, with the country in no desperate need for the services of the dockyard artisan. Had the Navy Board attempted to force the issue one year earlier, with the war in America still undecided, a unified workforce threatening a strike would have achieved a very easy victory. But, of course, the Navy Board was aware of that, choosing to confront the issue only upon the conclusion of that particular war.

The emerging unity, as witnessed at the time of the dispute over the carrying of 'chips' out of the yard, was in sharp contrast to an earlier dispute, this taking place in August 1739, when the shipwrights failed in an endeavour to gain support from other artisan groups. On this occasion the issue was one that affected only shipwrights, with other artisan groups seeing no advantage to the lending of their support. An argument, of course, might have been made for those of other trades offering the shipwrights a favour on this occasion, tied to the returning of such a favour in the event of a later need. However, there is no evidence of such thinking. Instead, when fines were imposed upon five Chatham shipwrights, the Master Shipwright having concluded that they had performed insufficient work, this particular artisan group, in vehemently opposing this action, found themselves completely on their own. Nevertheless, the shipwrights still considered themselves to be in a strong position, war having recently broken out with Spain, and proclaimed a strike on 29 August. A picket line was established early in the morning, this to discourage both shipwrights and others entering the yard. According to a letter written by the Commissioner of the yard, Thomas Matthews, the rope makers were approached, but 'would not be stopped by them and are at their duty'. As for the sail makers, Matthews further reported that they also showed no inclination to provide support. Instead, the Master Sailmaker asked the shipwrights at the gate why they attempted to stop 'his people [as] they did not belong to them nor had they any grievance'. In response, and again according to Matthews, the shipwrights 'behaved with all the insolence imaginable'.[18]

Ultimately, the shipwrights at Chatham did not require the support of other artisan groups; their own peculiar industrial muscle, through the use of the strike weapon during a time of war, being sufficient to force the Navy Board to pursue a policy of pacification. A delegation from the Board arrived on the evening of 30 August and from Hill House they observed a number of shipwrights milling around the Main Gate. According to the Board minutes:

> They gave us an opportunity to talk to them; upon which they seemed much pleased at Our Coming; and on our answering them, that we would do them justice; they promised that they themselves would go to work, and give notice to as many as the workmen, as they should meet with.[19]

News of the Board's arrival soon had the desired effect as, early the following morning, most of the yard's shipwrights had gathered outside the dockyard gates. They were reluctant to enter until the two members of the Board had spoken with them, but upon being given the same assurances as on the previous evening, the shipwrights entered the yard.[20] Following a brief enquiry that included interviews with several of the yard officers, the delegates determined the fines to have been unfair and that too much had been asked of that one particular shipwright gang. In rescinding the fines, the delegates did add that the shipwrights had been 'extremely wrong' in not having gone to the Commissioner of the yard 'as they and all others ought to do, when they thought themselves injured'.[21]

A show of complete inter-trade unity was most certainly expressed on two clear occasions during the years of the French Revolutionary War (1793–1802). This was not unconnected with a general growth in political radicalism, with a particular coalescing factor being opposition to new legislation being discussed in parliament, known by some as the 'Convention Bills'. Between them, and once passed, they would make it illegal for political meetings to exceed fifty in number, unless a magistrate had been advised, while making it an offence to incite people to hate the established constitution. The introduction of the new laws had come as a direct consequence of a massive anti-government demonstration in London. The King, on his way to open parliament, had been assailed by shouts of 'Down with Pitt', 'No War' and 'No King', while a window in his carriage was shattered.

Among the advantages of working in the yard was the right to medical care in the event of an injury sustained while carrying out yards duties. Often this might involve transfer to a naval hulk moored in the Medway and converted to use as a hospital ship. However, following the end of the Napoleonic Wars, Melville Hospital was constructed close to the Main Gate and upon that area now occupied by the modern-day Melville Court.

Throughout the country numerous radical societies had come into being, including a branch of the London Corresponding Society that was formed in Brompton, within the very shadow of the dockyard wall. John Gale Jones, a leading opponent of the new legislation, made a point of visiting the Medway Towns and must have addressed a number of meetings attended by dockyard workers. He also left an impression of a unique occasion in which the entire workforce of the dockyard expressed their absolute opposition to the proposed legislation:

> At Chatham, Commissioner Proby, it is said, called together all the workmen (near seventeen hundred in number) of the dockyard, and desired them to sign their names to an Address to His Majesty, congratulating him on his late happy escape, and praying him to pass the Bills. By a singular circumstance, however, the men unanimously declared they would not sign away their liberties, and, rushing out of the yard in a body, went to the place where a Petition against the Convention Bills laid, and every one instantly subscribed his name.[22]

The action taken by the workforce on this occasion, described by Jones, provides a rare example of total and absolute unity of both the skilled and unskilled employed in the dockyard. Knowledge that they would be mustered for purposes of signing an address in support of the new legislation was known several days beforehand. The Mayor of Rochester, considered by Jones to be 'a good patriot' for the cause of freedom, had a number of handbills posted. Entitled 'A Caution', they appealed to the yard workers not to sign:

> Being informed this evening that the Commissioner has requested a meeting of the workmen in His Majesty's Dockyard Chatham, and that the purpose of the said meeting is to request you to approve of the present Bill now pending in Parliament – I take this method of cautioning you against being entrapped to approve of measures which you are not acquainted. The present Bills in the state they now stand completely deprive the People of Liberty of Speech, of Writing, Printing, Preaching, or assembly in any respect of redress of Grievances however arbitrary or oppressive without the presence of a magistrate.

It was between 11 a.m. and noon on 17 November that Commissioner Proby assembled the workers and asked them to sign the address. In doing so, he made reference to the Mayor of Rochester's handbills:

> I understand a caution has been put up this morning in different places, to prevent you from being entrapped by me to approve of measures with which you are not acquainted.
>   I am of opinion, that you are, all of you, as capable of judging of any matters, which may be brought before you as any other person whatsoever, and therefore I shall read you the address, that you may form your own judgements upon it.

And this he proceeded to do:

> We have the fullest confidence that Your Majesty in conjunction with the Houses
> of Parliament will take the properest measures for the safety of Your Majesty's loyal
> person in future for the happiness of all Your Majesty's subjects, and for the good of
> the British nation in every respect.[23]

At the time, Proby felt his speech went down well, believing it probable that the mass
of men would sign. After all, they had no history of radical action, and could not be
considered in sympathy with the mob action in London.

No further developments, despite Jones' suggestion to the contrary, took place
on that particular day, although it can be assumed that a great deal of thought and
discussion took place. As Jones, in an account of his visit to Kent, later pointed out,
the Medway Towns were highly politicised and the workforce at Chatham was no
exception. Many, of course, would not have known the precise terms of the government legislation, but the Commissioner, in drawing attention to the Mayor of
Rochester's handbill, did much to publicise the negative aspects of the proposed
laws. Inter- and intra-trade discussions doubtless ensued and would have hinged
upon the bill and how it impacted on their own workplace situation. If, when the
Commissioner spoke, none had read, seen or heard of the handbill, all would be
familiar with its content by the end of the day. Having made the labourers and
artisans reflect on the two government bills, it is hardly surprising they reacted. On
the following day, while muster was in progress, Commissioner Proby related to the
Navy Board that:

> … the greatest part of them went to the ropeyard and took possession of the lower
> spinning house. The respective officers used their endeavours before and after break-
> fast, to indulge them, in vain, to go to their respective works. As the weather was
> exceedingly bad, I desired that Deputies might be sent to me, which they positively
> refused and therefore I went to them and made another speech.

In this, he expressed concern at their behaviour and asserted that his address was one
to which there could be no possible objection. To this, he further added that it was left
to each individual 'to sign or not', so giving no reason for them to have now assembled
in the spinning house rather than attending their place of work. Proby then went on
to make the following comments:

> They heard me with apparent quietness, when their spokesman said, that they all had
> determined not to sign either part of the address; and should proceed quietly out of
> the yard at 12 o'clock and go immediately to sign the petition, in consequence of the
> Mayor of Rochester's printed advertisement.[24]

The particular advertisement referred to had been circulated during the previous afternoon and had obviously much influenced all the artisan and labouring groups of the dockyard. Its content was as follows:

> The Mayor requests those of the Freemen and inhabitants who may be willing to petition against the Bills now pending; one in the House of Lords purposely to be for the better security of his most royal person; and the other in the House of Commons, purposely to be for the more effectual suppression of seditious meetings, to meet at the Guildhall tomorrow at one o'clock in the afternoon.[25]

As intimated, the various classes of workmen did leave the dockyard that afternoon, with large numbers signing the Mayor of Rochester's petition. They did not return to the dockyard that day, but having made their protest did not devise any further action. On 19 November, Proby was able to report:

> Of the artificers, workmen &tc who went out yesterday in the afternoon, to sign the Rochester petition, there have been only sixteen of them absent without leave, which is not uncommon at other times.[26]

As to the address congratulating the King upon his escape, this was duly sent to London four days later. Proby attached a short explanatory note detailing his interpretation of events:

> I am sorry it is not so fully signed, as I had every reason to have expected, which I trust would not have occurred, both from the steps taken by the Mayor of, and others in Rochester and Chatham … Many others would have signed if threats had not been held out to them.[27]

In his comments Proby felt a degree of force had been used. Such an accusation should not be discounted, as it seems highly unlikely that every worker assembling in the spinning house was fully in sympathy with the objectives of that meeting. Physical force was frequently used in trade disputes for achieving solidarity and it is possible that a degree of violence was offered to those who showed insufficient enthusiasm. But such an observation as Proby made must not be used to undermine the totality of the workforce action. A clear majority must have desired the eventual outcome; had it been otherwise, events on that day would not have run so smoothly. Furthermore, Proby was only in a position to surmise, as violence, if offered, would have been of a covert nature. Neither he, nor his officers, witnessed any violence, while informers reported no facts.

A second show of inter-trade unity was demonstrated during the early months of 1801 and prompted by a demand for a pay increase at a time of a dramatic rise in the cost of living. Within the various royal dockyards, including that of Chatham, local committees were established to coordinate the actions to be taken, with each yard also sending two delegates to join a central committee in London. Although the exact composition of Chatham's local committee is unknown, it seems to have reflected the size of each of the artisan and labouring groups within the dockyard. In May, when the Admiralty presided over discharges of such men 'as had composed the committee in Town [London], or committees of correspondence with other yards' the numbers discharged at Chatham included shipwrights, joiners, brick makers, sail makers, rope makers and labourers as well.[28]

The Committee in London was responsible for drawing up a number of petitions, with one that was submitted to parliament on 3 February declaring:

That the permanent daily wages of the artificers and labourers employed in His Majesty's Dock and Rope Yards has not received any augmentation since the settlement thereof in the reign of His Majesty Charles 2nd but the advance in the price of provisions, and the rise of house rent, with every necessary article of life, and advance of interest, upon the money which your petitioners are necessitated to take up, to supply the wants of their families since the period of time, have in most cases exceeded a triplicate proportion which circumstances combined together would have rendered it impossible for your petitioners to have subsisted themselves and families on the scanty pittance of their daily pay many of the families of your petitioners consume in the article of bread alone had it not been for the addition of extra work which the nature and urgency of the service of His Majesty's Navy ... have enabled us to attain.[29]

On 1 April 1801, and somewhat reluctantly, the Navy Board agreed to meet with the dockyard delegates. Most probably they would have preferred to have ignored the existence of such a committee but had been forced to take such action as a result of an increasingly turbulent situation within the yards. Furthermore, to placate the totally unified workforce, an offer was put forward, this deemed a special payment, restricted to married men without apprentices, and to last for the duration of the war, with amounts varying according to the size of families and level of skill. For a shipwright with four or more children an additional shilling a week would be allowed while for a labourer with a similar sized family it would be 10*d*. The amounts were approximately half for unmarried men and stood at the midway point for those with one to three children. Once informed of the offer, the delegates were ordered to return to their respective dockyards on pain of dismissal.[30]

Although the delegates favoured the Navy Board offer, the mass of yard workers, including those at Chatham, rejected them. It must be assumed that a ballot took place in all of the yards, with Plymouth and the various eastern yards proving considerably more militant than Portsmouth. Indeed, delegates representing Chatham are reported to have visited Portsmouth and to have referred to the possibility of a strike being called. Within the dockyard at Chatham, an orchestrated campaign was already underway, with bills opposing the Navy Board offer having been posted outside the dockyard gate. Indicating that the cost of living had tripled since 1775, it was a tentative reminder to the rest of the workers that the Navy Board offer fell far short of actual need.[31]

In mid-April, delegates once again met with members of the Navy Board. But time was running out. A number of factors were now operating in favour of the employers. First and foremost, the dockyards were operating under considerably less pressure. The Baltic fleet that was to engage in the Battle of Copenhagen, preparation of which had occupied much of the Chatham dockyard workforce, had sailed in March with much of the remaining work being routine. In addition, a split had occurred within the ranks of the various workers with a substantial minority in favour of accepting the wartime payment as offered. Furthermore, the Navy Board was being persuaded to take a much tougher line by the Earl of St Vincent who, since February 1801, had held office as First Lord of the Admiralty. He was an inveterate opponent of wage increases and favoured confrontation.

The outcome was that the Navy Board chose to make no further offer other than a promise to review wages. Following this, St Vincent came to the fore, getting it agreed by the Navy Board that they should form a committee to tour the yards and dismiss all workmen engaged in the recent dispute. At Chatham, which was visited during May, a total of seventy-nine artisans and labourers were dismissed, each told that they must present themselves at the dockyard gate on the following day that they 'might receive wages and collect chests and tools'.[32]

The dismissal of such a large number of leaders from among the workforce doubtless created a deep and memorable scar. While workers outside the naval yards might have treated dismissal as a temporary setback, such an occurrence within the dockyards was of a much more serious nature. Those employed in the yards had accepted lower wages while looking towards the long-term benefits of job security and a pension; should strike action threaten these advantages, then the majority of those employed in the yard would now choose to espouse this clearly blunted weapon. The outcome, therefore, was a more or less total rejection of strikes, replacing this weapon with a greater emphasis on the petition.

Throughout much of the nineteenth century, whenever the workforce had a grievance they produced a document, signed by as many employees as possible, which was submitted either to the officer in charge of the dockyard or to members of an annual committee of visitation. During the 1830s, over a fundamentally important issue of classifying workers by their levels of work output, they might have turned to a more militant form of action if petitions were never acted upon by those who managed the yards. But this was not the case. Petitions were responsible for bringing about a number of improvements, including several adjustments to individual trade pay scales. More important was the success of a series of petitions submitted between 1822 and 1823 to restore a 20 per cent pay cut in the wages of all artisans, imposed by the Admiralty to reduce the overall naval expenditure estimates. In December 1823, one of these petitions, from Chatham, resulted in the restoration of the earlier pay scales.[33] As for the unity of the dockyard workforce, fostered by the industrial disputes of the late eighteenth century, this was retained. In a number of the petitioning campaigns, there is clear evidence of these separate work groups coordinating their activities and working together.[34]

5

Building the Ships that Fought at Trafalgar

In total, the Royal Navy at Trafalgar assembled a winning fleet of twenty-seven ships of the line. Many of their names, including *Victory*, *Temeraire* and *Bellerophon*, have firmly entered into the annals of history and been accounted as among the most famous ships to sail the oceans of the world. Of significance, also, is that six of the battleships that fought at Trafalgar, including the aforementioned three, were all built on the river Medway. Of these, *Victory* (100), *Temeraire* (98), *Leviathan* (74) and *Revenge* (74) were all launched at Chatham, while *Bellerophon* (74), the 'Billy Ruffian' to her crew, was a product of Frindsbury, and *Polyphemus* (74) a Sheerness-built warship. In its own right, Chatham can rightly claim to have built more battleships of the Trafalgar fleet than any other royal dockyard while the Medway in general constructed more vessels of that same fleet than any other area of the country.

None of this was simple coincidence. Chatham was an industrial-military complex that had few rivals, with the dockyard having acquired a particular specialism in building those mighty wooden walls that were the nation's first line of defence. Although not the role that had originally been envisaged for the dockyard at Chatham, strategic needs had forced upon it this new arrangement. Situated on the east side of the country, and some sixteen miles up river, the yard at Chatham had proved itself increasingly unsuitable as a naval base – especially when the enemy was France or Spain. Much more convenient, and sheltered by the Isle of Wight, was the fleet anchorage and harbour linked to the dockyard at Portsmouth. With the Royal Navy beginning to range more frequently into the Mediterranean and across the Atlantic, it was this yard that had now acquired supremacy, supported in its efforts by the rapidly expanding and more recent yard that had been established at Plymouth.

While both Portsmouth and Plymouth had the facilities to build ships, this was not the major given task of these two yards. Instead, work undertaken was directed to that of supporting the fleet in operation. They were the yards that prepared new fleets when war was declared or carried out short- or medium-term repairs on ships that needed to be quickly got back to sea. When the nation was at peace, these two yards had harbours filled with ships in Ordinary, the workforce carrying out regular inspections and ensuring that these vessels were ready for a future conflict. It was also during such periods that Portsmouth and Plymouth were best placed to build new ships, these two yards then having the spare capacity to undertake such work.

At Chatham things were very different. It was no longer a first line operational fleet base. Apart from anything else, there were increasing problems with the Medway, this resulting from the continued silting of the river. Sometimes it might take two weeks or more for a large warship to successfully navigate the river from its mouth to the dockyard. Eating up much of this time was the need to await a suitable combination of wind and tides that would permit navigation of the various shoals and bends that permeated the river. According to one particular Admiralty observation made in 1774, 'there is only six points of the compass for a wind with which ships of the line can sail down, and ten to sail up and that only for a few days in the spring tides.'[1] In an examination of the problem that was undertaken in September 1790, it was found that numerous vessels had taken fourteen days to transit this stretch of the Medway, while others had taken in excess of a month. *Lenox* (70), a third rate drawing 21ft of water, had, during the year 1756, been detained in Chatham Reach for a total of six weeks, the tides too shallow for an earlier departure.[2]

At the very least, an operational naval base, in undertaking repair and maintenance work on urgently needed warships, should be in a position to provide a fast turnaround time. These extensive delays in navigating the Medway ensured that Chatham could not be relied upon to meet this basic requirement. Instead, the dockyard at Chatham had to be directed towards the equally essential role of both constructing new ships and undertaking more extensive repair work on a ship that was likely to be dry-docked for several months. A vessel that merely required careening and therefore needed only to be in dry dock for a few days, if sent to Chatham, might ultimately be out of service for several months, with much of this time taken by the lengthy delays in waiting for a suitable tide and wind.

The Earl of Sandwich, while First Lord, clearly recognised that Chatham was of great value to the Navy, but only if it was used for tasks to which it was best suited. In 1773 he wrote:

> I am now more and more convinced that if [Chatham] is kept singly to its proper use as a building yard, possibly more service may be obtained from it than from any other dockyard in His Majesty's dominions; the great extent of the yard that faces the river and the great length of the harbour which has the room to moor half the fleet of England of a moderate draught of water, are conveniences that are not to be found elsewhere; and it will appear by the repairs that have been carried on during the visitations I have lately made, that more business in the way of building and repairs has been done here than in any other one, possibly more than in any two of the other yards.[3]

These observations, as made by Sandwich, doubtless formed the basis of a paragraph which appeared in a general account of all the yards that was presented to George III in 1774. Once again they relate to the value of Chatham as a building yard rather than that of being an operational naval base:

Although from the alteration of affairs of Europe [Chatham] cannot now be called the great naval arsenal of the kingdom … yet it is of no less importance than it was in every respect except that for speedy equipment of great ships, the uses of it being in every other respect improved, such as for building and repairing even large ships, from where they may occasionally be moved to Portsmouth and Plymouth, and is the properest station for laying up and equipping the greatest number of smaller ships, of the line, frigates and as in cases of sudden and great armaments, the greater the number of ports the fleet is divided to the better for expeditious equipment and getting them round to the general rendezvous.[4]

As indicated, the most important of these various designated roles was that of warship construction. By 1772, Chatham had six building slips, a number only equalled by Deptford. The result was that during the final three decades of the eighteenth century, Chatham launched a total of thirty-five vessels; this far exceeded that of all other naval building yards in the country, in both number and total tonnage. Furthermore, due to this dedicated specialism, other shipbuilding yards were also attracted into the area, knowing that government contracts were easier to acquire if they were sited close to an existing naval dockyard. Apart from anything else, a naval warship that was constructed outside of a royal dockyard had to be regularly inspected by an assistant Master Shipwright employed in one of the yards. In addition, the vessel, once launched, would automatically be moved to a government yard for completion and final commissioning. For this reason, a number of private yards gravitated to the Rochester and Frindsbury area, these including Greaves and Nicholson, the yard that built *Bellerophon*. In being situated at Frindsbury, Greaves and Nicholson were immediately across the river from the naval dockyard at Chatham, a distance of less than 500 yards. Once constructed, *Bellerophon* had been taken across the river to the Chatham yard and immediately dry-docked for the purpose of tarring the hull prior to transfer to the dockyard Ordinary for fitting out.

With Chatham having become a significant building yard, as opposed to an operational naval base, there was a considerable financial downside. Government expenditure on the improvement of shore-based facilities was invariably directed to Portsmouth and Plymouth, with both these yards the recipient of major improvement programmes that were undertaken during the mid-eighteenth century. At Chatham, the workforce had to make do and mend, with only relatively minute sums being directed to their yard. Instead, older buildings that might have been replaced if found at one of the two strategic yards, were retained through the undertaking of frequent repair work. Although it was recognised that something eventually would have to be done, with the already cited report that was presented to George III in 1774 making the following point:

Those [buildings] now there have been very good when first built but as this was the yard that had any considerable building in it such as remain of those that were the first built are in a very decay'd state and must by degree as money can be spared from other services, be pulled down and rebuilt.[5]

Little, however, was to be done at that time, Chatham having first to weather the War of American Independence (1775–83), with new building work only being undertaken on two new building slips and a number of timber drying sheds.

However, the inadequacies of Chatham were clearly demonstrated at this time. In September 1770, when a controversy arose over the frequently contested Falkland Islands, war with Spain was viewed as a distinct possibility. Orders were given for the fleet to be mobilised, with Chatham receiving instructions to prepare nine ships for Channel service. Despite the urgency, Chatham was quite unable to respond, with three of the dry docks already occupied while the fourth was out of use due to a long-term repair need to its own timberwork. Matters were further compounded by the absence of a masting hulk, a large vessel fitted with lifting gear and used to step into position the masts of warships being prepared for service. At that time, and serving as additional proof that facilities at Chatham needed considerable updating, the ageing Chatham mast hulk was itself occupying one of the dry docks, being also in considerable need of repair.[6]

The ill-preparedness of Chatham at the time of the Falklands crisis was duplicated at the outset of the American War in 1775. Even before the actual declaration of hostilities, complaints were voiced that the dockyard was behind with work that had been allocated to it, a situation made worse by a shipwrights' strike earlier in the year over the imposition of task work.[7] With the situation in America rapidly deteriorating, the workload at Chatham increased. By the end of October warrants had been received from the Navy Board for the fitting out of eleven ships 'for foreign service', with three of the four dry docks allocated to this work. All seemed to be going reasonably well until the following summer. Upon examining the Old Single Dock in June 1776, a structure that had now seen 150 years of usage, extensive areas of wood rot were revealed. This had caused 'the apron', the ledge upon which the entrance gates rested, to start breaking up so that 'the whole must be taken up, and piles drove to secure the groundways'.[8] It was determined that this work must be immediately undertaken, with all available house carpenters transferred to the task and so delaying work due to have been undertaken on the thirty-two-gun *Montreal*.

With regard to Chatham's important shipbuilding role, it was much easier to plan ahead, a sudden emergency less likely to impact upon plans that had often been agreed several years in advance. Indeed, those employed in building a particular vessel, in the event of a sudden fleet mobilisation could be moved from the construction of a new vessel to that of helping prepare a vessel that had been newly taken from the Ordinary. Most new construction work was undertaken on a building slip, this ensuring that all dry docks were available for the repairing and maintenance of ships as and

Opposite: *Victory*, Nelson's flagship at the Battle of Trafalgar, is the most famous product of Chatham dockyard. Floated out of the No.2 Dock (then the Old Single Dock) in 1765, she spent many of her early years in the Chatham Ordinary before undertaking her first commission in 1778.

when required. However, there were exceptions, with the larger first- and second-rate three-decked warships often being built in dry dock. Nelson's flagship at Trafalgar, the 100-gun *Victory*, was one such example. She had been built in the Old Single Dock, having her keel first laid down in 1759 and eventually floated out in 1765. That she remained in dry dock for such a lengthy period underlines the problem of using the dry dock for new construction work, as it blocked use of this facility for the entire period of construction, including six months that was usually set aside for the vessel to season in frame. However, *Victory*'s long-term occupancy of the Old Single Dock was an exception, her period of seasoning having been extended by a change in the international situation. At the time she was laid down, the subsequently named Seven Years War (1756–63) was creating a considerable demand for such vessels and her construction was regarded as urgent. Following a series of stunning victories that took place in the same year as she was laid down, it was no longer felt necessary to complete her for immediate wartime service and for this reason she remained in dry dock for six years. In commemoration of those victories, the year 1759 became known as the Year of Victories, with the new first-rate under construction at Chatham taking her name from that particularly momentous year.

Three important documents relating to the construction of *Victory* are held at the National Maritime Museum and recently highlighted by the Chatham Historic Dockyard Society in their newsletter *Chips*. One relates to the naming of the ship and the other two to her successful launch. On 30 October 1760 the Navy Board informed the officers at Chatham dockyard:

> The Right honourable the Lords Commissioners of the Admiralty having directed us to cause the ships and sloops mentioned on the other side to be registered on the list of the Royal Navy by the names against each expressed; We direct you to cause them to be entered on your Books, and called by those names accordingly.

On the other side of the document were listed three ships that were then under construction at Chatham, these of 100, ninety and seventy-four guns and to be named respectively, *Victory*, *London* and *Ramillies*. As to the launch of *Victory*, the officers at Chatham received a further letter, this dated 30 April 1765:

> The Master Shipwright having acquainted us that His Majesty's Ship *Victory* building in the Old Single Dock will be ready to launch the ensuing Spring Tides. These are to direct and require you to cause her to be launched at that time accordingly if she is in all respects ready for it.

Confirming that this was carried out according to those instructions, Commissioner Hanway wrote to both the Navy Board and Admiralty informing them that *Victory* had been floated out of the Old Single Dock on 7 May, with this reply received from Philip Stephens, Secretary to the Board of Admiralty:

I have communicated to My Lords Commissioners of the Admiralty your letter of the 6 & 7 inst. the former giving an Account of the Augusta being put out of the Dock, the latter of the Victory being safely launched yesterday.[9]

Following her launch (or floating out), *Victory* spent the next thirteen years in the Ordinary, there being no particular need for a ship of her size during the years of peace that had followed the ending of the Seven Years War and the immediate opening years of the American War of Independence. It was not, therefore, until 1778 that she left the Medway, going on to serve in the Atlantic and Mediterranean. Following a further period in the Chatham Ordinary, she was called upon to serve in 1793 upon the outbreak of war with Revolutionary France. A further return to Chatham saw *Victory* entering dry dock in 1800 for what was termed a 'middling' repair. On inspection it was found that far more work would have to be carried out than had initially been anticipated. The 'middling' repair subsequently became a rebuild, at a cost of £70,933, with much of the hull and stern replaced, rigging and masts renewed and modifications made to the bulwark. Undocked on 11 April 1803, she was immediately ordered to Spithead where she was to wear the flag of Admiral Nelson. Still flying his flag, she went on to gain immortal fame in October 1805 when she, with *Temeraire* immediately to her stern, led the British fleet at Trafalgar.

While Chatham had four dry docks, all of them dating back to the seventeenth century, the building slips were considerably more recent in age. Admittedly the oldest had its origins in the previous century, but a second building slip of the same period had been replaced in 1738. To this original pair, a further two dry docks were added shortly after the Seven Years War, with a final pair built between 1772 and 1774. The fact of Chatham having only two building slips at the time of *Victory* being laid down is a further factor in explaining why she was built in dry dock rather than on a building slip, there being at that time neither a sufficient number of slips nor one of a size sufficient to take the new vessel. With the construction of four new slipways in a relatively short period of time, it ensured that dry docks would now have to be used even more infrequently for the construction of new vessels.

Much more expensive than building new slipways, or adding the occasional work shop or timber drying shed, was the massive expenditure that would eventually be needed to renew much else that existed in the dockyard. Apart from the ageing dry docks, considerable attention would have to be given to the ropery, an area of manufacture within the dockyard that had also seen 150 years of service by the time of the American War. In 1785, with that particular war now concluded, an Admiralty visitation to the dockyard made a number of points relative to its renewal. Several buildings were condemned and a number of others viewed as in urgent need of repair. The plank house, armourers' shop, treenail house, main storehouse and Rope House were recommended for demolition while the mast houses, rigging house, hemp house and wharves were in need of repair. Regarding the house carpenters and joiners' shop, Commissioner Charles Proby was instructed by the Navy Board that:

These buildings being much too confined and very inadequate to the service of the yard, you are to consider and report to the [Navy] Board your opinion how they can be enlarged and whether extending the former into the Deal yard and lengthening the lot towards the present storehouse.[10]

Not surprisingly, as each year passed, increasingly large sums of money were required for the simple upkeep and repair of buildings that should either have been demolished or totally renovated. In 1784 alone, £20,000 was allowed for repair work at Chatham. At that time improvements were being carried out to the Anchor Wharf, with a new storehouse being built upon the wharf at a cost of £3,500.[11]

By 1786 plans were well in hand for a renewal of many of those buildings that had been highlighted as in need of demolition. At the beginning of that year work had started upon the Anchor Wharf Storehouse and designed to replace one that the 1785 visitation had considered 'too confined for the purpose intended'. In 1786, also, there was a further visitation to the dockyard, the main purpose of which was the finalisation of plans for a new ropery. A strict order of work was laid down, in which the old Rope House was to be completely replaced by a new double Rope House built to the same design as one already constructed at Portsmouth:

We propose to begin with the hatchelling, tarring and white and black yarn houses and to employ the rope makers in the present laying house. Then, to take down the old spinning house, hatchelling, tarring and black yarn house connected with it, and build the double Rope House, and afterwards to take down the old laying house and rigging house and build a new rigging house and in the meantime a temporary rigging house may be immediately prepared for employing the riggers whilst necessary.[12]

Reconstruction of the ropery was the most extensive of the new work to be undertaken. Originally established during the seventeenth century, the ropeyard had witnessed few alterations since the beginning of the eighteenth century. A particularly significant feature was that of the earlier ropery having separate spinning and laying houses, these respectively of 1,120ft and 1,160ft in length, resulting from the need of these buildings to be as long as the longest piece of rope manufactured. It was in the spinning house that hemp was continuously spun into yarn while in the laying house the yarn was first twisted into strands and then worked into rope. Prior to the yarn being transferred from the spinning house to the laying house it was initially stored in the white yarn house prior to being tarred. Serving as a preservative, the tarring of the yarn was carried out in the tarring house, with the tarred yarn, once dry, being stored in the black yarn house.

Apart from the Rope House and its various spinning and laying floors, other buildings associated with the rope-making process were the hatchelling, hemp and rigging houses. The purpose of each of these buildings was fairly straightforward, with the hemp houses, of which there were several at Chatham, being stores in which bales of hemp were first secured upon arrival in the dockyard during the autumn. As for the hatchelling house, this was where the hatchelling boards, used for the combing of the tangled hemp prior to it being spun into yarn, were located. Finally, the rigging house was where the finished rope was taken for cutting, splicing and dressing.

For a ropery there were two alternative layouts. Either there could be a separate spinning house or laying floor, as existed at Chatham, or the two could be combined under one roof. A double Rope House (the name given to a ropery that combined the spinning and laying floors), as now planned for Chatham, did allow for savings to be made in building costs but it would reduce output. Of late, two dockyards had received new Rope Houses, those yards being Plymouth and Portsmouth, with the former seeing construction of separate laying and spinning houses, and Portsmouth a double Rope House. It was the comparison of these that had led the Navy Board to adopt a double Rope House at Chatham: the two separate houses at Plymouth being capable of producing so much rope that it was constantly under-utilised.

In April 1787, detailed plans for the new Rope House at Chatham were finalised:

> Money being granted for the erection of a new double Rope House, tarring and white and black yarn houses and a hatchelling house connected with the Rope House in your yard, we acquaint you that drawings of such of them are due to be carried on by the artificers of the yard will be sent to you by the Brompton coach, in a day or two, and direct and require you to carry on the said buildings agreeable thereto.

The latter also went on to inform the Commissioner as to exactly how the work was to proceed:

> … as it is intended soon to contract for the carrying on about one fourth part of the Double Rope House in this year … you are to begin with the south end, and to take down the present spinning house immediately, as far as is necessary for carrying on the same, and to proceed therein accordingly, taking care to preserve the old materials as much as possible and make use of as many as may be applicable to the new building.

Although the new Rope House was to be built on the site of the old spinning house, the fact of it being of a greater length, the spinning house being 17ft shorter meant that it extended into ground belonging to the Commissioner's garden:

> And it being necessary in carrying this part of the building to take down and reinstate the Commissioner's garden, also a part of the south wall of said garden in order to extend the present range with the projecting part of the said wall westward of the ropeyard. [13]

A significant feature of the new building was that it was to be constructed of brick, whereas the spinning and laying houses that it was to replace were of timber construction. This made a good deal of sense as the ropeyard area was always at high risk of fire, this through the combination of highly combustible hemp and the open fire that was needed to heat the tarring kettles. At Portsmouth, where the new double Rope House constructed at that dockyard had also replaced an earlier timber Rope House, fires had struck on three occasions. The first two of these, breaking out in July 1760 and July 1770, were almost certainly accidental and aided by the heat of summer. However, the third fire, this occurring in June 1776, was certainly not an accident, deliberately started by James Aitkin, a sympathiser for the American cause. It was this latter fire that had led to the rebuilding of the Portsmouth ropery, the fire having destroyed much of the original building. The yard at Chatham had also narrowly escaped a similar fate, James Aitkin having visited Chatham for the purpose of starting a similar fire appears to have had problems in gaining access to the yard, turning his attention to Portsmouth. Eventually, Aitkin was arrested in Bristol where he was in the process of setting fire to a number of storehouses.[14]

Obviously this extensive rebuilding work would seriously interfere with normal dockyard routine. Yet, despite the immense upheaval that occurred within the ropeyard, it did not prevent the continued manufacture of rope. For one thing, a temporary rigging house was constructed close to the Commissioner's garden, while the laying house was not demolished until completion of the new Rope House. This meant that the laying house, for the next few years, could double as a spinning house. If additional rope was still required then this could either be transferred from one of the other dockyards, or manufactured under contract. For the actual building programme, few additional workers were employed, considerable use being made of the yard's existing force of labourers, house carpenters and plumbers. In April 1787, however, reference is made to the employment of two additional bricklayers who would be employed upon the yarn, tarring and hatchelling houses. They were to be dismissed once this work was completed.[15]

The double Rope House. Completed in 1791, it is an impressive brick structure that houses both the laying and spinning floors that had previously been housed in two separate wooden buildings. Following the closure of the dockyard, the building was substantially restored from 1984–87.

The double Rope House was substantially completed by December 1790. It was approximately 1,250ft in total length, with the interior divided into 100 bays and two separate sections for the accommodation of the laying and spinning floors. Of brick construction, it was given a lead roof, with much of the lead being taken from the old spinning house. Windows were originally unglazed, this to help in the extraction of dust from the working area of each floor. The entire building was of three storeys, each of which had a separate laying and spinning floor, while a cellar provided a storage space for tar. Attached to the north end of the Rope House were separate hemp and hatchelling houses.

Earlier, in 1786, the main storehouse was completed. Just over 600ft in length, it was of brick construction and stood to the south of the Rope House, being sited on the Anchor Wharf. To the west of the Rope House the new yarn and tarring houses were constructed. All were of similar design, being of brick and two storeys in height. The white yarn house was connected to the Rope House spinning floor by a wooden bridge, allowing the hauls of yarn to be taken direct from the spinning house floor. Each of these buildings was completed by 1789, with the tarring house put into use by May. A separate hemp house, two storeys in height and constructed of brick, was also erected and stood to the east of the Rope House.

Apart from that carried out on the ropery, only a limited amount of rebuilding work was undertaken, although a large number of the older buildings were either more extensively repaired or completely renovated. Such was the case with the older mast houses dating to the reign of William III. Between 1785 and 1787 both the plank house and treenail house were pulled down and re-sited, while the house carpenters and joiners' shops were enlarged and extended. In 1787, £1,440 was set aside for building two new storehouses over the south-west mast pond and £1,500 for two new mast houses sited next to this same mast pond. It is also recorded that in July 1787 work was in hand upon the renovation of the Commissioner's House.

All this renewal work meant that the dockyard, as a whole, was in a much better position to undertake demands that were to be placed upon it by the war with Revolutionary France that was to break out in February 1793. Certainly the docks and slipways were in a much better state of repair, with only repairs on the first dock required, but this was not undertaken until 1801 when the first period of a long, drawn-out war with France was within months of being temporarily concluded. With the dockyard entering the new century, a further series of buildings and other structures began to be added. Directly related to ship construction was the addition of three new building slips, these constructed in 1804, 1811 and 1813. In addition, two mould lofts were also added, these dating to 1804 and 1811. On the clerical side, and resulting from a set of offices constructed in 1750 having now been declared structurally unsafe, a new office building was constructed in the centre of the yard and subsequently known as the Admiral's Offices, this completed in 1808. To meet the spiritual needs of those employed at the yard, a chapel was added in 1808, this replacing earlier dependence on the parish church of St Mary's. Finally, but of considerable significance, was construction of a steam-powered saw mill, this built to a revolutionary design that transformed the means by which timber was both transported around the yard and cut to shape.

Reference has already been made to both Samuel Bentham and Edward Holl, individuals who were closely connected with civil construction works undertaken during the opening decades of the nineteenth century. Admittedly, as far as Samuel Bentham was concerned, he had already ceased holding office by the time that work began on the saw mill, but it was his foresight in recognising that steam power could be applied to the cutting of timber that directly led to its construction at Chatham. Of more significance, perhaps, was that Bentham, in attempting to apply the power of steam to dockyard manufacturing processes, acquired the services of Marc Brunel, an asylum seeker from France, whose genius in this area of engineering was unsurpassed. Successfully working on an Admiralty project at Portsmouth, Brunel went on to submit to the Navy Board a detailed paper that outlined the total savings that could be made from the construction of a mill at Chatham.

At that time Chatham employed about 150 sawyers, each normally paid at the rate of 4s 2d per 100ft sawn. Given that, on average, a pair of sawyers working in a sawpit could saw about 220ft, this meant they had a joint weekly wage of 55s with the dockyard's annual expenditure on this item approaching £11,000. Brunel, in his estimates, reckoned that the saw mill he advocated for Chatham could not only produce considerably more timber but would require, through a considerable reduction in the number of sawyers employed, only £2,000 for wages and maintenance of machinery.

The saw mill that Brunel designed for Chatham consisted of eight saw frames that each carried an average of thirty-six saws, so producing 1,260ft of sawing per minute. While it would be impossible to maintain such a rate throughout the day, the potential was so great that this one unit could meet the needs of all the nation's dockyards. Potential savings on sawing alone were enormous. In addition, though, Brunel planned further savings by giving attention not only to wood sawing but the means by which timber was conveyed across the yard. Prior to the erection of the saw mill, all log timber arriving at Chatham was landed at the dockyard wharf before being dragged to a convenient place for stacking. According to Brunel, in any one year:

> There is required at least 6,000 goings and comings of teams of horses, merely to lay the timber for survey – 6,000 times to and from the stacks – at least as many more times one hundred yards in aiding the lifting on the stacks.[16]

From the timber stacks, the logs, once surveyed, would have to be removed to the point of cutting and then, once sawn, to a new stacking area. All this movement of timber, when the cost of wages and the employment of horses were included, amounted to a further expenditure of £14,000.

Instead of continuing such an uneconomic system within the dockyard at Chatham, Brunel proposed to extend the use of the steam engine to be installed in the mill, so it could also assist in the transporting of timber across the yard. The process would begin with construction of an underground canal that interlinked with the river and connected to a stacking and timber-surveying area sited close to the mill. Along this canal, the newly arrived timber would be floated. Apart from savings in the cost of moving the newly arrived timber, there was an added advantage of using the canal; the timber was freed from the sand and gravel that collected during the dragging and which impeded the operation of the saw. Once the timber reached the end of the canal it entered a reservoir from which a mechanical lift, also powered by the saw mill steam engine, removed each log. As soon as it reached the surface, the arm of a moveable crane on rails grabbed it. Having seized the log, the crane then descended a gradual incline before gently depositing its burden on the drying beds where it would be surveyed. In the meantime the crane would be drawn back to its original position by a chain once again operated by the saw mill steam engine. The same crane was also employed in conveying the dried timber to the saw mill where, once converted, the scantlings, or sawn timber was conveyed to any part of the yard by single horse trucks.

The mill, which was completed in June 1814, immediately brought about considerable financial savings that resulted from the sharp reduction in the number of sawyers employed in the cutting of planks and horse teams used in the movement of timber in both its sawn and unsawn state. In addition, because of its innovative design, it became a notable attraction, with a number of foreign dignitaries brought to the yard for the purpose of viewing its various component parts. One who was particularly impressed was William Wildash when writing a history of the area that was published in 1817:

> These saw mills, as the name imports, are employed in converting the fir timber used in the service of the yard into planks or boards; and are erected on an eminence about 35 feet above the level of the lowest part of the yard. To the ground on the north side of the mill; which is appropriated to the stowage of timber, balks are floated from the river by means of a canal which runs open about 250 feet; this canal on entering the rising ground becomes a tunnel in length about 300 feet, and empties itself into an elliptical basin the length of which is 90 feet, the breadth 72 feet, and the depth 44 feet. The operation of raising the timber from this basis is worthy of observation; and the steady, though quick motion with which it ascends is truly astonishing. We have witnessed a balk of 60 feet long, and 16 inches square, raised to the top of the standard 60 feet in the space of 60 seconds! The saw mill is constructed on a very extensive scale; and the mechanism of it may be reduced to three principle things; the first, that is the saw drawn up and down as long as is necessary, by a motion communicated to the wheel by steam; the second, that the timber to be cut into boards is advanced by a uniform motion to receive the strokes of the saw; for here the wood is to meet the saw, and not the saw to follow the wood, therefore the motion of the wood and that of the saw immediately depends the one on the other; the third, that where the saw has cut through the whole length of the piece, the whole machine stops of itself, and remains immovable; lest having no obstacle to surmount, the moving power should turn the wheel with too great velocity, and break some part of the machine.[17]

Edward Holl's association with the saw mill was that of overseeing the construction and approving the plans submitted by Brunel. As a civil architect, rather than an engineer, his interest was in the structure of the building rather than that of the machinery that it housed. With regard to the other major construction works that were undertaken at this time, the chapel and the office building were based entirely on plans produced by Holl. Both are still features of the dockyard; substantial and pleasant in design, they clearly reflect the undoubted talents of this particular architect. The chapel, which stands immediately north of the Main Gate and on land previously used for the storage of timber, is a rectangular building of yellow stock brick with details of Purbeck marble. It has a light and spacious interior with cast-iron columns supporting a tiered gallery. The offices, designed initially for use by the Commissioner and the principal officers of the yard, were located in a central position, which was close to the dry docks and building slips. Of brick construction and two storeys in height, it has an east-facing main entrance that leads directly to a corridor that interlinks with all of the separate internal offices. This, in itself, was something of an innovation, earlier offices at Chatham being grouped in separate parts of a building and provided with separate entrances. Administratively, this reinforced the independent authority possessed by the principal officers and helped create barriers in the smooth day-to-day operations carried out within the yard.

Prior to the construction of the dockyard chapel, only limited attention had been given to the spiritual needs of the workforce. Although the yard had long possessed a chaplain, services were normally performed on board one of the many ageing hulks that were moored in the Medway. In 1773 it was reported that *Revenge* 'has divine service performed in it by the chaplain of the yard regularly every Sunday.'[18] The growth of Methodism in the Medway area, a denomination that was attracting into its ranks some of the artisans and labourers of the yard, resulted in more attention being given to the construction of chapels funded by government money.

As a means of countering Methodism, the new chapel was hardly likely to attract into the ranks of the established church those it had lost to the particular tenets of that movement. Methodism had a certain openness that tended towards democracy, something far removed from the thinking that clearly underpinned the seating arrangement established for the new dockyard chapel upon its completion in 1808. Every member of the congregation was accorded a seat in the building based on rank, with the Commissioner and his family provided with a high-sided box pew at the very front. Around him were positioned the principal officers, also in high-sided box pews. Artificers not of officer rank were seated much further back, with a final row of pews reserved for the officers' apprentices. The gallery was similarly reserved, seating given over to those of the Ordinary and officers of the Royal Marines. This strict recognition of rank was hardly likely to counter the growth of Methodism, a sect that attracted those who saw all as equal in the eyes of the Almighty.

Departing from the architectural contributions made by Edward Holl, it is useful to direct further attention to Samuel Bentham. This is because of an additional contribution that he made to the yard and one so important that, without it, there was every certainty that the yard at Chatham would have been closed and replaced by an entirely new dockyard. Bentham's achievement was that of overcoming the problem of shoaling and the consequent difficulty of getting ships to the dockyard. First explored as an issue at the beginning of the seventeenth century, it had gained, as already noted, increasing severity throughout the following century and by the year 1800 there was a definite fear that larger ships would be completely unable to reach the yard.

In deciding to construct a considerably enlarged dockyard at Chatham during the early years of the seventeenth century it had been assumed that the river might actually have been gaining in depth. This, of course, had proved itself to be a completely false assumption, with the Navy having to now live up to the consequences of this error. One of the first pieces of evidence to reveal that serious problems lay on the horizon was produced in 1724 by the yard Commissioner, Thomas Kempthorne. He complained that larger ships were unable to move up river other than on a tide that was between half flood and half ebb. As a result of Kempthorne's concern, a careful survey was undertaken, with numerous soundings taken at various points of the river. In West Gillingham Reach, where a number of larger ships were moored, it was discovered that on a spring tide, the greatest depth of water was 27ft but this fell to 17ft during a neap tide. Even less favourable was the deepest point of East Gillingham Reach where there was only 19ft on a spring tide, this falling to 16ft. As a point of reference, it should be noted that the larger warships of this period generally required a depth of between 21ft and 24ft.

By the 1770s the situation had become even more serious. Instead of ships being able to move up river when between half flood and half ebb, such was now possible only on a spring tide. In other words, ships that were once able to navigate the Medway on tidal conditions occurring twice in every 24 hours, were now restricted to a particular tide that only took place once every lunar month. Furthermore, mobility of shipping on the Medway continued to decline, a survey of 1763 showing that since 1724 the depth of water on a spring tide in Cockham Wood Reach had been reduced by 2ft, while the area between Chatham Quay and Upnor Castle had seen a reduction in depth of 4ft.

As well as presenting a problem for navigational purposes, the increasing shallowness of the Medway also undermined its value as a naval harbour. To allow larger ships to continue using the river for this purpose they had either to be deliberately lightened, to reduce the draft that each required, or ran the risk that the keel or lower hull timbers would suffer damage by scraping the bottom of the river. Neither alternative was acceptable, as a deliberately lightened ship would have timbers that were normally submerged in seawater now constantly exposed to the sun. As a result, the consequent drying process would lead to this part of the ship becoming subject to dry rot.

The problem of mooring ships in the Medway was highlighted in 1771 following an Admiralty inspection of the dockyard and harbour that found:

On enquiry that the depth of water in this port is scarcely adequate for the draughts of the capital ships built according to the present estimates, as few of them can have the proper quantity of ballast on board, and remain constantly on float. The consequence of which is very apparent … [and] which weakens them greatly and makes them sooner unfit for service.[19]

Two years later, during a visitation to Chatham, the Earl of Sandwich, in his capacity as First Lord, added:

It must be allowed that this port is not so useful as formerly from the increased size of our ships, so that there are few above five places where a ship of the line can lay afloat properly ballasted.[20]

The problem was effectively put on hold until the early years of the following century when John Rennie was requested to view a whole range of problems associated with the further development of the royal dockyards, including that of warships finding it difficult to both navigate the Medway and use these waters for long-term harbouring. Working closely with John Whidby, the Master Attendant at Woolwich, and William Jessop, a consulting engineer, he began to unravel the problem as to why the Medway was subject to such an alarming degree of shoaling. Noting it to be a problem that was not simply restricted to the Medway, they settled upon the notion that it was a result of recent industrial and agrarian developments. Further up river, and beyond where the dockyard was sited, towns and villages were expanding. As they did so, they caused deposits of mud to enter the rivers and feed into the navigable channels and dockyard harbours. Additional deposits also found their way into these same rivers from agricultural improvements and land drainage. Specifically, for the Medway, much of the blame was placed on Rochester Bridge, a point Rennie included in his report:

If Rochester Bridge had been pulled down some years since, and a new one built in the line of the streets through Strood and Rochester, with piers of suitable dimensions, instead of repairing the old one, the large starlings of which act as a dam, and prevent the tide from flowing up to the extent it otherwise would do, the depth of water in front of Chatham, Rochester, and in Cockham Wood Reach, would have been greatly improved. The trustees unfortunately determined on repairing the old bridge. This nuisance still remains and no advantage whatever has been gained. Unless, therefore, something is done to preserve at least, if not to improve the navigation of the Medway, the soundings will go on diminishing in depth and the dockyard will become less useful. In its present state, vessels of large draught of water must have all their guns and stores taken out before they can come up the dockyard and be dismasted before they can be taken into the dock.[21]

At that time, Rennie could see no real solution to the problem and favoured construction of an alternative yard at Northfleet, this to replace not just Chatham but also the yards of Woolwich and Deptford.[22] The only drawback, however, was that of the likely cost of such a project, with Rennie suggesting a sum of £6 million. Others disputed this figure, with the Admiralty suggesting that this sum might well double upon construction work getting underway. The project got as far as having outline plans drawn up and the appropriate land purchased. Indeed, the entire Northfleet complex might have been constructed, and Chatham dockyard closed, if it had not been for Samuel Bentham developing a super-efficient dredger through the adoption of steam power. A dramatic improvement on the hand dredgers previously used and operated by dockyard scavelmen, its use resulted in the rapid clearing of many of the problematic shoals. Those hand dredgers had been hopelessly inefficient, removing from the bed of the river no more than a few tons of mud each day. In contrast, a steam-powered dredger based on Bentham's original design was removing, by 1823, as much as 175 tons of mud per day.

Inevitably, it was Bentham's development of the steam dredger that saved Chatham from an ignominious closure during the early decades of the nineteenth century. Instead this valuable military complex was not only to continue in its important shipbuilding and repair role but was to enter into a new period of supremacy. Within forty years of those closure threats, Chatham had been earmarked for a programme of expansion that was so massive in scale that it actually quadrupled the land area of the existing yard. Furthermore, it took on its very own specialism through the building of ironclads. Not only was Chatham the first royal dockyard to build an ironclad, but it also became the lead yard when any new class of ironclad battleship was laid down. Although his name is rarely spoken in Chatham, Samuel Bentham was the man who saved Chatham Dockyard – that is, until Margaret Thatcher arrived on the scene some 140 years later.

While Nelson's original *Victory* is dry-docked at Portsmouth, Chatham can at least lay claim to this model of the same vessel and one which itself has an interesting history having been originally constructed for the Alexander Korda film, *That Hamilton Woman* (1941).

6

THE ERA OF REFORM

The dockyard at Chatham had a much rosier future in the 1820s than it had possessed at any point during the previous fifty or so years. In that earlier period, the yard had even found itself under threat of closure, this a result of the increasing difficulty faced by larger ships attempting to navigate the Medway. With this problem now solved through the introduction of steam dredging, a series of further improvements were under consideration, these designed to allow the yard to both operate more effectively and also to expand upon the work undertaken.

One such project, although dating to the final years of the Napoleonic Wars, was put forward by George Parkin, the Master Shipwright at Chatham. This was in 1813, with Parkin wishing to see a general improvement to the yard's river frontage, including the various dry docks that occupied this same area. At the time Parkin was concerned with the markedly decayed state of the river wall and a general need to improve and lengthen all of the existing docks. In essence, he suggested a complete rebuilding of the central section of the yard's river frontage, with part of the wall moved forward several yards and onto an area of land that would be reclaimed from the Medway for this purpose. This would not only have the advantage of increasing the acreage of land within the dockyard, but would allow, at little additional cost, for the lengthening of the two most northerly docks.

The Navy Board appears to have been favourably impressed with Parkin's scheme, choosing to employ John Rennie, the leading engineer of the age, to undertake a feasibility study. Despite a clear statement that Rennie was only to give his opinion on Parkin's projected improvements to the dockyard river frontage, the engineer devoted most of his attention to a number of alternative ideas for the general improvement of the entire yard. These were presented to the Admiralty during the summer of 1814, with Rennie both outlining the general defects of the yard and how these might be overcome.

In his report, and given that the problem of silting was at that time unresolved, Rennie not unnaturally devoted a fair amount of attention to this particular issue. In addition, however, he also drew attention to other weaknesses in the usefulness of the yard, these relating to the limited value of some of the existing building and repair facilities together with a general lack of storage space. With regard to the former, he specifically drew attention to the dry docks, these having seen no substantial improvements since the beginning of the previous century. Built for warships of an earlier age, they did not have

Still used in the manufacture of rope is this forming machine that dates to 1811 and was the product of Henry Maudslay, a leading engineer of the age.

sufficient depth for the accommodation of the much larger warships that were now regularly being brought to Chatham. According to Rennie's calculations it was the Old Single Dock that had the greatest depth of water, this being 18ft 3in on a spring tide and 14ft 9in with a neap tide. Yet, with that additional depth acquired at the height of a spring tide, this dock still required a further 3ft of water for a first rate to make an unobstructed entry. As it happens, such vessels were brought into dry dock at Chatham, but to do so these ships had to be heaved on to blocks that were often 3ft above the base of the keel.

A further factor that counted against the efficiency of Chatham's existing dry docks was that they were constructed of timber rather than stone. Originally this had made a great deal of sense, it being cheaper and easier to build in timber. However, docks constructed of timber lacked durability, with those at Chatham, as already demonstrated, sometimes needing to be repaired at times that proved less than advantageous.

Although it would not have been impossible to completely modernise the dry docks at Chatham, any proposals were normally pushed aside on grounds of expense. The Chatham dry docks, as they stood, were of a very simple design, their shallowness partly resulting from the method used for their drainage. Unlike a series of dry docks that had been recently built at Portsmouth and Plymouth, those at Chatham had no attached pumping system. Instead, all four of Chatham's dry docks relied upon gravity drainage, with water receding from these docks during the normal fall of tide. To provide the necessary additional depth, these docks would not only have to be rebuilt (preferably in stone) but the increased depth would have taken them to a point that was beneath the river Medway's low tide level. As a result, a sophisticated pumping system would have to be introduced in order to remove large amounts of accumulated water. Rennie, aware of all this as he was, made a proposition that looked for a series of gradual improvements, rather than a dramatic and immediate wholesale rebuilding of the dry docks in the yard:

[As to] the shallowness of the dry docks, the plan I propose will not alter them; but as the docks are generally in a bad state, they must ere undergo a thorough repair, and when this is done, it will be the proper time to lay the floor of them sufficiently deep to take the largest ships to which their respective lengths are adapted; and such additional docks may be made as the demands of the public service may require, which perhaps may be to double the number of the existing docks.[1]

The Admiralty concurred, agreeing that one dry dock should be built immediately with its construction placed under the overall supervision of Rennie. This new dock was to be of a much greater depth than the four existing docks and would be built of granite rather than timber. To be sited immediately to the north of the Old Single Dock, it would eventually be known as the No. 3 Dock. At this point, some reference needs to be made to the overall numbering of docks, as the names originally used to distinguish each of the docks had ceased to have any relevance, leading to each being consecutively numbered. Thus, the original Double Dock (renamed the South Dock during the early eighteenth century) was now the No. 1 Dock and the Old Single Dock was the No. 2 Dock. In turn, the First and Second New Docks, situated further to the north and subsequently known as Nos 3 and 4 Docks would eventually be renumbered as docks 4 and 5, to make way for the new stone dock that was now to be built between the old Nos 2 and 3 Docks. For a time, this also meant that Chatham had five dry docks not four. This was only a temporary situation as, shortly after, the Old No. 4 Dock (new No. 5) was converted into a building slip. In turn, this also resulted in a consecutive renumbering of the slips, with the former dock having become No. 3 Slip. From now on, therefore, all docks and slips will be referred to by the numbers that they had acquired following both the completion of Rennie's new stone dock and the conversion of the No. 5 Dock into a building slip.

Rennie provided a description of his proposed design for the new stone dock in a letter sent to the Navy Board in August 1815:

A view of the interior of the ropery, looking along the length of the laying floor.

The size of the dock is conformable to dimensions furnished me by the Surveyor of the Navy. The floor is proposed to be 4 feet under the level of low water of an ordinary spring tide, which according to Mr Parkin's information rises 18½ feet, thus giving 22½ feet of depth at the high water of a spring tide, which I am informed will be sufficient not only to float a first rate but also admit of the proper sized blocks under her keel. At this time therefore there will be 4 feet of water to pump out of the dock at low water Spring Tides, and about 9 feet at neap tides, and for this purpose a steam engine will be required.

To this he added a series of estimates as regards its overall cost:

First, supposing the whole of the altars, floor and entrance to be made of Aberdeen granite. In which case the probable expense of the dock, admitting the whole to be set on piles, which from Mr Parkin's borings I fear will be necessary, amount to £143,000. The steam engine, engine house, well and drain, amounts to £14,700; and working her for two years while these works are in hand £2,000.[2]

Work on constructing the new dock was undertaken by John Usborne and Benson, a privately owned construction company, with John Rennie given access to the work at all times. The contract was signed on 16 February 1816 with payments made by the Navy Board at the rate of £1,000 for completion of each of a series of stipulated units. A separate pump house, this to accommodate a 50hp Boulton & Watt steam engine to be used in draining the dock, was also to be constructed. Situated immediately behind the new dock and on land formerly used for the storage of timber, this building was to be constructed by the dockyard's own workforce. Originally it was hoped that the new dock would be available for use during the early part of 1819, or even earlier, but a number of delays, primarily due to the contractors under-ordering materials and scrimping on the number of artisans employed, meant that it was not to be finally completed until 1821 and resulting in a total cost that amounted to £182,286.

Rennie's dry dock must be considered an important and significant feature of the yard, being the first to be built in the yard of a material other than timber. As such, it also paved the way for the complete rebuilding of three of the original docks, the No. 5 Dock having been deemed better suited to conversion into a slip. The new No. 3 Dock had a length of 225ft and a maximum width of 90ft. Internally it was characterised by stepped stone sides, these rising from the base of the floor to the ground level of the dockyard. Essential features of the dock, the steps were used both as a working area and as wedges to hold the shores resting against the sides of the otherwise unsupported vessel that stood within the dock. Divided into an upper and lower set, the top section of four steps was much steeper than a lower group of thirteen. Dividing the two sets was a broad central step that was primarily designed as a walkway. Access to the dock was by means of six sets of stone staircases, these positioned at the head, mid and aft sections of the dock. Finally, for the easy delivery of material to be used in the repair and building of ships, there were a number of stone slides (or ramps) which, at varying intervals, ran over the top of the stepped sides.

A particularly unusual feature demonstrated by the draft plan of the new dock was the use of a comparatively sophisticated entrance arrangement. As far as the existing docks were concerned, the entrance of a vessel was through a single pair of gates that were set either side of the slightly narrowing aft end of the dock. Held shut by a series of timber shores wedged between the gates and side walls of the dock, these gates were opened and closed through the application of manual power. The new dock dispensed with such a simple, if labour-intensive arrangement, introducing an entry neck that could be sealed at both ends. On the side of the neck closest to the dock was a pair of timber gates that could be opened and closed through the use of a capstan and chain device. The capstan was turned by only a small number of labourers, while the chains adhering to the gate held them firmly closed and overcame the necessity of using numerous timber shores for wedging purposes. According to Rennie's draft plan, these gates spanned an entrance area of 57ft and opened out on to a special recess that prevented them becoming accidentally entangled with any vessel floated into the dock.[3]

The river side of the short entry neck was sealed by a floating chest known as a caisson. Filled with water, a caisson would rest on the bed of the river, but once pumped free of water, could be floated and repositioned. Fixed into grooves that ran along the sides and bottom of the entry neck, it had the advantage of being completely removable and so allowed for the creation of a much wider entrance which was free of the additional need for a gate recess point. The use of a caisson was, during the second decade of the nineteenth century, a fairly novel innovation but, over time, completely

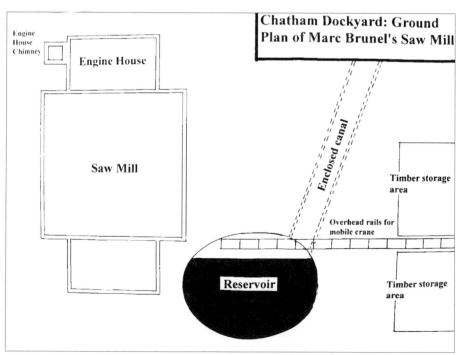

Ground plan of Brunel's saw mill, which dates to 1814.

replaced the earlier entry gate system. That Rennie chose to use a caisson as the first of two entry seals results from a further drawback in the use of gates, this being that no matter how well they were sealed, water always leaked both through the central join and hinged sections. By introducing a short neck, any water gaining access past the caisson could be drained away before it reached the gates.

By way of his illness and eventual death in October 1821, Rennie was never to see the first stone dry dock at Chatham completed. Yet its continued existence within the historic dockyard serves as a suitable tribute to this great engineer and the frequent visits he made to Chatham to ensure its overall progress. Without his insistence that the dock was to be built entirely of stone and finished to the highest standards, it could not possibly have survived in virtually its original state for over 180 years. Indeed, even at the time of writing, the dock is still in use, having been engaged in the repair of naval warships up until 1984; it currently accommodates the nineteenth-century sloop, HMS *Gannet*, brought into the dockyard for permanent display.[4]

Following completion of the new No.3 Dock, work commenced on lengthening and improving the Nos 1 and 2 Docks, with the work carried out from 1824 onwards. In both cases the design of these two docks, as reconstructed, was to be similar to that of Rennie's earlier dock, in that they were also of granite, possessed stepped sides and were provided with a caisson at the entrance. The contractor, once again, was Usborne and Benson, with complaints again received about the tardiness of the work performed. In July 1825, for instance, Charles Cunningham, resident Commissioner at Chatham between 1823 and 1831, felt constrained to write to the Navy Board in the following terms:

> Adverting to my former correspondence relative to the works carrying on in this yard at the Dock No.2, I think it proper to acquaint you that, not withstanding, there are only thirteen masons employed thereon. It appears by a report from the Master Shipwright that the quantity of stone in hand is not more than sufficient to keep them employed for about a fortnight but that the contractors stated to him on Saturday last another vessel was loading with that article and might be shortly expected. I suggest the propriety of the contractors being urged to send timely supplies of stone, in order that no impediment on that account, may take place in carrying on the works in question, with the few hands that are employed upon them.[5]

To save costs, and ensure the docks were adequately pumped, the steam machinery built for the first new stone dock was also used for pumping the other docks.

An additional problem to which Rennie had alluded in his comments of 1814 was the deficiency of space for the storage of timber and other materials. As it stood, and according to Rennie, 'the timber is obliged to be stacked wherever room can be found to lay it, by which the expense of teams [of horses] becomes very heavy'.[6] To his mind, the solution was for all matters relating to shipbuilding to be transferred to the Frindsbury side of the river, so providing additional storage space for timber dedicated to this task.

However, Rennie did not simply propose that the peninsula should become an adjunct to the existing yard but that it should be entirely incorporated into the existing complex. This would be achieved, so Rennie suggested, through the rerouting of the river by way of a channel that could be cut across the northern arm of the Frindsbury Peninsula. In turn, the existing channel, namely Chatham Reach, would be dammed and converted into a series of basins that would usefully serve the needs of ships being repaired and fitted out. In Rennie's own words:

> I propose to make a new channel or cut for the River Medway, from the bend below Rochester Bridge, opposite Frindsbury Church to Upnor Castle, forming a regular sweep, that it may join in an easy curve with the head of Cockhouse [sic] Reach, and to throw a dam across the old channel, from the north-east corner of Rochester Marshes to the Frindsbury side between the two shipyards, and another across at the north end of the dockyard and above the Ordnance floating-bridge, thus making the old river between the north end of the dockyard and the north-east point of Rochester Marshes into a wet dock, which, taking the surface covered at low water, will be upwards of 150 acres, leaving a space of land between the new proposed cut and the present channel of the river, on the Frindsbury side, of nearly the same extent, and which I proposed shall be purchased and taken into the dockyard.
>
>   At the northern end of the dockyard I propose that a new cut shall be made from the dock I have described, across Frindsbury to Gillingham Marshes, south of the line of St Mary's Creek to the head of Gillingham Reach adjoining the fort, and at its lower end I propose a lock to communicate with the Medway, having a small basin at the head for the convenience of vessels going into or out of the dock or Medway.[7]

A secondary advantage to the scheme, and referring to the hazards of navigating the river, was that in creating the new cut, the river would be considerably straightened, so allowing a greater quantity of tidal water to flow and 'deepen the river between the head of Gillingham Reach and Long Reach, and thereby further lessen the difficulties and detention in the navigation of these reaches'.[8]

    The Admiralty, for its part, was not sufficiently impressed. Noting that it would require a quite considerable financial outlay, they looked to a much cheaper, if less imaginative, approach to an overall expansion of the existing facilities at Chatham. In rejecting the idea of extending across the river, various purchases of marshlands immediately adjoining the dockyard and within the parish of Gillingham were undertaken. Formally authorised by Act of Parliament, these purchases included Fresh Marsh (18 acres) and Salt Marsh, the marshlands variously owned by Elizabeth Strover, Samuel Strover and John Simmons. The intention at this stage was to use these parcels of land for timber storage and depositing mud dredged from the river Medway. Later, however, this same land formed the basis for a further extension of the dockyard as carried out later in the century.

    Concurrent with these significant changes to the yard was that of the provision of roofs to the new docks and slips. The value of roofing was outlined to the Admiralty in a report

Holding its first service in July 1808, the Dockyard Chapel provided a discrete place of worship within the yard. Prior to its construction, officers of the dockyard, together with those artisans who chose to attend religious services, had to direct themselves to St Mary's, the parish church on Chatham Hill (Dock Road).

of 1817 in which it was claimed that in building and repairing ships under cover there would be a much diminished threat of dry rot. The report went on to suggest that the measure 'should take precedence over all other objects because there is none other to compare with it as so immediately and permanently affecting the public purse'.[9] By the time of that report, and providing some of the evidence for the necessity of covering all of the yard's docks and slips, both the No.1 Dock and the second slip had already been covered, a procedure that had been carried out in 1817. While the various docks were given coverings in the manner of an open-sided timber structure with a pitch copper-covered roof, those given to the slips were much grander. For one thing, they had to rise to a much greater height; this to give sufficient clearance to the entire hull that was building on a slipway that was at ground level. The estimated cost for the work of constructing these two covers was £1,165, but to this was subsequently added the sum of £5,630 for the coppering of the two roofs. The covering given to the No.2 slip not only rose to a considerable height but swept out grandly on each side, this to provide a sheltered working area for those employed on constructing new vessels. Unfortunately this particular slip cover was destroyed by accidental fire in 1966, but it had much in common with the covering placed over the No.3 Slip in 1838. The adjoining Nos 4, 5 and 6 slip covers, also extant, are very different in style. Designed by Captain Thomas R. Mould of the Royal Engineers, they are of cast- and wrought-iron construction with a corrugated ironclad roof. The final slip to be covered at Chatham, the No.7, was a considerable further advance in design. Authorised in 1851, it was designed by G.T. Green. Another work constructed from iron, it incorporated travelling cranes operating on rails built into the roof structure.

In the ropery, during the 1830s, steam power began to be introduced. But it had been a long time in coming. In fact, it should have been introduced in 1811, the year in which jack wheels, originally designed to be powered by steam, were first introduced into this area of the yard. Used in the process of laying the strands together to form (or close) the rope, five in number had at that time been purchased from the Henry Maudslay Company. Despite this, the Navy Board at that time had failed to support the purchase of the supporting steam engine, resulting in these expensive and intricate devices having to be operated manually. Not until 1836 was this ruling over-turned, with the sum of £2,500 placed in that year's naval estimates and earmarked for the purchase of a 14hp steam engine to be manufactured by Boulton & Watt. To provide the necessary accommodation, the hemp house adjoining the north wall of the ropery was to be partially demolished and replaced by an engine house.[10]

The arrival of this machinery was to completely revolutionise the process of rope making at Chatham. On the laying floor it immediately reduced the necessity of employing such a large proportion of the workforce during the final closing of the heavy ropes. Furthermore, it paved the way for the introduction of much larger and heavier jack wheels, these more able to handle the heavier ropes. Brought to the ropery during the 1850s, these particular jack wheels were constructed to run on newly intro-duced sets of rails that ran the length of the laying floor. At the same time, thought was given to making greater use of steam power, with a second engine providing power for the process of hatchelling and spinning, a series of spinning jennies installed on the top floor of the remaining hemp house. This machinery, which required of the opera-tors only limited skills, saw both the hatchelling and spinning processes undertaken by semi-skilled labour together with part-trained spinner apprentices. They in turn were themselves to be superseded, the work of spinning given over to women in 1864.

The employment of women in the spinning process was not the first employment of female labour in the dockyard, women having been employed in the colour loft, manufacturing flags, since the end of the eighteenth century. However, there was a dis-tinct difference between the two groups, with employment in the colour loft restricted to the wives and daughters of those either incapacitated or killed in naval service. As a result, those employed in the colour loft were treated with a good deal of respect and were referred to as 'the ladies of the colour loft'. The newly employed females entering the ropery were not accorded this same level of respect, referred to as 'the women of the ropery'. This reduced level of status resulted, in part, from their social background, not being widows or daughters of those in Admiralty service. In addition, less value was placed on the work they were performing, especially when compared with the skill of producing an intricately patterned flag, the ropeyard workers seen only as machine minders. In keeping with nineteenth-century views of morality, the women were strictly segregated from the men, with female employees having separate entrances, staircases and mess room. They also worked different hours, so as to enter and leave the yard at different times to their male counterparts. The only contact with a man was that of their overseer. As for the reason for the introduction of women in the ropery, this was strictly an economy, it being possible to pay them less than men.

Hand in glove with ensuring that the facilities in the dockyard and those employed were fit for purpose was that of also ensuring managerial efficiency. Of particular note was that the resident Commissioner had only limited authority, in that he merely served as a link between the Navy Board and the dockyard. In addition, there was the notable surfeit of officers, at both the principal and inferior levels, with many undertaking tasks

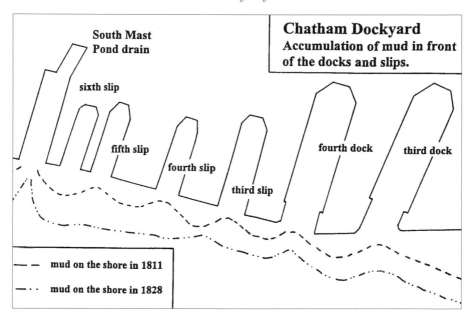

Chatham Dockyard
Accumulation of mud in front of the docks and slips.

South Mast Pond drain

sixth slip

fifth slip

fourth slip

third slip

fourth dock

third dock

— — mud on the shore in 1811

—·· mud on the shore in 1828

A problem that had to be confronted during the early years of the nineteenth century was the slow strangulation of the dockyard by large quantities of mud that was accumulating in the Medway. The rapidity of its accumulation can be appreciated by this comparison of mud in front of the dockyard in 1811 when compared with 1828.

that could easily be merged and performed by a single appointee, rather than two. In 1822, a partial attempt at reform was undertaken when the duties of the Clerk of the Ropeyard were absorbed by the Storekeeper and those of the Clerk of the Cheque by the Commissioner. In one sweep, therefore, two of the more senior posts in the dockyard were removed, with an immediate annual saving of several hundred pounds.

The reforms of 1822 had also seen abolition of a number of trade masters together with foremen of trades and quartermen. Quartermen had been attached to gangs of twenty working shipwrights and had been responsible for ensuring the quality of work performed. They had taken their instructions from one of the foremen of the yard. However, in abolishing this one group of inferior officers, another group of officers replaced them, these officially known as leading men.[11] They differed from quartermen in respect of being raised workmen who carried out the same tasks as those overseen. At the same time, the number of yard foremen was increased, these officers being relieved of clerical duties that they might be more proactive in the inspection of working gangs. Both the removal of quartermen and the introduction of leading men proved controversial, not least from one outspoken anonymous critic, possibly a clerk employed at Chatham Dockyard, who forwarded a printed volume of his views to the Board of Admiralty:

[It is] with extreme concern that I find so respectable and useful a body of officers abolished; and the places supplied by an inferior class, denominated leading men. Each [Leading Man] has charge of ten working men; whose workmanship he must superin-

Chatham Reach. If John Rennie's plans had come to fruition, this area of the Medway would have been locked into the dockyard with a new cut for shipping created on the far side of the Frindsbury Peninsula.

> tend the due execution of; the stores for whose use he must draw (that is obtain officially from the storehouses) and have the charge of; as also of whatever conversions of materials may be required for him to attend to (so that no wasteful expenditure of the one, nor improper conversions of the other may take place). At the same time, that all these important duties, are required from him (for which additional duty he is allowed only six pence per diem extra) he is to perform the same quantity of work, as each of his men, or otherwise, will be paid as much less, as his work may fall short thereof.[12]

The remaining trade masters were all abolished seven years later, replaced by foremen.

The years 1832–34 witnessed a further series of reforms that tackled the central weakness of dockyard management, the limited authority of the Commissioner. Under a Parliamentary Act of 1832 Superintendents replaced them, with the Act suggesting that these new officers would perform the same duties as the Commissioners they were replacing. But this was not to be. The subsequent general instructions, empowered by an order-in-council of 18 July 1833, made it clear that the Superintendent had full authority over all yard officers. Furthermore, all correspondence ceased just passing through his office; instead it was directly addressed to him with any returning correspondence, whether from the officers or workmen, having to be approved by him. The introduction of the new title also meant that those styled Commissioner would now cease to hold office, so that the Whig administration was able to make its own appointments. At Chatham, the newly appointed Superintendent was Sir James Alexander Gordon, the warrant for this appointment being dated 9 June:

> By the Commissioners for executing the office of Lord High Admiral of Great Britain and Ireland to Sir James Alexander Gordon, KCB, a Captain in His Majesty's Navy, hereby appointed Captain Superintendent of His Majesty's Dock Yards at Chatham and Sheerness by virtue of the power and authority to us given we do hereby constitute and appoint you Captain Superintendent of His Majesty's dockyards at Chatham and

Sheerness to be employed in conducting the business of the said dockyards during our pleasure willing and requiring you to take upon you the charge and duties of Captain Superintendent of the said dockyards accordingly and to obey all such instructions as you may from time to time receive from us for your guidance in the execution of the said duties strictly charging and commanding all persons employed as subordinates to you to behave themselves jointly and severally with all respect and obedience unto you as their Captain Superintendent and for your care and trouble in the execution of the duties of your office you will be entitled to receive a salary of £1,000 per annum until further orders and for so doing, this shall be your warrant.[13]

Totally omitted from the Act, and resulting from an 1831 policy document, was the recommendation that appointed Superintendents should retain their naval rank. Like the former Commissioners, they were to be drawn from serving naval officers, but unlike Commissioners they were not to lose their seniority. For this, there were sound reasons. Those who had been appointed to the post of Commissioner, and so without naval rank, had frequently found their authority undermined when working with those of naval rank, the latter sometimes countermanding their instructions.

With regard to the reforms of 1833–34, a backward step concerned the reading of instructions to the officers. Prior to 1833, the principal officers of the yard had collected together, listened to the Commissioner reading the instructions from London and had then jointly discussed how these duties might be performed. From July 1833, those meetings were to cease. Instead, the Superintendents were merely to read the orders of the day, the officers being immediately despatched to their duties. Unable to share their problems with each other, they were forced to approach the Superintendent as individuals, communicating with him in private. As was noted by Bromley, a senior clerk of the Admiralty, this situation not only prevented the superior officers from working in concert, but created 'petty jealousies'. A further retrograde step created by the instructions of 1833 was the ending of the daily meetings that once took place between the superior and inferior officers.

Relations between the Admiralty and Navy Board during the period 1816 to 1832, despite a potential for animosity, was one of relative tranquillity. In part, this was a result of the extraordinary longevity of the Tory administration under Lord Liverpool with Robert Dundas, 2nd Viscount Melville, the longest serving First Lord. Having taken office in February 1812 Melville had, by 1816, not only appointed the Comptroller, Sir Thomas Byam Martin, but the majority of those who made the Navy Board. Through a number of careful selections, Melville created a politically allied body that had every reason to make the system work. Nevertheless, members of the Navy Board were still intent upon upholding their own professional opinion. In particular, differences occurred over the extent to which the dockyards should economise following the conclusion of the war with Napoleon. Melville proposed that the workforce should both receive a wage cut and work longer hours, a view supported by Robert Barlow, the Chatham resident Commissioner from 1808–23. However, Martin, as Barlow's senior, was quick to take issue, unhappy that he so freely supported the view of the Admiralty against that of the Navy Board:

> Our friend Barlow seems to think that if we have the right to keep the men in the yard ten hours we have an equal right to demand ten hours active hard labour or a scheme of task, when the very Commissioners of Naval Revision admits that the extension of the men working by task shall entitle them to earn half as much again, and in the merchant yards double. [14]

In his efforts to maintain artificer numbers within the dockyards the numbers that he considered adequate for the works to be performed, Martin appears to have received the support of a former First Lord, the Earl St Vincent:

> I agree with you *in toto* as to the rapid ruin of the British Navy. Instead of discharging valuable and experienced men, of all descriptions from the dockyards, the Commissioners and secretaries of all the boards ought to be reduced to the lowest number they ever stood at and the old system resorted to. One of the projectors of the present diabolical measures should be gibbeted opposite to the Deptford yard and the other opposite the Woolwich yard, on the Isle of Sad Dogs. [15]

In general, Martin was highly critical of those who called for excessive economies and supported measures that protected the most skilled workers from dismissal. Nevertheless, during the years that followed upon the ending of the wars against Napoleon, numbers employed at Chatham were dramatically reduced. Whereas in 1814, the total workforce at Chatham had stood at 2,600, the number employed by 1832 was much nearer to 1,300.

The ability of the Admiralty and Navy Boards to work in harmony during the years that followed the Napoleonic Wars did not extend to the Whig-led coalition that entered power in November 1830. Having experienced, while First Lord between February and September 1806, the difficulties that could result from a hostile inferior Board, the new Prime Minister, the 2nd Earl Grey, was intent upon abolishing the Navy Board. Shortly after his accession to office, the new First Lord of the Admiralty, Sir James Graham, with the help of John Barrow, the senior permanent Secretary to the Board of Admiralty, put together a discussion document that outlined the reasons for abolishing the Board while indicating how it was to be replaced. Instead of an inferior Board, a number of principal officers were to be appointed, these to carry out tasks previously performed by the Navy Board. These officers were neither to act in concert nor have any form of executive authority. Instead, a naval lord was to be placed in immediate authority over each of them, with each principle officer having only the power to refer matters to his directing naval lord for discussion by the Board of Admiralty. It was upon the terms of this discussion paper, with but a few amendments, that the Naval Civil Departments Act, which reached the statute books on 9 June 1832, was ultimately based and which was responsible for the complete abolition of the Navy Board.

An important addition to the yard during the early nineteenth century was this building, standing at the head of No.4 Dock and which contained the pumping machinery that was eventually to allow Chatham to acquire docks of greater depth. Prior to the arrival of steam pumps, the dry docks had been gravity drained and could not have a depth below that of the low tide level.

A major problem for the newly reformed system was the general expansion of dockyard business and a consequent growth in correspondence directed to the Admiralty. According to Barrow, there was a 33 per cent growth in letters received and despatched from the Admiralty during the period 1827 to 1833. Graham had believed the opposite would take place. In 1836 Barrow went so far as to indicate that the Admiralty was being simply overwhelmed by becoming directly involved with all matters directly relating to dockyard matters.[16] A reference to the Admiralty minute books confirms this: one entry indicates that the principal officers were not to oversee the accounts without these being examined, on a quarterly basis, by members of the Admiralty Board – even though that Board had no understanding of accountancy matters.[17]

A further aspect of the Whig-led coalition reforms of this period was a desire to ensure that every member of the workforce worked with the highest possible levels of efficiency. In particular, the Whigs were unhappy with payment by task and job (piece rates), believing that this particular means of remuneration led to work being rushed. Conversely, they also questioned payment at a fixed daily rate, believing that this failed to encourage anything other than work performed at a most leisurely pace. The solution adopted was a complete revamping of the wage system through the introduction of a scheme known as 'classification' and by which artisans and labourers were paid according to their perceived merit. Introduced in 1834, it divided the workforce into three classes, with the most efficient placed into the highest, or first class, and paying them at a higher rate than other members of the same trade group who had been placed in either the second or third class. Designed to encourage higher rates of work output, it was supposed to encourage those in the second or third classes to work with a degree of efficiency that would eventually lead to promotion into the class above.

The No.2 Slip at Chatham was the first to be covered, with the roofing added in 1810. Unfortunately, this slip cover no longer exists, having been destroyed by fire in 1966.

In completely overturning the existing system of wage payment, classification was seen by the mass of the workforce as distinctly unfair. Previously, two factors had governed wage rates. First and foremost was the distinction between workers of different skill levels or trades. Within each of the yards a shipwright, the most skilled of all dockyard workers, was guaranteed a higher wage than that of either a caulker or an anchor smith. Similarly, the anchor smith earned more than a rigger or yard labourer. However, the precise wage earned was further determined by whether the worker concerned was paid by the day or had been placed on piece work. To ensure fairness, a book of prices had been maintained and frequently updated, this indicating the monetary reward attached to items of work agreed and completed.

Upon the introduction of classification, the amount of work paid by piece rate was restricted with differentiation by skill distorted. Under the scheme of classification it became possible for a labourer appointed to the first or highest class to receive earnings that paralleled many of those who performed a skilled trade. Similarly, a lesser skilled artisan might find himself in receipt of earnings considerably in excess of a large proportion of shipwrights. However, it was not the partial ending of the pre-existing differential wage structure to which the dockyard workforce was primarily opposed. Instead, it was the divisive nature of the scheme that permitted only a small select group of workers to earn the highest possible wage. While the right to work 'task' and 'job' had, under the old system, been strictly limited as to numbers, it had at least been operated on a 'turn and turnabout principle'.[18] In other words, within any given year, most would have participated, with annual earnings more or less equitable between those of the same trade.

Workforce opposition to classification was total and unremitting. Using the petition as the chief weapon in the campaign, the system of petitioning was to be developed and strengthened over the seven-year period in which classification governed the system of wage payment. From a fairly unsophisticated device, albeit frequently supported by considerable organisation, for the simple submission of requests, it was to become the means by which the entire dockyard community was drawn into a major political campaign.

Initial opposition to classification, however, did not give a hint as to this later transformation. Indeed, the earliest petitions from Chatham were fairly unremarkable, emanating from artisans placed in the third class and requesting promotion to a higher class, a concern that for some continued into the late 1830s. This was much to the Admiralty's liking, indicating a willingness to work within the imposed system. In each case, the Admiralty indicated that promotion was certainly possible but would depend entirely upon their future endeavours. Signs of a more orchestrated campaign began to appear in 1835 when a series of petitions emanated from the various trade groups employed both at Chatham and the other naval dockyards. In all cases, these were fairly general, listing a range of grievances that included the general depression of wages brought about by the loss of piece work and classification. Both the timing of these petitions and the similarity of content show they were the result of considerable organisation. Contact of either a direct verbal nature or through written communication must have been made. Possibly, some form of ad hoc committee might have been formed but there is no direct evidence. The failure of these petitions to move the Admiralty forced the leaders of the campaign to rethink their strategy. Instead, a more imaginative and forceful means of presenting the petition had to be devised. For this reason, in 1836, important allies were recruited into the campaign. Following considerable contact between the various yards, public meetings, towards the end of that year, were held in each of the major dockyard towns. At Chatham, a meeting was held at the Sun Inn during December and was addressed by, among others, William Evenden, a joiner in the second class. After explaining some of the past difficulties faced by those in the dockyard, he directed his attention to the system of classification, with his speech reported in the *Rochester Gazette*:

> The advocates for it stated that it was a stimulus for exertion, and he would ask the meeting what necessity there was for this, at a time when they had received a vote of thanks from the Admiralty for their exertions. It was a useless thing – it was an oppressive system – in as much as it deprived a man and his family of many of those comforts of which they had before been partaking. He had said it was a degrading system, and it certainly was so. He would appeal to any present, supposing they had been in the yard 20 years, and were put in the second class – how would they like to see a young man, who had been probably the apprentice, placed in the first class? Would it not be naturally supposed that the aged workman had done something whereby he had disgraced himself?[19]

The petition that was presented to the meeting and subsequently signed, either at the meeting or during the following week, by many thousands of local inhabitants, made it quite clear that the system of classification was primarily opposed because of its divisive nature:

> That your memorialists believe the system of classification adopted in His Majesty's dockyards was introduced with the earnest desire to reward merit and encourage industry, but are fully assured from observation and the testimony of the workmen, that it has signally failed to accomplish this object. They believe that it has created most invidious

distinctions amongst the workmen where no difference exists in merit. So much so as to cause in many instances the promotion to be deprecated rather than desired; that it is the cause of continual discord and jealousy, and tends to destroy that unity and good feeling which should at all times subsist between fellow-workmen, and that no beneficial effect has resulted, or can result there from, to the service of His Majesty.[20]

However, there was neither a resultant abolition of classification nor an increase offered in wages paid. But this failure does not appear to have undermined the general faith of dockyard artisans and labourers in the value of petitions. Over the next three years petitions continued to be submitted to the Admiralty on a regular basis, some of them from artisan groups while others carried signatures drawn from the wider community. In addition, increased involvement of Members of Parliament is also discernible. Often in attendance at these meetings, they also accompanied delegations of workmen who had been given permission to express their views to the Board in their London offices.

That the campaign to abolish classification was to meet with eventual success was only partly due to the on-going petitioning campaign. More important was increasing Admiralty awareness of the difficulties involved in both retaining and recruiting skilled artisans into the yards. During the latter part of the 1830s increasing numbers had chosen to leave, preferring employment in the private yards or working abroad, the situation reaching a crisis point by about 1839. Aware that something had to be done, Lord Minto, First Lord since 1835, determined on a major gesture to appease the workforce. In April 1840, it was announced that the hated third class would be abolished. Those currently rated to this class would, upon its abolition in January 1841, be raised to the second class. For the workforce, while not a complete victory, it was a move in the right direction. In May 1840 a delegation that consisted of two shipwrights from each yard together with thirteen Members of Parliament, all of them drawn from the dockyard towns, visited the Admiralty. Although a wide range of matters was discussed, including that of low wages, the system of classification was very much at the heart of the meeting. According to the *Rochester Gazette*, the deputation strongly protested 'against its continuance'.[21] Undoubtedly the matter that must have concerned members of the Board was a statement made by one of the deputation from Portsmouth. He strongly urged the necessity of a definite answer:

> … as he represented a body of six hundred of excellent workmen as could be found; and added that he did not wish to hold out anything in the shape of a threat, but he would tell his Lordship that 70 of them, and he was amongst the number, had resolved – unless something satisfactory was done - to quit the service, and they could at once obtain employment in a foreign country at double the rate of wages they were now receiving.[22]

While they were given no definite promises, the delegation 'left the Admiralty with full expectation that something will be done for them'.[23] It was at the beginning of September 1840 that the Admiralty finally announced an end to classification. For the men at Chatham, the news was given to a deputation of artisans who had waited upon visiting members of the Admiralty during the annual inspection of the yard. With the ending of classification, the men returned to being paid the day rate, the rates now being adjusted for certain groups. Only in war time, or emergencies, were piece rates to be reintroduced, this taking place at the time of the Russian War (1854–56) and brought to an end shortly afterwards.

A further reform that also came under such criticism that it had to be radically adapted after a relatively short period was the introduction, in 1833, of a specialised dockyard police force. Prior to that year, security within the dockyard at Chatham had been in the hands of porters, warders, watchmen and rounders. Each had a specific role, with the porter usually located at the Main Gate and rounders conducting regular patrols. The warders had general duties, assisting porters during times when men were leaving the yard while holding the keys to various buildings. As for watchmen, they carried out regular patrols of the yard each evening. The number of warders, watchmen and rounders tended to vary, influenced by the availability of a secondary security force, that of a military guard. As for anyone detained on suspicion of having stolen dockyard stores, they were usually brought before the Commissioner of the yard who, as an appointed magistrate, had the right to conduct an examination.

Generally, however, the system did not work particularly well. Whether working with a 'friendly' rounder or watchman or not, it seems that certain members of the workforce were particularly adept at smuggling useful items out of the yard. In addition, there are numerous accounts in the dockyard records of stores being taken by those from outside of the yard who simply clambered over the wall at night. Given that members of this loosely organised dockyard security force were frequently chosen from among the workforce and never received any training, it was unlikely to provide a solution to the security needs of such a large and potentially vulnerable industrial complex.

In theory, therefore, the introduction of a uniformed and purposely recruited body should have been a marked improvement over what had gone before. Yet the dockyard police force that first began to operate at Chatham on 26 July 1833 failed to live up

While the No.2 Slip may not have survived the vicissitudes of time, a number of other (albeit later) coverings do survive, with that covering the No.3 Slip (in foreground) being constructed in 1838.

to expectations. Its officers, usually retired naval lieutenants, lacked any training in their new role and were unable to instil any sense of real responsibility into those they employed as constables. As a result, pilfering of dockyard material continued unchecked with the force soon becoming a byword for inefficiency. Certainly this was recognised as early as 1840, when the dockyard police force at Chatham was placed under an efficiency review, with the Board of Admiralty's Secretary informing the Captain Superintendent at Chatham:

> I am commanded by My Lords Commissioners of the Admiralty to acquaint you that the Commissioners of the Metropolitan Police intend sending two of their superior officers to Chatham Yard for the purpose of ascertaining what arrangements are necessary for making the police force of the yard more efficient, and I am to signify their Lordships directions to you to afford them every assistance in the prosecution of their enquiry.[24]

Despite such efforts, no improvements in the system were discernible, with officers and constables of the dockyard force continuing to perform their duties in an inefficient and lackadaisical manner. Eventually, but not until 1860, this first attempt at the creation of a dedicated dockyard security force was replaced by a separate division of the Metropolitan Police. Serving as clear evidence that those responsible for this new force had little faith in those who had been previously recruited into the earlier dockyard force, very few of the officers and constables were allowed to transfer into the new body.

Despite the failure of many of these reforms, it did not prevent the yard at Chatham taking numerous strides forward and eventually allowing it to become the most

important of the naval dockyards for new construction of warships. While the era of reform had not necessarily been the most demanding in terms of vessels built and ships brought in for repair, something else of considerable importance was also occurring. In various ways, the yard was being prepared for a veritable revolution. Alongside those reforms, the yard at Chatham had steadily been moving from an age dominated by wooden-hulled sailing ships to one that would be dominated by steam and ironclads. In comparison, the various reforms and changes undertaken during the first half of the nineteenth century were to pale into insignificance when compared with the changes that were to be brought about during the third quarter of that same century.

Unicorn, which was originally launched at Chatham in 1824, undergoing renovation during the 1980s at Dundee.

7

THE SHIPBUILDING REVOLUTION

The middle years of the nineteenth century witnessed two major revolutions in warship construction: the introduction of steam as a motive power and the increasing use of iron in the construction process, with the latter culminating in the adoption of armour-plated hulls. As a major warship building yard, it was inevitable that Chatham would be at the forefront of these developments, frequently called upon to both construct radically new types of vessels while modifying those already under construction or about to be launched. Furthermore, it would eventually lead to a massively altered dockyard, with both new types of specialised workshops required and the employment of a workforce with skills significantly different from those required only a few decades earlier.

Paving the way for these later far-reaching changes were a number of adaptations to shipbuilding design and constructional methods that started to be introduced towards the end of the Napoleonic Wars. Among them was a system of strengthening the frame of a ship through the timbers being braced together by trusses laid diagonally, and forming a series of triangles rather than the existing method of laying frame timbers in a square and rectangular pattern. A method invented by Robert Seppings, and brought to perfection following his appointment in 1804 to the office of Master Shipwright at Chatham, its importance was that of countering a tendency for the keels of larger ships to arch. Technically known as 'hogging' it resulted from the irregularity, when at sea, of the weight occasioned by greater upward pressure placed on the centre of the keel when compared with the extremities. At Chatham, *Kent*, a seventy-four-gun third rate, while under repair and known for her tendency to warp along the keel, was the first ship to which this method was applied. Later, in 1810, Seppings was given permission to use the same system in *Tremendous*, but this time he also included cross pieces between the various gun ports and additional timbers in the spaces between the lower frames. *Howe*, a 120-gun first rate, launched at Chatham in March 1815, was the first ship laid down and wholly built on the diagonal principle.

Unicorn, a fifth-rate frigate and now a museum ship at Dundee, was launched at Chatham in 1824. The interior of the vessel is of particular importance, revealing the extensive use of iron work to replace knees and other supporting timbers.

A second improvement pioneered by Seppings during his period at Chatham as Master Shipwright was that of giving larger ships a round bow. This had the advantage of improving the strength of the ship while providing an enlarged area of space for the mounting of guns in this, a traditionally under-gunned area of a warship. Following the conclusion of the Napoleonic Wars, most ships under construction and vessels undergoing major repair were provided with this new design feature as laid down in June 1816 by the following instructions issued to the shipwright officers at Chatham:

> The Lords Commissioners of the Admiralty having by their Order of the 13th inst. approved of the general adoption of the round stern suggested by Commissioner Seppings in the construction of His Majesty's ships. These are to direct and acquaint you, pursuant to their Lordships' directions, to cause all ships of the line and frigates to be built with round sterns accordingly and also to put round sterns to such as may be repaired provided the repair may be such an extent as to justify the alteration. To enable you to do which, drawings are in preparation and will be sent to you for your guidance.[1]

By March 1822, a total of fifteen warships had either been newly built or converted at Chatham to the new arrangement. Members of the Board of Admiralty during an inspection of the yard at Chatham, some two years earlier, had made a point of commenting on the conversion of ships to the round stern:

The *Trafalgar* and *Prince Regent*, building in this yard, were inspected, particularly with regard to the formation of their sterns. Some observations were made with regard to the angles, which may be formed in pointing the guns in the after part of both ships, and the advantages of those in the ship with the round stern were very manifest. The ships appeared in excellent condition and the timbers well seasoned.[2]

At this period of time, both the Admiralty and Navy Board constantly expressed their concern at the need to examine methods that would not only provide greater strength to ships but also ensure that the timbers employed in their construction were more effectively seasoned and so less likely to be subjected to rot. A flavour of some of the other changes recently introduced into methods of shipbuilding practised at Chatham and the other royal dockyards, can be gained from this communiqué sent by the Navy Board to the Admiralty and explaining that considerable efforts were being made in these two areas of joint concern:

When ships are set up on the slips exposed to the weather, the Spring has been chosen as the best time for commencing operations in planking, the caulking of the wales and bottom has been deferred until the ships have been about to be launched and the painting (except upon the weather works) has been postponed as long as possible. The precaution of a temporary housing in midships and every other means of keeping the ships dry by caulking the topside weather decks &c have also been resorted to.

Another change to ships being built at Chatham during the middle years of the nineteenth century was the introduction of steam power, with the launch of one such vessel, *Cressy*, an eighty-gun screw ship, taking place in July 1853, seen in an illustration that originally appeared in the *Illustrated London News*.

To promote a circulation of air for the seasoning of the timber, a great proportion of the treenails has been omitted as long as possible, some strakes of plank left out, wind sails introduced into the hold and louvred boards fitted in the ships' ports. The system of covering over the docks and slips, which has been of late partially introduced, will no doubt effectively contribute to the duration of ships built and repaired by sheltering the frames as well as the converted materials and it will not only add to the comfort of the workmen but will also afford considerable facility in building and repairing ships. The rapid decay, which of late years has taken place in many ships built and repaired in the King's and Merchant Yards, may be attributed to the following causes: the want of a sufficient store of seasoned timber, the scarcity of English oak (a great difficulty which has rendered it necessary to substitute fir timber) and the necessity of fitting newly built and repaired ships for service without allowing sufficient time for seasoning them and also the want of a sufficient number of slips and docks at the dockyards to meet the increased demand for ships of war and to permit the frames &c to stand a sufficient time to season.

Within a few years several important changes have taken place in the mode of constructing ships that we expect will be found not only to give strength to the fabric but prevent premature decay by affording a free circulation of air in the upper parts, but this is not likely to be attended to with the important advantages expected, if care be not taken (when the ships are in commission) to keep the shelf pieces clear and the openings free from dirt, as has been done while they were building.[3]

These earlier changes to ship constructional methods, although considered radical at the time, were relatively insignificant when compared with the subsequent introduction of steam machinery into the hulls of warships combined with the eventual replacement of timber hulls with those of iron. In adapting to the use of steam as a motive power for warships, the workforce at Chatham was aided by their accumulated familiarity with the use of steam in certain of the manufacturing areas of the yard. By 1814, as already detailed, it had been introduced into the saw mill with a steam pump also having been introduced into the yard for the purpose of draining an increasing number of dry docks. Furthermore, steam was also being used afloat, steam dredgers now employed in clearing the channels of the river of those fast-accumulating mud shoals.

It was in May 1831 that the first steam vessel was laid down at Chatham, a timber-hulled paddle sloop named *Phoenix*. An event of considerable importance, she was one of four paddle steamers built in the naval dockyards at this time, the four vessels being among the largest and most powerful of the day. Each was the product of a different senior shipwright employed by the Navy Board, with *Phoenix* designed by Robert Seppings who, by that time, was serving out his final years as Surveyor of the Navy. Another former Master Shipwright at Chatham, John Fincham, explained the reasons that lay behind this particular decision to concurrently build four independently designed vessels:

The importance of employing steam-vessels led now to the adoption of measures calculated to improve their character. The Admiralty desired to engage all the talents in the service with the view to this end, and invited the several Master Shipwrights to send in plans which they respectively deemed best suited for steam vessels.[4]

To this Fincham added:

It is no disparagement of the talents of their respective constructors to say that these vessels shared in the imperfections which were almost necessary at a time when the conditions of excellence in steam-vessels were only in the course of development; at the same time it is fair and just to say, that they were all useful vessels, and they have been durable and permanent in their usefulness.[5]

In having decided that these vessels were to be built in the royal dockyards, the Admiralty was sending out a clear message that the private yards were no longer to have a monopoly in this area of shipbuilding. As for the fitting of engines, Chatham still had a clear area of weakness, newly constructed steamers having often to be towed to one of the several specialist marine engine constructors located along the banks of the river Thames. *Phoenix*, for her part, following her floating out of dry dock in September 1831 was taken to Lambeth where Maudslay, Son & Field were responsible for both constructing and fitting her engine. For this, they charged the Admiralty £10,781 for the machinery and a further £7,968 for its installation, with the total cost of the vessel amounting to £33,463.

From this initial experience, Chatham went on to build a total of nineteen paddle steamers, with the last of these a sixteen-gun sloop named *Tiger*, launched in 1849 and fitted with a 400nhp engine built by John Penn & Son at their Deptford yard. During those years of constructing paddle steamers, Chatham had taken on an increasing amount of work connected with the steam machinery, fitting the engines of some and acquiring the skills to construct and modify boilers and paddle wheels. In addition, the workforce at Chatham oversaw the conducting of trials upon vessels once the machinery had been installed.

A further important landmark for Chatham was the building of *Bee*, a composite vessel fitted with both paddle wheels and an underwater screw and both working off the same machinery. Launched in February 1842, she was very much an experimental vessel, designed to assess the screw as a means of propelling a vessel through water. While paddle steamers had proved themselves useful, towing large sailing ships in unsuitable winds or for the more rapid carriage of troops and supplies, they had only limited value as warships. Primarily this was because of the large paddle wheels that sat on either side, these having an immense vulnerability to canon fire while also restricting the number of guns that could be fitted. In moving away from the use of paddles and replacing them with an underwater screw, much experimental work was required, with *Bee* having an important part to play in this work. Not only did she permit those who crewed her to learn the characteristics of a screw-propelled ship but she also permitted a direct com-

Steam power was gradually introduced to the ships built at Chatham during the middle years of the nineteenth century. _Cressy_, an eighty-gun screw ship, was launched in July 1853 and is seen here in an image from the _Illustrated London News_.

parison to be made between the two types of propellants. Indeed, she had been so designed that paddles and screw could work in opposition, allowing a direct comparison to be undertaken and demonstrating with regards to this particular vessel that the paddle could continue to drive the vessel forward despite the screws running in reverse. According to one more recent commentator, 'this must surely be the most bizarre trial of all time!'[6]

In persisting with the screw as the motive force that would push a warship through water, Chatham was charged with constructing three gun vessels that were all entirely dependent on the use of underwater screws. To be named _Teazer_, _Boxer_ and _Biter_, only the first was actually completed. _Teazer_, which entered the Medway in June 1846, therefore represents the first pure screw-propelled vessel to be launched at Chatham, with the machinery for this vessel built and fitted by Miller, Ravenhill & Co. of Blackwall.

The value of the screw to the needs of a warship led to the Admiralty making the decision to convert to steam a number of its existing sail-powered warships. Initially these were vessels of some age, with the intention of using them as harbour block ships. In other words, vessels that could be used in defending ports and harbours from any threatened attack. It was never intended they should be on the front line, merely an adjunct to existing harbour defences. The value of fitting machinery, which at this time was heavy in its use of coal, was that these vessels could be moved relatively short distances in any weather. At Chatham, _Horatio_, a 'Lively' class frigate that had originally been launched at Bursledon in 1807, was pulled out of the Medway Ordinary for this purpose. Entering dry dock in November 1845, the work required was that first she should be made good of any defects prior to the clearing and redesigning of her interior for the insertion of the necessary machinery. It was a task slow in completion, with _Horatio_ to remain in dockyard hands for approximately four years. Eventually, towards the end of 1849 she was ready to be taken to the East India Docks where she was fitted with a 2-cylinder horizontal expansion engine producing 250nhp.

Given that _Horatio_ was one of the first ships to undergo this form of conversion, she was very much a trial ship. This goes some way to explaining the length of time it took for the work to be completed. It also meant that, upon her return to the Medway in the late summer of 1851, she was subjected to a robust series of seagoing trials (these consisting of a series of runs between the Mouse and Nore lightships) which revealed that the main shaft needed altering as it was subject to overheating. Even after this problem had been addressed by Seward & Co., the firm that had manufactured the machinery, a further series of trials showed that her machinery was still not performing to full satisfaction as explained in an official report submitted by Alexander Lawrie, the Chief Engineer of the dockyard and addressed to the Captain Superintendent, his immediate superior:

> I have the honour to report that on the trial of HMS *Horatio* yesterday difficulty was experienced in keeping up the steam and on this account as well as the frequent pruning of the boilers only 33 revolutions were obtained out of the engines, the screw shaft not having attained the ordinary velocity. I am not yet able to state whether the alterations made by Messrs Seward & Co. will have the effect of preventing the heating of the main shaft.[7]

Between 1852 and 1859, the workforce at Chatham carried out similar conversions on a number of much larger warships, these also being given steam machinery together with the addition of sails. However, with regard to these, there was one big difference to the earlier conversion of *Horatio*. While the latter had already served as a seagoing ship, this

Another task frequently undertaken at Chatham during the age of fighting sail was that of breaking up an ageing vessel, with the collected timbers often reused. The reuse of such material was no longer possible by the late nineteenth century, when this particular vessel, *Resolute*, a former Arctic exploring ship, was broken up at Chatham in 1879. Here, a couple of old salts, looking across the Medway, take a final view of the vessel before she is completely demolished.

new round of conversions involved vessels that were already under construction but had not yet entered the Medway. The vessels concerned were *Majestic*, *Irresistible* and *Cressy*, each of which had originally been designed as eighty-gun second rates, together with *Hood*, a ninety-one-gun second rate. In the case of each of these vessels, with the keel and part of the frame already assembled, work had been brought to a temporary stand-still, it being recognised that they were about to enter a world where sail power had now been effectively superseded by steam. With a subsequent agreement on how they should be redesigned, work upon their construction was continued with machinery eventually installed into these ships by John Penn and also Maudslay, Son & Field.

In contrast to the conversion of large warships to steam was that of *Euryalus*, a Chatham-built frigate that, from the time of her keel being laid, was designated to carry both a full rig of sail and steam machinery. Admittedly, she too, had originally been ordered as a dedicated sailing ship, but this had been quickly rescinded and instructions issued that she should be built to a new design. Launched in October 1853, her engines were supplied by John Penn and fitted at Chatham. Her subsequent acceptance trials, which took place in February 1854, were reported in the pages of the *Illustrated London News*:

> On the 17th ult. she [*Euryalus*] had her steam up, and worked her trunk engines, by John Penn and Son, for two hours, at moorings, in the Medway. At one o'clock next day, she left Chatham, for the purpose of being tried at the measured distance between Nore and Mouse Lights, when her speed was ascertained as ten knots per hour; the engines working admirably, and making from 58 to 61 revolutions per minute. She anchored about five o'clock, pm, at Sheerness; and next morning pro-ceeded under steam to Chatham, for the purpose of being made completely ready for sea at the port where she was fitted, and had her engines put on board.
>
> The *Euryalus* is now lying in dock bending her sails, and hoisting her boats in. She will come out of Dock on Tuesday next, and proceed to Gillingham to take her powder in; and she will be in the Downs to form one of the Baltic squadron on or before the 6th March.[8]

The dockyard at Chatham was now very successfully adapting itself to the needs of steam-powered warships, an increasing number of engines being repaired and serviced and also fitted into newly built ships. In addition, an increasing amount of iron work was also being used on ships, these often replacing knees and other supporting timbers where iron had both the advantage of greater strength and was not subject to rot. An interesting example of a Chatham-built ship where iron was used extensively in this fashion, is that of *Unicorn*, a fifth-rate frigate that is now a museum ship at Dundee. Launched in 1824, her carefully preserved interior reveals that not only are her deck beams supported by iron brackets (where timber knees would once have been used) but iron bolts have replaced her diagonal strengthening timbers.

A Navy Board instruction of May 1805 appears to represent the first formalised use of iron in naval dockyard building practices, with the document encouraging the use of iron knees.[9] In part, this was to reduce the pressures placed on existing timber supplies, as oak suitable for conversion into use as a supporting knee timber was always difficult to acquire. However, the general value of iron for both bracing the hull and as brackets for supporting stern timbers became widely recognised. In fact, the use of iron in strengthening a timber hull also played an important part in allowing such vessels to take on board the machinery necessary for adaptation or conversion to steam. Peter Goodwin, in an article written for *Mariner's Mirror*, points out that for the purpose of carrying the weighty boilers together with either 'extensive paddle or propeller shafts', it was required to have 'a stable platform to give it considerable support'. As Goodwin adds, this could only be provided by 'a rigid hull form braced by iron.'[10]

In reaching a stage where both steam machinery could be repaired and occasionally fitted together with the manufacture of iron work, it became necessary to employ an increasing number of artisans who possessed the necessary new skills while also reducing those who possessed the traditional skills and who had previously dominated most areas of dockyard work. In addition, new and specialised equipment was also required together with new workshops. The smithery was, of course, especially busy, this mainly responsible for manufacturing much of the ironwork now required, with a new and much enlarged smithery added to the yard in 1808. Designed by Edward Holl, it had the capacity to handle much greater quantities of iron, manufacturing the bracings and other strengtheners being added to ships at that time. In 1843, and indicating the continuing and even more extensive use of iron, this smithery benefitted from the addition of a steam-operated tilt hammer and Hercules hammer, supplied at a cost of £4,309. These could be used in constructing the largest iron items, including 20cwt anchors. In addition to the smithery, a metal mill was also added to the yard during the 1840s together with a forge shop containing a 50cwt steam hammer powered by two high-pressure boilers. In his *Reminiscences and Notes*, R.G. Hobbes, a senior clerk at the dockyard, mentions the smithery before going on to describe the workings of the metal mill. Although not published until 1895, his descriptions refer approximately to the year 1849:

> I loved to go to the smithery and watch the forging of the mighty anchors, and see the blows given whose thunder shook the solid earth around and might be heard afar off.

As for the metal mill, which produced among other things, copper sheets, bolts, nails and mast hoops, Hobbes went on to describe the process of manufacturing the metal:

> It was formerly called conversion, as the copper was not smelted from the ores, but from old sheathing and bolts from ships, sent to Chatham from all the other Royal Dockyards. Many tons at a time were delivered at the metal mills, where a suitable reverberatory furnace was used to melt the copper in quantities of from four to five tons at a time, which quantity could be melted once or twice in the twenty-four hours as required, the work going on day and night without intermission from Monday to Saturday, three sets of men being employed.[11]

To keep pace with these changing demands, an ever-expanding number of mechanists, millwrights and smiths had to be employed at Chatham, together with the appointment of a Chief Engineer at the head of a separate department. In February 1852, the officers of the yard made a request for an increase in the number of smiths and millwrights employed, giving the following reasons as to why they were needed:

> The immense increase of ironwork by the introduction of steam ships and the use of iron in the hull and fittings of all classes of vessels – and this, not only in quantity, but also of much more elaborate workmanship – the greatly increased demand for sea stores – such as iron bound blocks &c and, in this yard, the average employment of 4 or 5 smiths on the works pertaining to the Chief Engineer – are reasons for the increased proportions we have recommended. [12]

At this stage, however, the main component of a ship, even if it was given steam machinery, was still timber, with the frame and planking laid along the side of this material. Shipwrights, therefore, still predominated and took charge of all ships while under construction. However, developments in gunnery and the arrival of the explosive shell required that warships should be considerably strengthened against such an onslaught. [13] At first, this need was restricted to ships that would operate in-shore and close to the heavier guns that were usually associated with harbour defences. It was a requirement that was spurred by events in the Crimea with ironclad floating batteries specifically built for the conflict that spanned the period October 1853 to February 1856. One such ship was *Aetna*, constructed at Chatham and launched in April 1856. As such, she was the first armoured vessel built at the dockyard, possessing a timber hull that was clad with 11.4cm iron plating.

The work performed on *Aetna* placed Chatham on course for the next great revolution in warship construction, building ocean-going armoured battleships that would soon entirely replace their unarmoured, wooden-hulled predecessors. First to develop such a vessel were the French, with *La Gloire* launched at Toulon in November 1859. Designed by the French naval architect Dupuy de Lôme, she was a 5,630-ton broadside battleship with a timber hull of 43cm in thickness covered over with the addition of 12cm-thick iron protection plates. To this extent she was similar in some respects to *Aetna*, in that she was clad in iron rather than her hull being constructed entirely of metal and her outer cladding having only a limited backing of timber. Through *La Gloire*, the French gained an initial lead in the construction of such vessels. Britain, having both a greater level of available resources and being more technically proficient, soon overtook the French with the launch of *Warrior*. She was a vessel that was not only twice the size of *La Gloire* but outclassed her in both speed and gunnery while also having a fully armoured hull that supported an 11.4cm armour belt with a 43.2cm teak backing. Built by the Thames Iron Shipbuilding Company, two further 'Warrior' class broadside ironclads were also launched that same year and from privately owned shipyards, namely those of Robert Napier in Glasgow and Palmer Bros of Jarrow.

Construction of the hull of a warship either on a slipway or dry dock was only part of the work that was undertaken on new warships by the artisans of the dockyard. Once launched she had to be fitted out, with dockyard workers here seen employed upon the fitting out of *Euryalus*, a steam frigate launched at Chatham in October 1853.

For Chatham and the other royal dockyards, all this was proving something of a threat. If such vessels were only to be built within the private sector, the value of Chatham and the other naval yards would quickly diminish. Indeed, a degree of pressure was beginning to emerge for these yards to be either closed or seriously reduced in scale, it being suggested that the largely privately owned yards would be much more adept at meeting the needs of the Navy. Among those who took this view was Patrick Barry, a London-based naval correspondent, who went so far as to suggest in 1863 'that we [Great Britain] cannot ever be possibly strong under the existing system' and that upon 'the lifeless dockyards the treasure of this great country is poured out in vain'. His particular solution was a 'complete overthrow of the whole system' and its reorganisation on commercial principles.[14] This was something against which the Admiralty fought, aware that the naval dockyards came significantly into their own during times of war. It was at such moments that a naval yard could be quickly mobilised and the necessary ships rapidly put to sea. If reliance, instead, was placed on dockyards organised on a profit motive basis, it seemed unlikely that such facilities would be so readily available, the existing facilities simply unable to meet the new demand. Admittedly, the royal dockyards might be under-utilised during times of peace, but that was because of a proportion of their resources being on standby for a sudden (and sometimes totally unexpected) outbreak of war.

To ensure that the royal dockyards did not continue to be overshadowed by the private yards, an important experiment was put in hand. It was decided that two very different vessels should be built and both fully incorporating the use of iron. Moreover, it was Chatham, due to the skills already developed and a sufficiency of available space, that was chosen to undertake this work. The first of these was *Royal Oak*, a conventional ninety-gun warship that had been radically redesigned while in frame, to facilitate the addition of iron cladding. The second was *Achilles*, the first true iron-hulled battleship to be launched in a royal dockyard. *Royal Oak* was officially ordered by the Admiralty in April 1859, with her keel laid thirteen months later. For *Achilles*, the lead time was not quite so extensive, for she was ordered in October 1860 and her keel laid six months later. In neither case was it possible to start immediate construction as a considerable amount of preparation had to be undertaken. If nothing else, a considerable amount of new machinery had to be brought to the dockyard, this included specialised bending, cutting and drilling equipment. However, little of this would have been of value for construction of one of these vessels, *Achilles*, if it had not been for an earlier lengthening of the No.2 Dock and completed in October 1858. In itself, this had been necessitated by the increasing size of ships with this dock subsequently selected for the construction of *Achilles*. Despite being the largest dry dock in any of the naval yards, having a length of 395ft, she was still not of quite sufficient length for the new ironclad, with the altars at the head of the dock having to be cut away prior to the keel of the new ship being laid. It was a point picked up by Patrick Barry, who claimed that the dock was still not of an adequate size, with her construction undertaken 'in a dock barely large enough to hold the ship'. According to Barry, who was writing while construction of *Achilles* was underway, possible defects in the construction of this ship were being concealed by the dock providing a glove-like fit:

> Few care to undertake the descent to the bottom of the dock, and of that few, not many are disposed to pursue knowledge under circumstances so embarrassing and filthy. Going down in a diving-bell to the foundations of Blackfriars Bridge is on the whole a more inviting undertaking than going down to the lower part of the *Achilles* among the blocks, props, smiths' fires, ashes and other things below.[15]

In addition to the ordering of machinery, working sheds had to be erected for its accommodation with this including the conversion of the No.1 Dock into a giant covered workshop. Here, metal plates were to be assembled with these transferred to where the two ships were being built by means of a newly installed tramway. As a completely new venture for the dockyard, work upon *Achilles*, not unnaturally, did fall behind. Constantly the delivered iron plates had to be rejected, failing to meet the high standards demanded by the Admiralty. Yet every effort was made to maintain the most rapid building pace possible. All other work in the dockyard was frequently brought to a standstill, absolute priority given to the two ironclads. If shipwrights were unable to be employed upon one ship, they were simply transferred to the other. Such was the situation in February 1862 when the majority of shipwrights were engaged upon the building of *Royal Oak*. According to the *Rochester Gazette*, 'the officials of the yard being apparently determined to spare no effort in order that she may be as far as possible advanced by September, the time fixed for launching her.'[16]

Interest in progress upon these two vessels was by no means restricted to the local press, with both national and specialist newspapers and journals also keen to report progress on their construction. Some two months after the previously quoted *Rochester Gazette* report, the *Illustrated London News* was in a position to inform a much more geographically dispersed readership:

> The construction of this gigantic iron frigate [*Achilles*], under the superintendence of Mr O.W. Laing, the Master Shipwright of Chatham Dockyard, is proceeding with the greatest rapidity towards completion: the vessel is nearly in frame, and the progress day by day is something wonderful. The *Royal Oak* wooden frigate of 51 guns is now ready for plating; and the forward state of everything in connection with the new fleet at this establishment reflects the highest credit on all the officials

Reopening of the No.2 Dock, as depicted in the *Illustrated London News* of 13 November 1858. Work on lengthening this dock was commenced in October 1855 and completed in October 1858. The work was carried out by Messrs J. and C. Rigby, from the designs of the director of engineering and architectural works of the Admiralty. The dimensions of the dock were:

Length from the caisson to the coping	395ft
Length on the floor from caisson to head of dock 3	60
Depth from coping to floor	31
Width on the floor	30
Width between coping	85

The dock was to prove an important addition to the yard at Chatham as, without this extended dock, it would not have been possible for *Achilles* to be laid down just three years later.

connected with it. The stem of the *Achilles* is a splendid specimen of iron forging; it was furnished by the Thames Iron and Shipbuilding Company, the builders of the *Warrior* &c., and weighs upwards of twenty tons.

The projected launch date for *Royal Oak*, early September 1862, was indeed met, with this vessel entering the Medway on the tenth of that month. The *Rochester Gazette* duly reported this important event:

> As this was the first launch of a vessel of this class from Chatham dockyard – and in fact from any of the royal dockyards – great interest has been excited by the event … An immense staging was erected in the head of the slip; it was tastefully decorated with flags. Admission to this was only to be gained by ticket … At half past one o'clock labour was suspended in the Yard, and already a large crowd was greatly increased by the flocking to the spot by hundreds of workmen. [17]

Once launched, and having a length considerably less than *Achilles*, she was transferred to the No.3 Dock where she was comfortably received. Here, she was fitted with an 800hp engine supplied by the Henry Maudslay Company, with *Royal Oak* finally completed in April 1863.

With the launching of *Royal Oak*, a large proportion of the workforce was transferred to *Achilles*, with 1,300 eventually employed on this one ship. As new processes were involved, the Admiralty had been forced to engage an even greater number of ironsmiths together with an increased number of boilermakers. In particular, the ironsmiths were called upon to train some of the existing dockyard shipwrights into the skills needed for the construction of these new-style ships. This was regarded by them as unacceptable with about ninety ironsmiths downing their tools shortly after lunch on 3 July 1863. They also complained they were not getting a promised advance in their pay. A basic account of the event that followed was later given in a pamphlet memorialising the life of John Thompson, a Chatham dockyard shipwright, and reproduced by the *Chatham News* in May 1893:

> After dinner every man and boy [employed as ironsmiths] turned out on strike, and the scene was indescribable. The Captain Superintendent, noticing an unusual gathering of the ironworkers after the dinner hour in front of his office, despatched a messenger to the Chief Constructor [the Master Shipwright, Oliver Laing] for his immediate attendance. On arrival he was asked the meaning of that large concourse of ironworkers there. The chief said it was a great surprise to him to hear them state that they would do no more work until they got an advance of money, on what was originally agreed upon. This naval captain was moved with indignation at the course the men had adopted, for which there was no precedent but the great mutiny at the Nore and Spithead on April 28th, 1789 [sic]. He said, 'I cannot find language strong enough to condemn the means employed by these men.' My

orders are, 'Give them fifteen minutes to decide whether they will leave the yard or return to their duty; failing this, call on the whole force of police to be in readiness to drive the whole of them out of the gate, which they shall never enter again. Should there be any resistance, call to your aid the armed military guard.' The chief, on putting in his appearance, replied to the men. He said he had but one request to make, 'that they were all to return to their duty at once.' Furthermore, he could give them no assurance whatever that their grievances would be considered. They would have fifteen minutes given to them to leave. Those who were disposed to return to duty at once could do so, and those who declined would be removed by force.

Conceive, my readers, what a consternation this must have caused throughout the dissatisfied ranks. One quarter of an hour to decide a question that might affect them the whole of their lives. Eyes were fixed upon the large clock just where they stood, until it chimed the quarter. The chief of the police at once emerged from the rear of the office at the head of a strong and powerful force. 'Forward,' was the order given in a loud tone of voice. There were but two only who had the moral courage at once to return to duty, Bill Morgan and Welsh Bob, both powerful men; these men have ever since been cared for by the authorities. The gate being reached, many went there for the last time with a sad heart. Many lessons may be learned from this for the consideration of our workmen.[18]

Although fundamentally correct, it does miss out the all-important issue of the ironsmiths having to train the shipwrights, this being the real cause of the strike. As to the importance of the event, particularly for Chatham, is that of what followed. The Admiralty, in needing to replace the dismissed ironsmiths, sought help from those who had not chosen to continue the strike, persuading them to train, with the help of the dockyard engine smiths, a much larger number of shipwrights. Eventually reaching 500 in number, these newly trained shipwrights were employed in plating and marking while the work of drilling and riveting was given over to yard labourers. Henceforth, this latter group, who were granted a higher rate of pay, became known as 'skilled labourers'. Within the Medway Towns, these dramatic events were considered a victory by the local community. Many of those shipwrights transferred to *Achilles* were on the verge of redundancy, the Admiralty about to replace them by a larger influx of ironsmiths. John Thomson also makes reference to this in his memories of working at the dockyard:

The question may be asked: Did the ironwork remain at a standstill? Oh dear, no. The Admiralty wired, 'try and get your own shipwrights to take the entire ship in hand.' No sooner was this known throughout the yard, than immense numbers of volunteers came forward, and with a little instruction from the two men named, they succeeded. Riveting and plating was taken up by the shipwrights, while the drilling was kept exclusively for the labourers, who were then styled for the first time 'skilled labourers.' The work went on with amazing rapidity. So great was the change that

A further view of the No.2 Dock in October 1863, with work upon *Achilles* well in hand.

their Lordships on their visitation frequently alluded with delight to the shipwrights in Chatham yard so nobly responding to their call.[19]

Through the employment of shipwrights trained in ironworking, progress on *Achilles* continued without any further major interruption. Often neglected is that of the impact of these changes upon the environment of the yard. The clatter of steam-powered machinery now reverberated around the various factories and workshops within which they had been installed. Outside, the sounds of hammering on metal and various industrial pollutants were also transforming dockyard life. Dickens, in revisiting the yard after nearly fifty years' absence, was particularly struck by these changes, emphasising the distinctly different sounds that were produced by those engaged upon the construction of *Achilles*:

Ding, Clash, Dong, Bang, Boom, Rattle, Clash, BANG, Clink, BANG, Dong, BANG, Clatter, BANG, BANG, BANG! What an earth is this. This is, or soon will be, the *Achilles*, iron armour-plated ship. Twelve hundred men are working at her now; twelve hundred men working on stages over her sides, over her bows, over her sterns, under her keel, between her decks, down in her hold, within her and without, crawling and creeping into the finest curves of her lines wherever it is possible for men to twist. Twelve hundred hammerers, measurers, caulkers, armourers, forgers, smiths, shipwrights; twelve hundred dingers, clashers, dongers, rattlers, clinkers, bangers, bangers, bangers![20]

Eventually, shortly before Christmas 1863, *Achilles* was ready to be floated out of the No.2 Dock. However, things did not go according to plan. R.G. Hobbes, as a clerk in the dockyard, was able to provide a first-hand account of a floating out that was beset with difficulties:

> On the 22nd the tide at Chatham was one of the highest that had occurred for years, and, had everything been arranged for it, she might have been launched at noon that day. That night, however, several hundred workmen began to make the usual preparations. But it was found that the caisson at the entrance to the dock could not be removed without great difficulty, and that the exit of the ship would also be impeded by the projecting ends of the dock itself, which it would be necessary to cut away. At midnight the tide was high again, and the *Achilles* floated, but could not be launched in consequence of the removal of the impediments not having been completed.

Having been allowed to settle back into the dock, it was planned that she should be floated out on the next high tide that was due on the afternoon of 23 December. However, a change in wind direction resulted in a much lower than predicted tide, forcing the launch to be delayed. All the hands required for the floating out were ordered to stay overnight. Returning to the account given by Hobbes, he states that *Achilles* was once again afloat in dock just an hour before midnight and was immediately towed out by five steam tugs that had been kept in readiness. Then another mishap occurred:

> Near the entrance to the dock a bank of sand and mud had accumulated, and in consequence of the length of time the *Achilles* had been in dock, and the impossibility of removing the caisson, it had gone on increasing. At the moment the *Achilles* cleared the dock, the tide, which at that part of the harbour is always of great force, caught her broadside and forced her round on the sandbank, where she grounded. The tide had now ceased flowing, and it was greatly feared that with the falling tide it would be impossible to get her off. Notwithstanding the united efforts of the five steamers, she at first defied all attempts to remove her; and it was only by the exertions of several hundred men, who manned the capstans on the sheer-hulk in the middle of the harbour, and the full steaming of the tugs, that she was ultimately got safely off the bank.[21]

Having so narrowly avoided a serious disaster, *Achilles* was successfully towed to her moorings in Gillingham Reach. Here she was to remain for much of the following year, this for the purpose of fitting out. Since the very founding of the dockyard in the sixteenth century, this had been the adopted practice, the yard having no enclosed area of water for it to be carried out under more controlled conditions. Rennie, of course, had produced plans for enclosing Chatham Reach, but nothing had come of this proposal. With the not inconsiderable growth in size of ships, and the increasing size and complexity of steam machinery, the existing arrangements for fitting out vessels at Chatham were recognised as quite unacceptable. Indeed, the officers at Chatham estimated in that being forced to convey every item of furnishing to *Achilles* by water, it added approximately £50,000 to her overall construction costs. Materials having to be brought out and fitted while she lay at her moorings in Gillingham Reach included 50,000 sq. ft of canvas, thirty miles of rigging cordage, the various huge timber sticks that made up her four masts, all items of her steam machinery that had been manufactured by John Penn & Son, a 12.5-ton screw propeller, two funnels and the twenty 100pdr muzzle-loading guns (together with shells and gun carriages) that made up her armament. In addition to all this, other items included coal, food supplies, steering gear, general items of interior furnishing and much, much more. Not until September 1864 was she finally out of dockyard hands, commissioned at that time into the Channel Squadron.

Immediately following upon the floating out of *Achilles* from the No.2 Dock, the workforce became available for the construction of two further ironclads, *Lord Warden* and *Bellerophon*. Significantly improved over the two earlier ironclads built at Chatham, both were designed to carry their guns, numerically reduced but more powerful in weight, in a central armoured citadel rather than on the old-style broadside pattern. In turn, this permitted a reduction to be made in the length of these vessels, so increasing their manoeuvrability. A further important point as regards these two vessels, was that both had timber hulls that were clad with 4.5in armouring, this to use up the vast stocks of timber that had, over the years, been accumulated in the yard. While *Bellerophon* was laid down in the No.2 Dock on the day immediately following the floating out of *Achilles*, *Lord Warden* was laid down in the No.3 Dock on 24 December. As with the two earlier ironclads, there was a similar level of interest in the progress of their construction and how any difficulties were overcome. *The Times*, for instance, carried this report in August 1864:

> The delays which have taken place in the progress of the ironclad frigate *Bellerophon*, 14 [muzzle loading guns and of] 4246 tons now building at Chatham Dockyard, in consequence of the non-supply of angle and plate iron from the contractors, are likely to be effectually remedied, arrangements have been completed by which at least 100 tons of iron will be sent into the dockyard weekly by Messrs. Cheney and Co., who have the contract for supplying that description of iron for the vessel. Notwithstanding, however, the delays which have taken place in the construction of *Bellerophon*, which are attributable solely to the non-delivery of the requisite material from the contractors, the most marked progress has been made on the construction of the frigate, which will not occupy one half the time in building that was consumed in the construction of the *Achilles*, built at the same dockyard.[22]

Chatham was now the recognised lead government dockyard for the construction of the new ironclad battleships. However, the improvements to the buildings of the yard were small compared with what was actually required. First and foremost, of course, was the need for an enclosed area of water where vessels could be fitted and refitted more conveniently. Plans were certainly in hand to ensure that such facilities would be brought to Chatham, this through the purchase of St Mary's Island and the resulting construction of a massive extension that would more than quadruple in size the existing yard. In the meantime, with such work taking many years to complete, attention was given to the newly created iron shipbuilding areas adjacent to the Nos 2 and 3 Docks. Work undertaken in this area, and underway while *Achilles* was still under construction, included an enlargement to a number of the workshops and the erection of a large workshop for machinery required for preparing armour plating, with this latter being undertaken by Messrs Foord & Sons of Rochester.

However, all of this work was merely a long-term stop gap, designed to ensure that Chatham could continue in its work of building ironclad ships prior to the completion of the massive St Mary's Island project. Although construction work effectively began on this vast open area of land in 1862, it was not to be finally completed until 1885. The largest civil engineering project undertaken in the southeast corner of England until the building of the Channel Tunnel, it was to allow Chatham to retain that newly claimed role of being the leading naval dockyard for construction of Britain's most important warships, with any new class of battleship being first laid down at Chatham. Seemingly neglected it may have been during much of the eighteenth century, with the development of the ironclad, the dockyard at Chatham had once again come into its own.

QUADRUPLED IN SIZE

The origins of the massive extension that was to utilise the full extent of St Mary's Island and effectively quadruple the area occupied by Chatham dockyard can be traced back to John Rennie and the report he submitted to the Board of Admiralty in August 1814. Among the problems he had highlighted was that of the yard having insufficient space for the storage of timber and other materials. For him, the solution lay in the acquisition of the Frindsbury side of the river and its integration into the existing dockyard facility through the damming of Chatham Reach and its conversion into a series of basins. In rejecting this proposal, the Admiralty accepted that an increased storage area was necessary, choosing to undertake a series of purchases of marshlands more immediately adjoining the dockyard and lying within the parish of Gillingham.

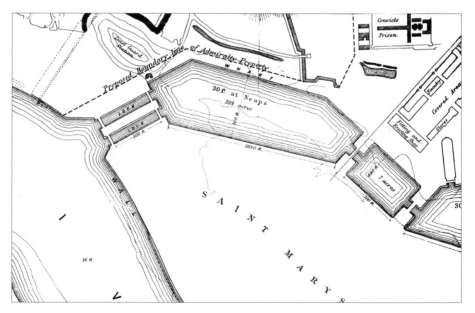

An early version, dating to 1861, of the planned layout of the three basins that were to run the length of St Mary's Creek, thereby forming the main feature of the massive extension that was to effectively quadruple the size of the existing dockyard. As eventually built, the basins were not to vary substantially in size and were also to adopt a uniformity of shape.

The intention at this stage was to use the new land not only for timber storage but also for depositing mud dredged from the river Medway. Later, however, this purchased land was to form the basis for that massive extension of the dockyard with further and even larger tranches of land being added during the 1860s and facilitated by legislation brought before parliament for this very purpose. Given the significance of that early first purchase of land that was undertaken in 1821, it is worth examining it more closely. In a note sent by the Navy Board to the Admiralty in June 1817, a full description was given, including the names of its then current owners:

Lands and houses at Chatham proposed to be vested in the Crown:

Fresh Marsh	18 acres	0 rods	39 perches
Salt Marsh	7 acres	2 rods	3 perches

Both belonging to Elizabeth Strover of Brompton (widow) and Samuel Roger Strover (Capt. of Bombay Artillery now in the East Indies). On lease from them to Peter King and released by him to John Baseden.

Fresh Marshes 7 acres 1 rod 35 perches
Belonging to John Simmons and in the occupation of John Bader junior.

Two tenements belonging to Richard Webb of Luton near Chatham.

Five tenements lately belonging to Ann Hughes:

She took them under the will of her father Robert Simmons of Brompton in Gillingham, dated 7 May 1776 and proved in the Probate Court of Canterbury 14 June 1776. She died on 23 May 1816 in Ireland, leaving four or five children by her last husband, Hughes, a Chelsea Pensioner, and Richard Finch by her former husband. The residences of her children are now not known and would be very difficult to find out.

One tenement belonging to Thomas Clark.
One tenement belonging to Thomas Elvey
One tenement belonging to George Clerk
One tenement belonging to James Clerk
One tenement belonging to the denizens of Thomas Milton[1]

In addition to these initial land purchases, a second factor that played a significant role in the construction of the extension can also be traced back to the early years of the century. This relates to the employment of convicts on a sizeable proportion of the construction work associated with the extension. It was a practice that dated back to

1810 when convicted felons, as opposed to prisoners of war, were employed upon the construction of a new river wall for the dockyard at Sheerness. Housed in *Zealand*, an ageing Dutch third-rate that had been captured in 1796, other similar hulks were soon being set aside for the housing of prisoners undertaking work at both Sheerness and Chatham yards. Apart from building work, they were employed on the vital task of dredging the river, many of them soon to be digging mud out of the barges for disposal onto the newly acquired land that made up St Mary's Marsh.

While the government, in using hulks for the housing of convicts, gained a seemingly endless pool of cheap labour, the law-abiding workers of north Kent were the losers. With hundreds of convicts soon employed at Chatham, the number of ordinary labourers was greatly reduced. In particular, those who had been employed on the mud-dredging barges were the first to suffer, but as the use of convicts was extended, many others also began to lose their jobs. By 1831, the nature of the work being undertaken by convicts was quite considerable, with Commissioner Charles Cunningham providing the Navy Board with details of the nature of work undertaken and the number of working days that convicts were employed on each task for the week ending 9 July 1831:

Loading and unloading mud barges	51
Excavating and driving piles at engine house (well)	8
Getting materials into and clearing out ships	30
Filling in earth &c at culvert drain to docks	19
Assisting riggers on works in Master Attendant's Department afloat	47
Excavating for burying masts in mud	15
Excavating at mast pond	10
Boathouse storing boats, gear &c	16
Carting and clearing timber for survey	11
Clearing docks and slips	21
Mast houses storing gear &c	7
Shipping, landing, weighing and housing stores	22
Stowing, spreading, fitting, carting &c timber	213
Beating hemp	6
Sweeping, weeding and clearing the yard	30
Stacking old timber for monthly sale	6
Sorting chips from rubbish	12
Picking oakum	7
Picking nails from dirt rubbish	7
Total	538[2]

Cunningham appears to have been quite an advocate for using convict labour, but admitted that there were a number of tasks for which they were not suited. These he listed for the convenience of the Navy Board in a letter written in January 1828:

There are many services, where it would be impossible that labour and men could be supplied for that of horses: drawing the timber from the wharf to the pickling pond (a distance of at least half a mile) and from thence, after being immersed, to the pits for conversion; removing the larger pieces (such as beams, stems, stern posts, keels &c.) to the docks and slips and other heavy stores from place to place (such as lead, chain cables, mooring chains, anchors &c. &c.). Likewise tarring of yarn.[3]

Overall, and where the work was directly comparable, Cunningham estimated that forty convicts were required to equal the efforts of one horse.[4]

The working day for those convicts in the dockyard was long and arduous. Employed six days a week – Sunday only being a day of rest – they were employed for the maximum time that daylight permitted in winter, this extended to 10 hours in summer. A lunch hour was permitted, with convicts returning to the hulks for an hour. For work performed, the convicts did receive a small remuneration, this enabling the men with full exertion 'to earn four pence a day while pile driving and three pence a day when excavating' and of which only part was immediately paid with the remainder 'reserved until the time of their liberation'. In addition, each convict, when undertaking such work, was permitted 'two pints of beer and four ounces of bread'.[5]

Having spent most of their daylight hours labouring in the dockyard, the convicts returned to the less-than-welcoming conditions of the prison hulks. Here they were accommodated in the dark and damp conditions of the lower deck and allowed to occupy themselves until lights out at 9 p.m. Unfortunately, guards rarely observed what was taking place during these hours of association, with gambling, rape and bullying all known to have been

It is interesting to compare this plan of the extension, which shows it after completion, with the earlier planned layout of 1861. In fact, this plan dates to 1943 and shows a number of additional buildings that were added both during the nineteenth century and later.

rife. Among those concerned about this latter aspect of prison life was Thomas Price, a chaplain who demanded that juvenile offenders should be removed from the system. In 1823, and as a result of his campaign, the former seventy-four-gun Frindsbury-built warship *Bellerophon* was set aside for convicts aged under twenty-one. Two years later she was replaced by *Euryalus*.

The use of hulks on the Medway as penitentiary ships was to continue until 1854 when they were replaced by a purpose-built prison, this also constructed by the convicts. Positioned just outside the dockyard on a site later occupied by HMS *Pembroke*, it was the building that housed the convicts when employed on constructing the dockyard extension. Taken out of the prison gate each morning, they were marched to their respective work areas, usually somewhere on St Mary's Island, undertaking the more menial tasks associated with excavation and laying of foundations.

William Scamp, the Board of the Admiralty's Deputy Director of Engineering and Architectural Works between 1852 and 1867, was one of the major advocates of the scheme that was to extend the dockyard on to St Mary's Island. In doing so, he gave specific attention to the employment of convicts, believing this to be an important factor in holding back the overall financial outlay that would be needed to undertake the mass of construction work. Having previously been employed in overseeing a number of dockyard expansion programmes undertaken at some of the overseas bases, particularly Bermuda and Malta, he felt that the use of convicts would be a considerable asset, but only if the system of managing the convicts was generally improved. In January 1857, Scamp elaborated on this:

> By a judicious method of employing the convicts, and one, which I believe may without difficulty be introduced; the whole scheme, large as it may appear, may be carried out to completion within a moderate time, and at a small cost.[6]

And to this he further added:

> What appears to be wanting are a general system of mechanical management and a method of qualifying men and applying their labour to duties for which they are practically qualified.
>
> The general management as regards the discipline of convicts will necessarily require being under the control of the convict department but the direction of the men in the execution of their duties may, I imagine, be under the control of this department [Engineering and Architectural Works].
>
> This being established, a method should be adopted for raising the men from a state of worthlessness to useful labourers, from labourers to artificers, and from artificers to leading men. I most successfully adopted a similar method for qualifying men for executing difficult engineering and other works of great magnitude at a foreign station; and some years ago prepared a form for the guidance of officers in accomplishing the same object with convicts at Gibraltar and Bermuda, and which is still successful in use.[7]

Scamp, over a long period of time, gave attention to how the facilities at Chatham might be adapted, giving particular attention to layout and efficiency. In 1849 he put forward a fairly revolutionary concept that would not only have considerably reduced the time taken in preparing a ship for the Ordinary but also completely reduced the reliance of the dockyard upon the river as a working area. In essence, it involved the construction of a camber, where masts and other furnishings would have been removed, with the vessel then raised and moved to a dry berth and secured for the length of time it was to remain in the Ordinary. It was not an idea pursued by the Admiralty, it being feared that in lifting and transporting the vessel, damage would be inflicted on the structural integrity of the vessel.[8]

As for the extension that was to be built at Chatham, it was initially intended that it would simply provide the dockyard with a few additional docks and slips, these to be built upon the land that had been acquired on St Mary's Marshes where it immediately adjoined the existing yard. By the mid-1850s, these initial thoughts were accompanied by the possibility of constructing an enclosed basin in which warships built at the yard could be more efficiently fitted out and completed, rather than this being undertaken in a mid-river position. Scamp, who in association with Col G.T. Greene, his immediate superior, carried out much of the original design work, in producing an important discussion document in January 1857, was concerned that in setting out to provide Chatham with such an enlarged new facility, 'ample basin space' should be provided, this being 'useful at all times but essentially necessary to meet the demands of a great war'. Scamp noted:

> At Deptford some basin space is being added while at Woolwich the basin space was twice increased. After the works were commenced at Sheerness, much more basin space [was and still] is required. At Portsmouth though, 100 feet was added to the breadth of the basin during the time the works were in progress, yet this establishment is still deficient in basin space. At Devonport the basin will chiefly be used as a boat basin and at Keyham a suggestion that I made some years ago for increasing the north basin from 700 to 1000 feet, was approved from a conviction that more basin space would be required. Having all these examples, it would be a great misfortune should another mistake be made at Chatham.[9]

Indeed, it was eventually settled upon Chatham having 67 acres of water enclosed by these basins, this considerably in excess of that existing in all of the other yards combined. In design, they were to follow the length of the creek that had once separated St Mary's Island from the mainland, with a total of three being built and interconnected. The influence of Scamp is clearly discernible. In all of his major design undertakings, Scamp had looked at efficiency savings through the creation of properly integrated work spaces. In laying out these basins, each was to have a specialised role that hinted at a production line process. Once launched, or floated out of dry dock following underwater repairs to the hull, a vessel would be released into the No.1 (or repairing) basin for the completion of work upon her upper deck before being taken to the No.2 (factory) basin for the installation or repair of machinery and boilers. Finally, the vessel would be moved to the No.3 (fitting

Before work could begin on the extension, convicts were first employed on construction of both the prison that would house them and construction of a masonry wall that would surround St Mary's Island. Here, in this engraving from the *Illustrated London News* of March 1861, convicts are employed on the carriage and breaking of stone for the sea wall.

out) basin for rigging, coaling and the mounting of her guns. Surrounding each of these basins were the various factory buildings, storehouses and workshops that were necessary to support the dedicated tasks undertaken upon ships brought into each of these basins. As for the repairing basin, on its south side there were four graving docks, each 420ft in length, with 28ft 6in over the sill at high water neaps, and 31ft 6in at high water springs.

Before any of these works could begin, not only had much of the land on St Mary's Island to be purchased but a further Act of Parliament had to be passed to allow the Admiralty the right to both acquire and block from public use the creek that separated St Mary's Island from the area currently occupied by the dockyard. This was duly brought before parliament during the summer of 1861 and, in particular, dealt with the need to compensate the Mayor and Aldermen and Company of Free Dredgers of the City of Rochester for the destruction of the fishery in the creeks. While the area of the planned extension had first been marked out in December 1860, construction work could only begin during the following year when the new Act had come into force. To begin with, and not unnaturally, this was construction of a river wall and embankment, this having an estimated cost at that time of £85,000. Whether that particular cost was adhered to is uncertain. But more definite was the fate of the overall estimate for the entire project, this standing at £943,876 at this particular point in time. By 1865, the overall cost had risen quite steeply and was then being estimated at a final figure of £1.25 million. Even this figure was to prove hopelessly inaccurate, with the final cost of the project reaching in excess of £2 million.

Not surprisingly, given that it ensured the future of Chatham dockyard, and would bring a great deal of work and prosperity to the area, the *Chatham News* was in a celebratory mood when plans for the extension were publicly announced in November 1860:

This is an important fact for our Towns. An augmentation of our Dockyard must, in the first place, cause a great increase in the amount of employment, and sensibly swell the amount of expenditure of various kinds in the Towns. With an enlarged Dockyard must come increased employment for officers, clerks, artificers, labourers; a larger demand for residencies, increased trade, augmented prosperity for the locality. It is believed that these Towns are making an advance in almost every direction; and this scheme, if carried into effect, will give a great impetus to that progress.

To this was further added the comment:

Though, unfortunately, of late the Towns, in common with most places, have suffered from the generally depressed state of trade, and the failure of a Kentish staple – hops, and though they will, like other towns, feel the effects of the short harvest, we may reasonably expect that, from the greatly increased Government expenditure – a kind of expenditure on which the locality must greatly depend at all times – which we may look for in the future we may safely prophesy a large increase in the prosperity of our Towns.[10]

During the 1860s, the island site was completely drained and then built up an additional 8ft, with sure foundations being dug for the numerous projected buildings. This was all carried out by convict labour, with over 1,000 employed on the site. Another task given to the

Not surprisingly, in constructing the mid-Victorian dockyard extension that was built at Chatham, a massive amount of material was required. Not least was the need for bricks, with more than 110 million having gone into its construction within the first ten years of the project. For the most part, these bricks were manufactured on site, a further task being undertaken by convicts. This *Illustrated London News* engraving from April 1867 shows the brick field on St Mary's Island and which had, during that year, produced 10 million bricks for the works that were then underway. The first brick had actually been produced in March 1866, the convicts having first drained and levelled a 21-acre site of marshland before installing six brick-making machines that had been supplied by the Atlas Works in London.

convicts was that of preparing and then operating a 21-acre brick field built at the north end of St Mary's Island. This produced most of the bricks used in the extension and is said to have been responsible for the manufacture of 110 million bricks by March 1875.

The first phase of the extension was completed in 1871. At that time two of the dry docks were complete, while in June of that year the No.1 Basin was officially opened. This was the basin immediately opposite Upnor, designated as the repairing basin, and built with an entrance into the river Medway. The entrance, sealed by caisson, separated the two bodies of water. As part of the opening ceremony, the ironclad *Invincible*, built at the Napier yard a few years earlier, was brought to Chatham to demonstrate the advantage of the new basin, with the *Chatham News* duly reporting the event:

> As she passed through none who saw her grand and graceful proportions – her deck alive with officers and men – but must have admired the spectacle. The great ship had her course turned when she had entered the basin, and she proceeded towards the No.1 Dock [sequentially the No.5 Dock]. In short time with hauling and very slow steaming, she was got safely into the No.1 Dock where she will undergo repair. The dock will henceforth be 'the Invincible Dock'. The fine ship having been placed in dock, the caisson to close its mouth was placed in position, and preparations made for emptying the water in the dock – a process which at present takes a considerable time, as there are only temporary engines for the dock; hereafter all the docks can be emptied in four hours by the powerful machinery to be provided.[11]

In its comment column, the *Chatham News* carried a further item, this continuing to extol the virtues of the extension scheme:

> Those who do not love Chatham, or who have a jealousy of her have been ever ready to prophesy that the new dockyard must be a failure – that the works created must tumble in – that if the basins and docks were made ships could not get up the river to enter them, and so on. Well – a grand basin, 21 acres in area, with a depth of 33 feet of water, has been successfully constructed; ships have steamed through it; a fine ironclad vessel with her guns etc., on board, has safely come up the Medway, has passed through the wide and deep entrance of the uppermost basin, has traversed the basin, and is now in one of the enormous graving docks which abut on the basin, another dock is ready to receive the largest ship in the Navy; many ships of the first class could lie in the far stretching basin. This much HAS BEEN accomplished. There have been difficulties but they have been overcome. At no distant period a second basin of nearly the same size will be completed. The two great docks in hand will be finished rather later – a glance at these in their present state impresses one with the magnitude of the work, and proves how much time must necessarily be occupied in carrying it out.[12]

As noted by the *Chatham News*, work had begun on the two other basins as well as the second pair of dry docks. It was in November 1872 that the No.8 Dock was finally

A contemporary model of the No.2 Basin, showing progress on construction of the basin with work in hand pile driving and the removal of excavated mud and clay. The model was actually made by convicts held in the prison and dates to 1871 or thereabouts.

completed, with the No.9 Dock completed in 1873. Next was the No.2 Basin and finally, in 1883, the No.3 Basin. It was this latter basin that also provided a primary entry into the Medway, this through the caisson gates of the Bull's Nose – so named because of its shape. Although in this later construction work continued use was made of convict labour, the savings were not as great as had originally been expected. For this reason, much more of the work on both the Nos 2 and 3 Basins involved a large proportion of contract labour, with the employment of convicts subsequently reduced.

One particular attempted financial saving that did pay off, was the reuse of several buildings from the dockyard at Woolwich. Indeed, the fact of this dockyard, together with that of Deptford, having been closed in 1869 was a direct result of the expansion of facilities at Chatham, it no longer considered necessary to retain these two yards on the Thames given that they would also have needed a considerable updating of their facilities. In the case of Woolwich, two slip covers were identified as of future value to Chatham, these being iron-framed structures that could be taken apart and reassembled. In their subsequent life at Chatham, they were to serve as Boiler Shop No.1 and Machine Shop No.8, both reassembled alongside the No.1 Basin. While the cost of constructing such buildings can only be guessed at (it was probably in the region of £20,000–30,000), the amount needed for their removal and re-erection was a mere £6,000.[13]

Once completed, the extension works totally revitalised the dockyard, allowing the refitting of a greatly increased number of ships while encouraging the Admiralty to use Chatham for the building of numerous additional battleships. This, of course, led to a considerable increase in the dockyard workforce. Whereas in 1860 the number employed had stood at 1,735 it had, by 1885, and completion of the extension works, reached over 4,000. Of the ships built at Chatham, each class of battleship was larger than its predecessor. In

1875 Chatham launched *Alexandria*, the largest ship by that date to have been built in the yard. Displacing just over 9,000 tons, it exceeded by nearly twice the tonnage any vessel previously built at Chatham. Yet, not ten years later, *Rodney*, displacing over 10,000 tons, was launched. Others followed in quick succession. Fourteen thousand tons had been reached by 1891 with the launching of *Hood*, followed by the 15,000-ton *Venerable* in 1899.

The construction of one vessel, *Magnificent*, is associated with an experiment that had less to do with ship design and more to do with the ever more important panacea of financial savings through increased speed and efficiency. As a result of a report issued in 1888 by a committee established by parliament to look into the management of the home yards, it was revealed that idleness within sections of the workforce was 'practically unchecked'. In particular, reference was made to the practice of 'keeping crow', whereby a look-out was kept for supervisors while the rest of the gang idled. As for the inferior officers, the ones directly appointed to supervise the gangs, they were considered to be 'either apathetic or too much in the hands of the men' while the superior officers were found 'to be power-less'. The Admiralty reacted by introducing a few poorly thought out ideas, which included the removal of a number of less competent and ageing inferior officers together with the introduction of chargemen, promoted workers who were to ensure that those they worked with were fully employed. In addition, a newly devised method of payment by results, this time known as 'tonnage payments' was also temporarily adopted, with each man paid according to the weight of the material built 'into the whole of a section of a ship'. However, as the majority of those employed in the yards worked in gangs, it was

An engraving from *The Graphic*, dating to December 1871, showing excavation work being undertaken on the No.2 Basin. Viewed from the south-east, work is very much in a forward stage, with much of the depth of this 20-acre site having already been reached. The similarity between the engraving and the dockyard model are remarkable and suggest that either the model was based on this engraving or that both the model and the engraving were executed at a more or less identical point in time.

One of the last of the buildings belonging to the extension to be completed was that of the lock pumping station that stood between the North and South Lock on the Bull Nose. The distinctive chimney immediately adjoins the Boiler House with the Engine House distinguishable as the raised part of the building furthest from the camera. Following the closure of the Upnor Gate, that gave access into the No. 1 Basin, the two locks were the only means of bringing warships into the three basins and were regularly pumped to ensure a safe and easy entry and exit.

impossible to reward individual output. As a result, tonnage payment, which had not noticeably increased work output, was rapidly abandoned.

Undoubtedly the Admiralty was hamstrung by its own parsimony. If the workforce was to be motivated into increasing its output then the rewards, however allocated, would need to be of a sufficient level. Indeed, there was much evidence to suggest that those employed in the naval dockyards failed to work harder because they believed their pay to be inadequate. Should the Admiralty choose to correct this, so that wages reflected the private yards where the average wage was sometimes 30 per cent greater, then levels of efficiency might improve.

Given that the Admiralty was ill-prepared to increase wage levels to those found in the private yards, the Board decided upon a more imaginative approach. It would institute a race in which two identical ships, one at Chatham and one at Portsmouth, would be laid down together. Using the age-old rivalries that existed between these two yards, those building the ships would be encouraged into a maximum effort. To ensure fairness, those managing the two yards were given a completely free hand in deploying the workforce. Indeed, the only stipulated condition was that the two ships should be completed in as short a time as possible.

For Chatham, the race officially began on 18 December 1893 when the keel of *Magnificent* was laid down. She was a 'Majestic' class battleship that would eventually displace 14,900 tons. Meanwhile at Portsmouth, just twenty-eight days later, the name ship of this class was also laid down, with the intervening period having been used to prepare some of the plates and frames that were needed for her construction. In itself, this had marked an interesting departure from normal shipbuilding practice, it having previously been reckoned more efficient to carry out all construction work wherever the keel was to be laid. In the light of this venture, which made considerably better use of facilities at the dockyard, other ships were also to have preliminary work performed upon them prior to the official keel laying. At Chatham, meanwhile, everything was moving forward with great rapidity. In the same week that *Majestic*'s keel was laid, it was confidently reported:

> The construction of the *Magnificent* is being pushed, and already the frames amidship have been put in place to the height of the armour deck.[14]

However, it was not long before similar reports were made on the progress of *Majestic*, with this vessel having possibly overhauled *Magnificent* in early May. At least this was the optimistic assumption made by the Portsmouth correspondent of *The Naval and Military Record*:

> The *Majestic* at Portsmouth is now 400 tons ahead of the *Magnificent* at Chatham, and instead of floating her out next February, the officials hope now to celebrate that event this side of Christmas.[15]

It appears that the two ships continued neck and neck for much of the rest of the year, with both superintendents allowing a huge proportion of yard workers to attend to their respective charges. At Chatham, in September, it was reported that 1,200 were employed upon *Magnificent* and that the vessel was 'completely plated from stem to stern'. Furthermore it was indicated that the engine contractors, Messrs Penn, would soon commence work on the fixing of her engines. At Portsmouth meanwhile, the first indication of a serious problem was just emerging:

A modern-day view of the No.1 Basin, which officially opened in June 1871. To facilitate its use for the repairing of ships, it had a total of five dry docks leading away from the basin. Of these, the No.5 Dock, originally known as the Invincible Dock, can be seen immediately to the right. It was so named because the first vessel to enter this dock was the ironclad battleship *Invincible*. With such a grand name for this historic feature, it seems unfortunate that this is not recognised within the Chatham Maritime development.

An unexpected delay has occurred in the delivery of the armour plates for the *Majestic*, and this may prevent the floating of the ship out of the dock early in December. [16]

This was only seen as a temporary setback, with twenty-one gangs, besides other trades, working on *Majestic* by the end of November. By then, so it was estimated, *Majestic* had 5,335 tons built into her while *Magnificent* could only boast 5,140 tons.

However, the delays in the delivery of armour plating were proving problematic. At Portsmouth there was increasing concern that Chatham would eventually win the race, not through greater effort, but as a result of contractual delays. It appears to have been a subject of much comment for, while there was only one contract for *Magnificent*'s armour plates, the *Majestic* at Portsmouth had two suppliers. This, so it was felt, gave Chatham an advantage, orders for this yard being fulfilled with greater promptness. In fact, it even appears that Chatham was managing to acquire armour plating that was destined for Portsmouth. Of this episode, Lord Charles Beresford, then Captain of the Steam Reserve at Chatham, later wrote:

> During 1893–4 the *Magnificent* was being built by Chatham in rivalry of Portsmouth, which was building the *Majestic*. It was becoming a close thing, when the *Magnificent* received from the manufacturers a lot of armour plates which might have gone to the *Majestic*, and which enabled us to gain a lead. [17]

The delays in delivery of armour plating appear to have caused insuperable problems for the early completion of *Majestic*. The result was that *Magnificent* was not only launched before *Majestic* but a total of forty-three days separated the two occasions. Without doubt, therefore, Chatham had won the first part of the race – the race to get the two battleships into the water.

The final part of the race, completion, continued to be enthusiastically supported. At both Portsmouth and Chatham, it was fully intended that the vessels should be out of dockyard hands by the end of the year, so setting a record for both yards. On board *Majestic*, following an initial flurry of activity, during which the main engine and masts were shipped, something of a lull set in during March. Again, this was no fault of Portsmouth, but the result of a non-delivery of boilers. Once these arrived, so it was confidently reported in the pages of *The Naval and Military Record* in April, 'the energies of the builders will be considerably increased'. At the same time, delays were also taking place at Chatham, a result of severe cold weather and the freezing over of the fitting-out basin.

By spring, the race to complete both ships was again in full swing. Chatham yard was first to get the 6in gun casements fitted, this completed by the end of June. Not surprisingly, there was a certain amount of rejoicing, this reflected by the resident Chatham journalist of the *The Naval and Military Record*:

> So overpowering is the desire to score over the *Magnificent* that the turn-tables have been placed on board without having been taken to pieces – incomplete as they are.

It need scarcely be added that the corresponding work is already complete on the *Magnificent*, the forward and after barbettes are ready for mounting the 12-inch guns as soon as they arrive from Woolwich.[18]

However, this fine fellow was soon forced to regret these particular comments, the long-awaited barbettes for the 12in guns seemingly having disappeared. At the very least they had still not arrived by October, leading to a suspicion that Portsmouth was receiving undue favouritism:

> During the process of manufacturing the gun shields for the *Magnificent*, one of the foremen of the Yard made five or six visits to the contractor's works to ascertain if the order was being carried out according to the moulds and drawings, and to ensure that no alteration would be required on their arrival; but, although they were to be sent to Chatham, the contractors, for some reason not yet explained, delivered them to Portsmouth.[19]

Despite this setback for *Magnificent*, both ships were able to undertake their sea trials during the latter part of 1895, with these vessels both commissioned into naval service on 12 December. Although a contrived end to the race, it was the only fair result. Such competitions were quite meaningless. Whether one yard was in a position to launch or complete before another (or even at the same point in time) was entirely dependent on materials outside the dockyards. Furthermore, such races did not really help create efficiency, they merely caused delays elsewhere. For a dockyard such as Chatham to have a

Glatton, laid down at Chatham on 10 August 1868 and having been built in dry dock, is here seen on the occasion of her floating out of dock, this taking place on 8 March 1871. A particular feature of this illustration is that of it including the various covered slips of the yard, with the No.7 Slip nearest to where the artist is viewing the scene, while Nos 6, 5, 4 and 3 are sequentially located beyond.

fifth of its workforce dedicated to the building of one ship meant wholesale delays elsewhere in the system. While the Navy might receive one leviathan earlier than expected, it had to suffer endless delays upon other vessels entering the yard for repairs and refittings. Instead of a smooth and balanced work programme, such a meaningless competition resulted in the wholesale movement of hundreds of men in a frenetic roundabout that had nothing to do with the true needs of the Navy.

The changing nature of ship construction and the Admiralty's increasing desire for efficiency naturally had an impact upon the workforce. Much of this was fostered by a growth in private capital investment into the shipbuilding industry, with the government dockyards often forced to compete for the purpose of acquiring the right to continue building ships. The competitive construction of the two 'Majestic' class battleships was not unconnected with this changing situation, as was the considerable

A Chatham-built battleship, *Barfleur*, is here seen in June 1894 leaving the No.3 Basin, passing through the North Lock, following her completion. Weighing in at 10,500 tons, her main armament was that of four 10in guns. Laid down in October 1890 and launched in August 1892 she had subsequently been brought round from the No.7 Slip, upon which she had been constructed, to the extension on St Mary's Island for a completion programme that took just under two years.

reliance upon outside contractors. In an earlier age, the naval yards would have been virtually self-contained, able to manufacture all of the materials required for construction of a new ship. While this was no longer the case, the private sector having achieved for itself a secure position with regard to the manufacture of armour plating and many other heavy items of equipment, it was to the naval dockyards that new and experimental construction work was reserved. But to compete, the earlier practice of retaining an inflated workforce, sometimes treading water until an international situation brought on a sudden urgency, was most certainly abandoned. The proportion of hired men, those with no permanent contract and open to immediate dismissal, was increased, while even those on the establishment also found themselves open to dismissal during times of austerity. The late 1880s proved particularly horrendous, with hundreds of labourers and artisans discharged and the Medway Board of Guardians being overwhelmed by requests for help. Mavis Waters refers poignantly to one particular episode that took place in September 1887:

Magnificent, winner of the race against Portsmouth to be the first to launch a 'Majestic' class battleship, is seen here as she prepares to depart Chatham following her completion. Overall, from laying of keel to finally getting the two vessels to sea, the Admiralty inspired race between Chatham and Portsmouth yards was deemed a tie.

> Confronted with a woman who wanted assistance for herself and her family while her discharged husband was away in search of work, they [the Medway Board of Guardians] consulted in hushed tones about the possibility of giving out relief, officially prohibited, in the special circumstances of that winter; 'We are sure to have a number of cases of this kind', said the Chairman … 'I am sure the members will not wish to smash the homes up … we have not begun to feel it yet.' 'Have a thousand men been discharged?' asked the Reverend Whiston, 'Over a thousand,' replied Councillor Breeze grimly.'[20]

According to Waters, this particular crisis, which had passed by January 1889, had a profound effect upon the dockyard workforce. No longer were they prepared to put their trust in the protection of the Admiralty, something that in the past had brought them relatively secure work and the removal of occasional grievances. Organisationally, therefore, they had tended to veer away from involving themselves in nationally organised unions, creating for themselves a number of local associations. These had proved quite incapable of fighting their corner during that crisis period, with the artisans and labourers at Chatham dockyard beginning to look at the means by which those in the private sector were bargaining with their employers through membership of trade unions. Over the following decades, those employed in the various yard trades began to take out union subscriptions, with shipwrights ensuring that the national Amalgamated Society of Shipwrights rapidly replaced the dockyard-based Ship Constructive Association.[21]

9

GLOBAL CONFLICT

It was the launch of HMS *Dreadnought* at Portsmouth on 10 February 1906 that brought an end to Chatham's battleship-building pretensions. Controversially it was stated that Chatham was without the space and facilities to launch such a large ship, but this was always disputed by many of those who worked in the yard. In doing so, the older hands of the yard were often heard to argue the case in later years. And they had a point. Both the No.8 Slip, built adjacent to the north of the existing slips and completed in 1900 together with the No.9 Dock, built a few years earlier and annexed to the No.1 Basin, were both of a size that might easily have accommodated *Dreadnought* or one of her sister ships.

At the time of its construction, the No.9 Dock was the largest in the world, having a length of 650ft and a working breadth of 84ft. To support work upon ships being carried

When this photograph first appeared in the *Navy and Army Illustrated* in August 1899 it was entitled 'a busy scene at Chatham'. What it shows is the return of naval ships to the dockyard following an exercise, with various stores having to be offloaded while seamen are readying themselves for a spot of shore leave.

Africa, the last battleship built at Chatham and launched from the No.8 Slip on 20 May 1905. While the dockyard had once specialised in the construction of battleships, the arrival of the 'dreadnoughts' and 'super-dreadnoughts' resulted in Chatham transferring the major part of its skills to the construction of submarines.

out within the dock, both sides of the new facility possessed gantries for a 20-ton crane while nearby the No.9 Machinery Shop was added very shortly afterwards. As for the No.8 Slip, this was much larger than most other slips of this period, being 616ft in length and specifically designed for construction of large battleships. Due to that policy reversal, based on the supposition that battleships were now too large to be built at Chatham, the No.8 Slip witnessed the construction of only one such vessel. This was *Africa*, a battleship of the 'King Edward VII' class displacing 16,350 tons. Entering the Medway on 20 May 1905, she was launched by the Marchioness of Londonderry but not without a small amount of difficulty. On the chord being severed that then released two heavy weights that should have knocked away the dog shores, the vessel failed to move. Even upon the deployment of two hydraulic presses, each capable of moving 200 tons, the ship remained static. Finally, a lift frame hydraulic ram, exerting a pressure of 1,000 tons, managed to achieve the desired effect and sent the vessel into the water.

A new specialism soon followed – that of submarine construction. In all, a total of fifty-seven were to be built, with the last, an 'Oberon' class patrol submarine for the Royal Canadian Navy, launched in September 1966. First to be built at Chatham were four 'C' class vessels, *C17*, *C18*, *C19* and *C20*. Of a somewhat crude design when compared with submarines launched later in the century, they were of a mere 290 tons and carried a crew of only sixteen in number. Much more significant, and in keeping with the pioneering work usually associated with Chatham, they were the first submarines to be built in any royal dockyard, with the first of these, *C17*, launched from the No.7

Slip on 13 August 1908. From the Admiralty's point of view it was important that some of these craft should be built in their own naval yards, this to ensure that a check could be kept on the charges made when they were built in the private yards.

While submarines, especially those built prior to the First World War, may not have had the glamour of the large battleships and cruisers, the planned entry of *C17* into the Medway was still enthusiastically covered by both local and national newspapers, excitement fostered in the latter by a supposition that the launch was being conducted in a shroud of secrecy. The *Chatham News*, with its greater experience of reporting ship launchings at Chatham, attempted to put the matter into a broader context:

> The so-called moonlight launch of a submarine from the slipway at Chatham yard caused quite a commotion in the London Press, which appeared to have overlooked the fact that submarines were built at this port. As for the secrecy, this has been strictly observed at all the launches of submarines from the slips of private firms, whereas, at Chatham, the workmen employed in building them are bound to secrecy.[1]

After the launch, *C17* was taken to the No.2 Dock where she was fitted with engines and other machinery, all of which was constructed at Chatham. In September the *Chatham News* was reporting:

A turn of the century view of the colour loft and where a number of the 'ladies of the colour loft' are to be seen engaged in making flags for naval warships. Employing roughly twenty women, they typically produced in any one month some 1,200 flags of different size and purpose. This and the ropery were the only two areas within the dockyard, prior to the outbreak of the First World War, where women were employed.

The first two of the four submarines being built at Chatham, will be ready for trials in a few weeks, probably, and there will then be an opportunity of comparing the Dockyard work on this kind of vessel to that done by private firms. Chatham Dockyard was entrusted with the first pair of this type of craft to be built in the Royal Dockyards and apparently the Admiralty are quite satisfied with the progress that has so far been made, as a second pair of similar craft have been put in hand, and will no doubt be pushed forward as fast as possible.[2]

The outbreak of the First World War in August 1914 not unnaturally had a considerable impact on the yard at Chatham. Most obviously was the massive amount of new work directed to the dockyard, this resulting in the need to rapidly expand the existing workforce, with the number employed reaching 11,000 by November 1918. One way this was achieved was through the employment of women on tasks for which they had previously been thought incapable. On entering the yard, the newly recruited female workers were trained to undertake very specific tasks rather than the broad range normally acquired by an apprentice.

In contrast to those newly entering the yard to undertake the essential tasks associated with warship construction and repair were some of those already employed in the yard and who wished to enlist. If they were part of the established workforce they simply were not allowed to do this, the Admiralty wishing to retain their skills for the duration of hostilities. Some did so, but in so doing, they immediately lost their entitlement to a future pension and readmission to the yard at a later stage. Given this situation, it is not surprising that many of those employed in the yard were embittered by criticisms laid against them for not taking up arms. The *Daily Sketch* for instance, in December 1914,

Following the ending of the First World War there was considerable jubilation, with the Anchor Wharf Storehouse suitably bedecked with flags to celebrate the Armistice on 11 November 1918.

openly suggested that such workers, in failing to enlist, lacked patriotism. A remark clearly resented by those employed at Chatham, it naturally elicited an angry response from the central committee of the General Labourers Union. An apology was demanded from the *Daily Sketch*, it being pointed out that many of those employed in the dockyard had actually been refused the right to enlist. It was further pointed out that some had still left to join the Army, but in doing so forewent both a relatively secure job and a future pension.[3]

Certainly there was no shortage of work for the dockyard during those wartime years, with the yard responsible for the launch of twelve submarines and two light cruisers. Looked upon with special pride was the forming of *Zubian*, a tribal class destroyer that had begun life as two separate destroyers; *Zulu* and *Nubian*. In late October 1916 *Nubian* had seen most of her bow section destroyed when she had been torpedoed off the Belgian coast while *Zulu* had lost most of her stern when mined in the Dover Straits in November of that same year. Both ships being of the same class, it was decided to join the two between the third and fourth funnels, a task completed at Chatham by June 1917. Another major task undertaken was that of preparing a number of ships for the Zeebrugge raid of April 1918. Designed to strangle both Ostend Harbour and the Bruge canal at Zeebrugge through the sinking of several block ships, Chatham undertook work on six of the ships. On the cruiser *Vindictive*, to be used to land marines, additional armament was put in place, including howitzers, mortars and flamethrowers. More significant was work carried out on five block ships, *Thetis*, *Iphigenia*, *Intrepid*, *Sirius* and *Brilliant*, with each first gutted and filled with 1,500 tons of concrete. Lesser alterations were carried out on other ships, including the placing of explosives into submarines *C1* and *C3*.

A flavour of the intensity and urgency of work being undertaken in the yard during these wartime years was provided by R.C. Lockyer, in a subsequently published essay. First joining the yard in 1916 as a sixteen-year-old rivet boy, he began his working life in the No.8 Slip where *Hawkins*, name ship of a light class of cruisers, was under construction and not to be launched until the following October. The job of a rivet boy was to heat the rivets in a portable furnace before it was placed in a hole already drilled into the armour plate and then hammered by a riveter using a pneumatic riveter. As Lockyer explained, 'thousands of rivets were used' with 'many teams of workers employed'. It is his observations of the yard at this time that gives his essay a particular value, recording the everyday detail that is often lost over time. Of the yard in general at this time, he refers to being 'amazed' by the many sights he witnessed:

> Many of our ships were either sunk or damaged and lots of the latter were brought to Chatham for repairs. They were terrible sights when they either crawled into the basins or, more often, had to be towed in. The more badly damaged vessels were got into dry dock as soon as possible, some in fact nearly sinking.

Of one cruiser, which he fails to name, and returned to sea following repair to extensive torpedo damage, he recalls that within 24 hours she was back in dockyard hands, 'having been blown practically in two by enemy mines'.[4]

A danger that did present itself during the First World War was that of aerial bombardment. While Zeppelins and Gothas did pass close by, none actually deposited their deadly cargo of explosives directly on to the yard. In contrast, the nearby naval barracks did suffer horrifically from one bomb, this jettisoned by a Gotha bomber, with the raid occurring on 3 September 1917. Dropping a 110-pound bomb, the enemy aeroplane scored a direct hit on the naval barracks, this resulting in the death of 136 naval ratings. That the bomber, in company with three other aircraft, had located Chatham so easily was a result of the town lights not having been switched off. Helping ensure such a considerable loss of life was that of the bomb having hit the drill hall, this used to provide additional sleeping quarters. Having, as it did, a glass roof, the thousands of flying shards merely added to the number of victims. On another occasion, and as recorded by R.C. Lockyer, German aircraft were seen over Gillingham, with a number of anti-aircraft guns opening fire on them. In the dockyard, where Lockyer was then working on board *Erebus*, a large flat-bottomed monitor undergoing modification, he received a sudden fright when the guns of this vessel, despite her being in dry dock, were fired in the direction of the raiders. In his own words, Lockyer described what happened next:

> At its very first shell my forge fell over and hot coals scattered over the deck. A Master-at-Arms bawled out, 'Put that light out' and a frantic scramble then took place for buckets of water to douse it.[5]

While it was accepted that the bomber, through its growing speed and efficiency, was a threat in any future war, little thought during the inter-war period was given to ensuring the safety of the dockyard at Chatham. It was certainly accepted, and this beyond a shadow of doubt, that the yard would be a target, with its possible destruction a likely outcome. But instead of looking at the dispersal of its machinery and skilled workforce to potentially less vulnerable parts of the country, the entire facility was left 'in situ'. Nor was the opportunity taken to camouflage or conceal some of its more prominent structures. Only from 1938 onwards, with war absolutely inevitable, was a decision taken to cover some of the older and highly inflammable wooden buildings with an external layer of asbestos boarding, this to minimise the effect of incendiary bombs.

The years immediately following the end of the First World War were the post-war years, a difficult time for the dockyard. Previously issued orders for the construction of new ships that had not yet been laid down were immediately cancelled, while work on *Warren*, a W-class destroyer under construction, was suspended. This, the only destroyer ever to have been ordered for construction at Chatham, was never completed, being scrapped in 1919. At the same time the Navy was also being run down and the river Medway was crammed with ships being paid off. The numerous creeks were filled with unwanted torpedo boats, while destroyers and cruisers were anchored in mid-river positions, awaiting delivery to the breakers yard.

Members of the dockyard's Electrical Engineering Department pose for a photograph that was taken in 1919. A number of women are among those employed in this area of the dockyard but would soon be made redundant. It had only been a temporary wartime policy to bring women into a number of additional areas of dockyard work (over and above the colour loft and ropery) for the purpose of releasing men to enlist.

To provide some work, the yard labour force was employed upon completing a number of partially finished ships. These were vessels originally launched in private yards but having no engines or other equipment. In 1922 the cruisers *Enterprise* and *Despatch* came to the yard, as did the W-class destroyer *Whitehall*. The submarines *L23*, *L53* and *K26* were also fitted out at Chatham, while the submarines *K24*, *K25* and *K28* were to have been brought to Chatham, but were scrapped instead.

Many of the passing events of that period were recorded by Cyril Cate, a dockyard electrician who, from 1916 onwards, had begun keeping a regular diary of passing events. As with many employed in the dockyard, he came from a family totally immersed in dockyard matters, his father having been a shipwright while his sister Emily had joined the yard's Torpedo Department in 1916. Launchings, in particular, were well recorded in the pages of his diary, with one of the earliest that he mentions being *Kent*, a County class cruiser launched from the No.8 Slip in March 1926:

> I went to No.8 Slip and saw launched successfully HMS *Kent* by Lady Stanhope. Public allowed and crowds of people attended … *Kent* in the North Lock (for purposes of entering the fitting-out basin) by about 3.30 in the afternoon.

Launchings of vessels did not always go as smoothly as this one had done, with Cate adding this note to his diary on 23 September 1923:

Submarine O1 or Oberon to be launched but after the ceremony was performed and all was ready two blocks aft were found to be too firm to move and tide came in and hindered work of removal. Launch postponed [until the following day].

A large number of more general activities within the yard are also recorded within the diaries. In September 1926 he refers to the demolition of a dockyard hoist (known as sheer legs because of their similarity to a pair of shears) that had once been used for the fitting out of ships' engines:

[Saturday 4 September] Sheer legs on No.2 Basin were demolished. They are forty years old and condemned as unsafe. All ships were cleared from [the] basin and at 12.30 a charge fixed to lower part of back leg was exploded and the legs allowed to fall into water.

Moving a few years forward, Cyril gives a series of daily reports on the success of the annual Navy Week held by the dockyard during the summer of 1929. On the first day, Monday 12 August, Cyril indicates 'a good number of people to have been present'. As for himself, he was quite fascinated by the event. That evening he was at Wigmore where his father owned land which the family used for playing tennis. While there, he spent some time watching 'all the visitors' to the dockyard making their way home. On the following day he must himself have given the impression of being one of the

Kent, launched on 16 March 1926, was the largest cruiser to be built at Chatham. Of particular importance was that the order to build this vessel came at a time when many dockyard workers were being laid off, so ensuring that some of those who may well have lost their jobs in the yard were given a few years of respite.

exhibits on display. Helpfully reinforcing the public notion that yard workers rarely exerted themselves, he spent the entire day 'sitting on the foc'sle of [HMS] *Hawkins*'. For the rest of the week he continued to comment on the immense numbers visiting warships open to the public. On the Saturday, however, he rather reversed the situation. Instead of entering the yard as a worker, he joined the visiting public and boarded a number of the vessels.

Elsewhere in the diaries, numerous references are found to the various ships upon which Cyril was working. In 1919 alone he records the names of eleven separate vessels, these including destroyers, cruisers, a small monitor and a troop ship. As a rule, any vessel upon which he was working would be moored in the fitting-out basin. However, this was not always the case. Sometimes the vessel had already left the dockyard, with urgent electrical work having to be undertaken while the vessel was in the Medway or even lying off Sheerness. On one occasion in 1926 he was working on a vessel while it was in the process of leaving the yard. This was *Centurion*, a former battleship that had been converted into a target ship. On 16 August this entry appears, 'our boat *Centurion* placed in North Lock in morning and left at 3.45 for Sheerness.' On the following day he made a further reference to this vessel, 'caught the "*Advice*" [a dockyard paddle tug] in morning at 7.15 and went to "*Centurion*". Worked on fire pump and got back to locks at 3.30.'

As with the vast majority of the population, the coming of war in 1939 proved something of a watershed in Cyril's life. The number of hours he was expected to work dramatically increased while Winnie (whom he had married in 1930) together with Sylvia (their five-year-old daughter) and Derek (a son of three months) were evacuated to Sellindge. On Saturday 3 September, the day war broke out, he noted 'war commenced with Germany at 11 a.m. I had to work until 7'. This, in itself, broke a carefully established routine. Cyril was a committed Christian, a member of the Plymouth Brethren, who always made a point of attending Sunday service at the Gospel Hall in Gillingham's Skinner Street. In addition to this, he was a Sunday school teacher. Having to enter the yard on Sunday and return to an empty home (for his family had been evacuated on the previous day) must have been an extremely unsettling experience. Nor could matters have been helped by the alien environment of a blacked-out Gillingham. He had already confided to his diary on 1 September, that the entire Medway Towns were under 'complete black out at night' adding that 'sandbags were everywhere'. To this he added a few days later, 'everywhere looking warlike'. As for the dockyard, '[4 September 1939] Maidstone and District buses in yard being converted to ambulances. Police patrolling sheds with metal helmets'.

That the dockyard did not succumb to aerial bombardment, although it underwent numerous attacks, was more by luck than judgement. Easily located from the air and within short flying time from the Continent, it seems surprising that Chatham, when compared with the yards at Portsmouth and Plymouth, received relatively small amounts of damage. Nevertheless, lives were lost and a number of structures were destroyed. In late 1940, the Factory, a large building which housed the engine fitters and lay alongside the No.1 Basin, received a direct hit, this resulting in the loss of twenty-three lives. On later occasions, both the smithery and saw mill were to be bombed. One incident often recalled by those who worked in the yard during those years is that of *Arethusa*, while in dry dock, using her 4in anti-aircraft guns against bombers seen to be approaching London. Reminiscent of the actions taken by *Erebus* some twenty-three years earlier, a curtain of exploding shells proceeded to force many of these bombers to alter course. If nothing else, it raised the morale of those working in the dockyard.

With its workforce brought up to 13,000, of whom 2,000 were women, the output in these years even exceeded that of the First World War. In all, twelve submarines, four sloops and two floating docks were laid down during these years, while 1,360 refits were carried out. Additionally, the dockyard supplied stud welding equipment for tanks and other fighting vehicles, fitted out over 1,200 shore establishments and, in December 1944, supplied and started a shore carrier service to naval bases and parties on the continent. A number of two-man submarines were built at Chatham, fitted with lorry diesel engines and dustbin-like torpedo tubes. Of the larger refits, the cruiser *London* was plated with armour and *Scylla* was converted to an escort carrier flagship. The final months of the war also saw Chatham busily engaged in fitting out part of a fleet destined for the Far East and the continuing war against Japan.

For those employed in the dockyard during the Second World War, a particular fear, and on a par with being caught in an air raid, was that of post-war Britain turning against those who had secured the victory. Reflecting on the years that followed the ending of the First World War, they remembered how numbers employed in the yard had been mercilessly slashed, with thousands forced out of the yard to fend for themselves as best they might. Some, indeed, saw it as not unlikely that the dockyard, upon the ending of the war against the Axis powers, might even be closed. After all, both Pembroke and Haulbowline had suffered this fate immediately after the First World War, although the former had been reopened upon the outbreak of the Second World War. As it happens, nearby Sheerness was certainly closed, although not until 1956, with the temporarily reopened Pembroke also finally abandoned. Chatham, however, avoided the dreaded axe, successive Conservative candidates in seeking out the dockyard vote promised that only with that party in power would the dockyard be secure. Of course, the irony was that under Margaret Thatcher, the 'Iron Lady' of the Conservative party, the yard was finally closed. In the meantime, Chatham remained open, seemingly defying the odds, but bringing a degree of prosperity to an area of Kent that was entirely dependent upon this one major employer. Life in the Medway Towns, apart from those who commuted to London or in some other way were insulated from their neighbours, was the naval dockyard.

10

WITHIN LIVING MEMORY

In the years that immediately followed the Second World War, Chatham dockyard hit the news headlines on two occasions, but for completely the wrong reasons. It resulted from two dramatic accidents that took the lives of a number of those employed in the dockyard. The first of these occurred during the afternoon of 14 January 1950. In the Thames estuary, *Truculent*, a submarine returning to Chatham following successful sea trials, collided with the SS *Divinia*, a 640-ton Swedish tanker. As well as her normal crew of sixty-one, the submarine also had on board eighteen dockyard workers who had been monitoring her machinery during that final day of her sea trials. While *Divinia* suffered relatively little damage, the submarine was badly holed and immediately began to sink. While those on the bridge were thrown into the sea, those below were able to make the vessel watertight aft of the Control Room with many later exiting through the aft escape hatch. Tragically, in the darkness, most were swept away by the tide and died of either hypothermia or drowning. In all, only fifteen survived, the tragedy taking the lives of forty-nine sailors and fifteen dockyard men who had been on board.[1]

The second tragedy took place on 15 December 1954 and resulted from the caisson that was holding back the river at the head of No. 3 Dock giving way. Recent work on the caisson had resulted in her being insufficiently flooded to meet a tide that was 3ft higher than the norm. The result was that instead of remaining fast the caisson rose up and allowed water to pour into the vast area of the dock. Inside, the submarine *Talent*, undergoing repairs, was swept to the end of the dock before being washed out into the Medway and coming to rest on the opposite bank. As for the caisson, which also collided with the submarine, this reared some 2–3ft into the air and onto the side of the dock. Those working on the submarine were also swept out into the river, with a number of them desperately holding on to the submarine's deck. While most were subsequently rescued, three were later found drowned and a fourth died in hospital. A communiqué, issued on the evening of the flooding by Rear-Admiral G.V.M. Dolphin, stated:

> Some 31 men who were working on the submarine have received attention at the dock-
> yard surgery. Three were taken to Chatham Naval Hospital, two of whom were seriously
> injured. Civilian divers have been working in the dockyard since the accident and sal-
> vage equipment is available for use in the river. The salvage vessel *Swin* is standing by.

Investigations were made on board the submarine. Because of the fact that it might have rolled over these men were withdrawn. Since then the submarine has settled on a more even keel and the men will return to continue their investigations as soon as possible.

More recently, to mark the sixtieth anniversary of the sinking of the *Truculent*, a memorial service was held by the Medway Branch of the Submariner's Association at the St George's Centre (the former chapel of the Royal Naval Barracks). In reporting the service, the *Kentish Express* carried an interview with ninety-year-old Charles King, who had been coxswain on *Perseverance*, one of the vessels that had helped raise the submarine some three months after the disaster. 'It was a horrific accident,' he said. 'I was not there when the sub was hit but it was terrible as the majority of those on board were killed.'

Over the years I have talked to many former yard workers about their time in the dockyard. Those that were there during the 1950s frequently comment on these two tragedies before moving on to happier times and the certainty of employment that kept them at work throughout the two following decades. As an outsider, not as a dockyard worker but as a Medway resident and historian, I too have memories of the yard. These date back to the late sixties, a time very different from now and one in which the entire Medway area was completely dominated by this one centre of industrial output. In approaching Dock Road on any weekday late afternoon it was impossible to ignore the seething mass of humanity that was making its dash for freedom from both Pembroke and Main gates. First came the cars, but these could

A special memory that many have of the dockyard is that of visiting it during Navy Week (later becoming Navy Days). It was particularly exciting during the inter-war years, as a much larger number of vessels were normally open to the public while regular displays were to be seen of some of the most modern equipment available to any warship.

have emanated from anywhere. Less mistakable were the hundreds of cyclists, each following the quickest homeward route, oblivious to those attempting to cross that busy thoroughfare at a time when the pedestrian should have known better. Buses, also, were part of this singular one-way movement, with almost the entire local bus fleet given over to the needs of the exiting workforce. To assist them, and to ensure that none mistakenly boarded the wrong bus, the on-board destination signs were assisted by stone plaques affixed to the wall towards the lower part of Dock Road and proclaiming the adjacent bus to be bound for Jezreels, Waldeslade, Luton or the Davis Estate. Was there nowhere in the area of the three towns that didn't possess a minimum of at least one bus load of naval dockyard workers?

So proud of its dockyard, and the massive workforce employed on maintaining the Navy, that local papers were always a-thirst for news and ready to print the latest happening of a newly arrived ship or another that was soon to tumble down the launch ways. On occasions, and often stretching across the year, full-page feature articles would also bring some extra detail, each internal dockyard department having the spotlight turned upon it, so that those outside might learn more of what happened inside. Two particularly informative series graced the pages of the long-since-vanished *Chatham Observer*. The first of these appearing, somewhat irregularly, throughout much of 1955, concentrated on the various departments within the yard. In doing so, it served as a useful reminder that modern technology had not only brought numerous changes to working practices but also to the way the dockyard was organised.

Not surprisingly, it was the Constructive Department that first came under the spotlight, this being the largest employer of labour within the yard. As the *Chatham Observer* described it, this was the department that undertook 'the structural work involved in the building, conversion and repairing of HM Ships of all classes'. In former times, due to whether a ship in dockyard hands was afloat or in dry dock, the undertaking of such work had been overseen by either the Master Shipwright or the Master Attendant. However, since the late nineteenth century, all such work was simply managed by the Chief Constructor. Under his authority, as a divisional manager, there were numerous specialised workshops that included the heavy and light plate shop (where metal used in the building and repairing of ships was prepared), the smithery (used for forging and galvanising), the ship fitters' shop (where work was undertaken on auxiliary machinery such as steering gear, winches, windlasses, valves, gear rods and rudders), a joiners' shop (where work on furniture for both ships and shore establishments was undertaken) and a drawing office (where draughtsmen and tracers were employed).[2] In 1955, A. T. Lemman held the post of Chief Constructor, responsible for 3,200 industrial workers together with additional managers, supervisory staff and ninety draughtsmen.

The second largest department in the yard was that of the Engineering Department, this having broken away from the authority of the Master Shipwright during the nineteenth century and now directly supervised by the Engineer Manager. Within the department there were some 2,700 industrial workers, with the largest proportion employed in the Factory. This was an extensive and noisy building where the engine fitters, who fitted ship's engines and other mechanical devices on ships, undertook their work. The foundry and pattern shop also fell within this department with the foundry producing metal items needed on a ship and made through the process of pouring molten metal into a mould and the product ready when the metal had cooled. As for the pattern shop, it was here that patternmakers made the moulds for use in the foundry. Other working areas that fell within this department included the boiler shop, coppersmiths shop and ropery. In the boiler shop, boilermakers built and repaired the boilers used both in the dockyard and on board naval warships, this work included the funnels, the only part of a ship not built by shipwrights. As for the coppersmith's shop, where coppersmiths were employed, copper piping for ships and shore establishments was made. Both the boiler shop and coppersmith's shop were situated alongside the foundry close by the No.1 Basin. The ropery, the oldest section of the dockyard, which had been manufacturing rope since the seventeenth century, still employed spinners and rope makers in the manufacture of naval rope, this rope ranging from five-eighths to 20in in circumference. A final and distinctly different working area within this department was that of the optical shop and metallurgical laboratory. Of these two areas, the *Chatham Observer* noted:

> In complete contrast to the hum drum of the busy factory, there are the optical shop and metallurgical laboratory, two very important features of the department. Such instruments as range finders, direction finders and gun sights, as well as binoculars are repaired and tested in the optical shop, while members of the Royal Naval Scientific Service physically test and analyse materials and Service failures in the latter laboratory.[3]

While the Constructive and Engineering Departments could both trace their genesis back to the previous century, or even beyond, the Electrical Manager's Department had only been formed in 1903. In June 1955 it had a complement of 1,750 industrial workers and 180 non-industrials and had responsibility for the whole of the electrical installations and power to both the dockyard and the adjoining naval establishments that included the Ordnance Wharf and Royal Naval Barracks. At the heart of this department was the main generating station, located 600m south of the No.8 Dock, it could provide some 15,000kw when required. Technically, nearly all the employees in this department were known as electrical fitters, with most employed in electrical workshops.

Responsibility for the construction and maintenance of all buildings in the yard, including the dry docks, jetties and the twenty-four miles of rail line that ran through the yard, was the Civil Engineering Department. Consisting of 850 personnel, this department was also responsible for all Admiralty establishments throughout the whole of Kent and part of Sussex, with work in 1955 being carried out on both a new barrack block for the Royal Marine barracks in Deal and on the reconstruction of the Royal Observatory at Greenwich. More locally, this department of the yard was also undertaking work in connection with a new Admiralty housing estate then being built in the Darget's Wood area of Chatham, with a 56-acre of woodland cleared for the erection of 500 houses.

A further dockyard department that had connections that took it well beyond the construction and repair of ships was that of the Naval Stores Department. This, of course, was a department long associated with the yard, the Storekeeper, one of the original principal officers of the yard, once having responsibility for this department. While in earlier times, stores accumulated at the yard were only for vessels fitting out in the Medway, this was no longer the case. Instead, the dockyard was now at the centre of a worldwide supply system that could provision any ship or overseas establishment with stores that ranged from a needle to a 9-ton mooring anchor. The No.3 Basin was the core working area for this department, but a number of storehouses existed throughout the yard, including the two eighteenth-century stores that stood alongside the Anchor Wharf. The motto of this department, suggested the *Chatham Observer*, was 'you want it we can produce it'.[4]

Underpinning the work of all these departments in the dockyard was the apprenticeship system. This had its origins in the very earliest days of the dockyard, with young boys once indentured to an artisan of the yard for a period of seven years for the purpose of learning the trade. Not always particularly well-regulated, the quality of the training varied considerably, with many of the apprentices, on completion of their training, often unable to carry out anything more than the simplest and most straightforward of tasks. Not until 1843, following the establishment of an apprenticeship school at Chatham, did matters really begin to improve, with 136 apprentices in that year beginning a more formalised programme of education.[5] Within the school a broad curriculum of subjects was studied on certain afternoons and a few selected evenings, while the practical skills of their trade occupied much of the rest of their work time. To begin with, selection for an apprenticeship in the yard had been heavily dependent on personal influence, with artisans employed in the yard usually able to gain an apprenticeship for their own sons. Only in the 1840s was an examination system introduced; this becoming more rigorous and competitive over the years. By the 1950s, when the length of an apprenticeship was no more than five years, selection was based on an annual Civil Service open competitive exam and limited to those aged between fifteen and seventeen years. The result achieved in this exam determined the trade that could be selected, with those of shipwright and electrical fitter among the most highly prized.

In its examination of the various departments of the yard, the *Chatham Observer* drew attention to an emerging problem within the dockyard apprenticeship system at Chatham: that of an increasing level of indiscipline. According to John Crawshaw, Head of the Apprenticeship Department at this time, it resulted from an increase in recruitment that had taken place from 1951 onwards, with a consequent lowering of standards. In his own unpublished account of these years, he refers to twelve apprentices appearing in court, four of them for theft of private property within the yard and the others for housebreaking or assault.[6] At the time, it was suggested that there was a lack of control of the apprentices within the yard, leading to Alfred Bottomley, the local MP, carrying out an enquiry into these allegations and which subsequently absolved the apprentices.[7] 'To clear the air still further,' declared the *Observer* in January 1955, it chose to 'carry out its own investigation of the "Yard apprenticeship scheme".' In doing so, the newspaper learnt that there was 'a surprisingly large number of more than 1000 apprentices' in the charge of 'competent instructors'. Of those apprentices, it had to be admitted that there was the occasional 'bad penny'. In general, however, the *Observer* concluded:

> It is only natural that some of the younger lads among the apprentices should occasionally engage in boyish pranks, but the instructors, who probably did just the same sort of thing when they were apprentices, know how to deal with these demonstrations of high spirits.

Clearly demonstrating its loyalty to the local dockyard and those connected with it, the newspaper went on to correctly conclude:

> One thing is certain, the Yard apprentices receive the finest training a boy can possibly get, be it in the field of shipbuilding and repairing, or in electronics.[8]

For its second glimpse into dockyard life, undertaken ten years later, the *Observer* adopted a much more informal approach, concentrating upon individuals and their immediate work areas. In October 1965, focus was on the drawing office and a few of the 300 clerks, tracers and draughtsmen employed in that section of the yard. At that time a team from this office was working on the development of catapult auxiliary loading equipment for aircraft carriers while another team had been responsible for designing the standard Admiralty Diesel engine that was then being installed into a number of submarines. Of individuals in the drawing office, sixty-five-year-old Don Edser was among those featured, it being mentioned that he had first joined the yard in 1916 as a shipwright and had transferred to the drawing office twenty years later. A natural artist, it was his responsibility for producing the drawings for ships' crests and badges.[9]

That the dockyard was a workplace with a strong community spirit is something that comes out very clearly in this series of articles. Many of those featured by the *Observer* had a long and very happy association with the yard. Indeed, thoughts of retiring and leaving this happy family were not high on the individual agenda. In the Factory, then employing 450 workpeople on a 6.5-acre floor area, could be found eighty-one-year-old Percy Kewell, an engine fitter. It might have been expected that he would have retired some sixteen years earlier, having first served in the Navy for nearly twenty-eight years before joining the yard in 1930. However, this he hoped never to do, declaring himself to be 'glad to return to work on Monday morning.' As with many other areas of the yard, the Factory, then manufacturing the Admiralty Standard Diesel engines that had been designed in the drawing office, had its own social club that organised outings and other family events.

Further helping foster this workplace community spirit was *Periscope*, the newspaper of the dockyard and naval base. First published on 29 October 1965, it was a monthly tabloid-style publication that continued in print until June 1983. In terms of editorial control, it was neither a mouthpiece for management nor the unions, although occasional management pressure was occasionally applied. Among regular features was the yard restaurant menu, a rundown of various social events and a written tribute with photographs of those eight or nine members of the yard who, in any particular month, had finally opted for retirement. Other, if less regular,

PERISCOPE

NEWSPAPER OF H.M. NAVAL BASE, CHATHAM

Vol. 18 No. 213   June 1983

Pickfords

REMOVALS LTD.

make regular runs
to all naval bases

Medway 48055

☆ FREE ESTIMATES ☆

"OUR LAST AND BEST" CHURCHILL COMPLETES

THE end of eight decades of submarine work at Chatham dockyard was marked as difficult as anything attempted by anyone anywhere.

"The fact that it was completed to a tight programme to every activity throughout the refit.

"Once we got in the refit phase the team was well settled both on the production

The last edition of *Periscope*, the naval base newspaper, was published in June 1983 and headlined with the completion of the yard's last submarine fit.

features examined aspects of the yard's history, including the ships that it had built and past memorable events. The front page, not unnaturally, was given over to important dockyard news stories, these often drawing attention to ships about to be brought to Chatham for a refit and so ensuring a goodly amount of work. Thus, the November 1979 front page headline proclaiming 'new refit will cure workload problem' might have seemed out of place in any other tabloid, but a vital lead story when appearing in *Periscope*. Sometimes also appearing on the front page, but always tastefully clothed, was the 'Maid of the Month', a female usually aged between eighteen and twenty-five and employed in a clerical position within the yard. Worryingly sexist, it nevertheless provided a further means to personalise those in the dockyard, with 'Maid of the Month' for May 1982, twenty-one-year-old Sue Taylor, a temporary clerical assistant in the drawing office, able to tell her fellow workers that she had always been a speedway fan; an interest that she then shared with her boyfriend!

Returning to my own memories of the dockyard while under Admiralty control, I made a point of attending numerous Navy Days. Whereas, during the 1930s, the event had lasted for a complete week, now it was restricted to the Sunday and Monday of the Whitsun bank holiday, with a run through of the main events practised on the Saturday of that same weekend. In looking at the souvenir booklets I purchased at these events, I note that many of them are rain-damaged, a reminder of the climatic conditions that inevitably seemed to accompany an otherwise very promising occasion. Of course, these same souvenir booklets also testify to the various attractions being put on by the Navy, with submarines, frigates and warships from other navies present and ready to be boarded. Regular in their presence for a number of years was the helicopter cruiser *Blake* and the ice-patrol vessel *Endurance*, while the No. 3 Basin was the scene of a simulated rescue or mock-attack carried out by the Royal Marine Commandos. The largest annual event to be held in the Medway Towns, Navy Days attracted many thousands of

The Nuclear Refit Complex that was added to the yard in the late 1960s and which continued
to operate until shortly before the yard's closure in 1983.

visitors, with the roads to and from the yard completely gridlocked as motorists in the
morning attempted to enter the yard and then exit during the late afternoon. [10]

While those, like myself, were permitted during Navy Days to take photographs of
some of the most modern ships of the fleet, it always seemed strange that the Georgian
end of the dockyard was completely off limits. While some of the most secret aspects
of the Navy were open to public gaze, the least modern area of the yard, including
its nineteenth-century ropeyard jack wheels and dock steam pumps, was completely
sealed. Was it possible that our Cold War enemies were incapable of laying a hefty cable
or sewing a decent flag? However, in writing my first history of the dockyard, I was
finally permitted into this area, allowed to gaze on the amazing scene of spinners and
rope layers at work in the dusty confines of the Rope House and of ships lying in the
nineteenth-century stone dry docks. The one proviso given was that no pictures were
permitted of underwater hull sections and the camera must never be directed to the
slightly more distant nuclear refit complex. But, of course, everyone knew that such
pictures were certainly available to the KGB, taken from the masts of Russian merchant
ships as they sailed past the yard and into the port of Rochester.

Of something else I noticed in entering the yard during a normal working day, and
when compared with the rival yards of Devonport, Rosyth and Portsmouth, life was
running at a very different pace. At these other yards, a careful glance over the shoulder
was constantly required, this a matter of safety as trucks and other loads passed by in
rapid and quick succession. Chatham, by comparison, was a haven of limited activity.
Clearly, for those who were responsible for the future of the nation's naval ship repair
facilities, Chatham was already being run down.

The threat of closure was one that slowly developed following the ending of the
Second World War. Certainly there was no hint of such a possibility in a top secret

memorandum addressed to the Prime Minister in August 1945. The most that was being talked about was that of dispersing certain naval facilities away from southern England to the yard at Rosyth.[11] Funny that! The Admiralty seemed to be ignoring the real lessons of the Second World War – that of the development of A-bombs and missiles. These, having seen the light of day, would leave no area of the country completely safe from an enemy in possession of such weapons. Seemingly, the Admiralty was planning to re-fight the Second World War on the basis of what should have happened prior to 1939.

By the late 1950s and early 1960s, the future of Chatham was a lot less secure, with considerably smaller amounts of work being sent to the yard. But this did not prevent Conservative Prime Minister Harold Macmillan, during an October 1959 electioneering visit to the Medway Towns, assuring the local yard workers, whose vote he was desperate to secure in this highly marginal seat, that the dockyard was safe from closure.[12] Nevertheless, and despite Macmillan's declaration, the odds, according to Emma Haxhaj in a carefully researched paper on the post-war dockyard at Chatham, were heavily stacked against the yard having a long-term future. In particular, she points to two important factors, both to do with location. Firstly, Chatham dockyard was 'situated in the relatively prosperous south-east, with easy access to London and a comparatively varied industry base'. This made it less burdensome to close the yard at Chatham, as under this reasoning, it would be easier for those employed in the dockyard to find work elsewhere. Secondly, according to Haxhaj, the Chatham yard was 'strategically ill-positioned for the needs of the post-1945 Navy' given that the Nore was no longer an operational naval command.

Only a few years prior to Macmillan's visit to the Medway Towns, the dockyard had certainly been marked down for possible closure, the Admiralty Way Ahead Committee, which had been formed in 1955, discussing it as a possibility. This was the committee that had recommended the closure of Sheerness and may well have brought down the axe on Chatham had it not been more expedient to recommend the closure of three overseas yards, those of Simons Town, Hong Kong and Malta. While the internal debates of the committee had not been publicised, the fear of the yard at Chatham being closed was certainly a topic of general discussion in 1963. Indeed, for Chatham, that particular year seemed to bring nothing but bad news. A specialism in submarine construction looked as if it was coming to an end. Having launched, between 1959 and 1962, three 'Oberon' class patrol submarines for the Royal Navy, with a fourth, Onyx, still on the slipway, there were no further orders in the pipeline. Worst still, the future Polaris submarine building programme, involving construction of a possible five nuclear-powered 'Resolution' class vessels, were all to be constructed in private yards.[13] This, indeed, was a considerable blow, Chatham most certainly having the experience and background to build such large and complex vessels within the time frame required. Finally, and seeming to confirm that a closure scenario was on the table, was that of the Admiralty announcing, during the summer of that same year, a decision to reduce the dockyard workforce by 500. That this was to be through natural wastage, rather than actual redundancies did little to soften the blow. In an attempt to raise workforce morale, Rear Admiral Beloe, the yard's Admiral

Superintendent, was reported to have declared that 'there had been some loose talk locally of the closure of the Dockyard which was of course nonsense'.[14]

The decision to build the 'Resolution' class submarines, albeit in the private sector yards, did permit Chatham one very big favour. In order to refit those vessels once they were in service, together with the six nuclear-powered hunter killer submarines that were also entering naval service, the existing submarine refit facilities were quite inadequate. A further facility was deemed essential to make good this shortfall, with Chatham regarded as the most appropriate yard. In part, this was because of its existing experience of building and repairing submarines but also because of Chatham having the necessary slack in its existing programme of works. The decision was officially announced in the House of Commons on 11 March 1965, with the new complex to be placed between the existing Nos 6 and 7 Docks and to be on stream by December 1970.

Constructed, therefore, during the late 1960s, the complex was officially opened by Vice Admiral Horace Law on 29 June 1968. Making use of the two adjoining dry docks, its most noticeable feature was a 120-ton hammerhead travelling crane that was easily visible from much of the area that surrounded the dockyard. Standing in the region of 50m in height, its purpose was that of lifting a portable refuelling workshop (the Reactor House) on to the submarine which would already have been brought into one of the two dry docks. Once attached to the submarine, and from within the Reactor House, an opening was cut into the hull for the purpose of removing the spent nuclear fuel and inserting new fuel. In addition to the crane, the complex was flanked by offices and workshops together with the various units that maintained the submarine while the reactor was shut down and which included core coolant, coolant discharge and electrical supply. Also playing its part in the refitting process was the Factory, this considerably modernised with the addition of air-conditioned clean rooms where equipment could be cleaned ultrasonically, washed with demineralised water and hot-air dried.

The first submarine to enter the complex was *Valiant*. Entering No.6 Dock in May 1970, she was finally returned to naval service some two years later. As well as being refuelled, she received a complete refit that included the stripping out and refurbishing of all her systems, the reinstallation of new equipment, rectification of known defects and general equipment modification. At the same time, tests were undertaken on the integrity of her hull, this involving non-destructive examination surveys. In total, and prior to her floating out from the No.6 Dock, this was to consume in excess of some 2 million hours of work, a sum total that represented some 50 per cent of the dockyard's total ship work capability. Apart from *Valiant*, the fleet nuclear submarines *Warspite*, *Churchill*, *Conqueror*, *Courageous* and *Dreadnought* were all to be refuelled and refitted at Chatham. In addition, and prior to the closure of the yard in 1984, *Sovereign*, a 'Swiftsure' class submarine was also refitted at the complex, with a number of additional dockings for essential refits also undertaken.

At the time of the building of the complex, and also during its period of operation, much had been made of its high levels of safety. This was to offset concerns within the Medway area that there was a potential for radiation leaks that could have a negative impact upon those employed in and around the site. One Admiralty-sanctioned publication, first issued during the mid-1970s, while accepting that there were potential dangers, attempted to allay concerns by providing an explanation of how uranium and other fission products within a submarine reactor core were handled:

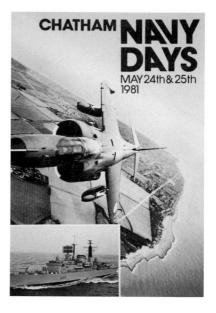

> Other fission products with much longer half-lives still remain in the core at the end of core life, and this highly concentrated source of radioactivity in all the structural parts of the core present a formidable problem when refuelling is carried out. Therefore remote handling techniques, heavy shielding, strict radiological controls and extensive operator training are used to make refuelling a safe operation. Loading the new fuel is relatively simple; although the new core contains a considerable amount of fissile material there is no radiation hazard from active fissile products.[15]

The last Chatham Navy Days took place in May 1981 with a full programme of events. This is the front cover of the printed programme for that occasion. A further Navy Days was planned for 1982 but unfortunately was cancelled due to the Falklands conflict placing other requirements on the vessels that would have been present on that final occasion.

Awareness of these locally expressed health concerns had also given rise to numerous official statements at the time that construction of the complex had first been announced, these indicating that safety was the major priority. During the summer of 1965, the *Chatham Observer* quoted dockyard managers as saying that two watchwords would govern how the complex would be run: safety and absolute care. They indicated that workers who came into contact with radiation would be checked and re-checked, with this all being overseen in a special Health Physic building that was to lay alongside the complex and which was, indeed, constructed.

Unfortunately, and as seemingly verified by former workers and their families, because of work within the complex often being under pressure of time 'proper monitoring and safety were not always in place'. At least this was the view of Jonathan Shaw, following his election to parliament for the Chatham constituency in 1997. In his maiden speech, he cited the case of David Spriggs, a refitter on the submarine *Dreadnought*:

> He was working deep in the heart of a reactor when a pipe burst above his head and drenched him in water. The supervisor reportedly told him to carry on until the end of the shift, when the Geiger counter showed alarming levels of radiation exposure. Following the accident, which the Ministry of Defence [MOD] called a serious incident, David Spriggs was told to take six months off, yet he was back at work within a couple of weeks because of pressure of work at the dockyard.

Later on in the same speech, Shaw added:

> A further concern to us in the Medway towns is that the MOD may not have done
> all that it could to ensure that all available safety systems were in place at Chatham.
> It failed to install the new safety system, Modex, an American invention, which was
> introduced in American yards in the 1960s and early 1970s. It was a significant devel-
> opment in dose abatement technology. According to the Defence Committee report
> of 1990, it reduces the dose burden within the reactor compartment by a factor of
> four to eight. Modex was introduced at Devonport and Rosyth in about 1979, but it
> was never installed at Chatham.

All of these concerns had first been raised in 1990 as a result of a number of former
dockyard workers having contracted various cancers. Tim Robson, at that time a
Rochester city councillor and, himself, formerly employed on nuclear submarines
within the complex, had begun to assemble evidence of these various shortfalls.
Unfortunately, a year after he had begun the campaign, he learnt that he had also
contracted cancer. Despite this, and prior to his death in August 1995 at the age of
just thirty-nine, he continued his campaign, winning the support of Rochester-upon-
Medway City Council in January 1994. From then on the council used its resources
to press the Ministry of Defence to provide annual health checks for former dockyard
workers, so that it would be possible for them to detect at the earliest possible stages
whether they had a cancer that could be attributed to radiation exposure.

In his speech to the House of Commons, Shaw was able to conclude that a considerable step forward on the issue had finally been made:

> After years of campaigning, a significant step was taken in June this year, when my hon.
> Friend the Under-Secretary of State for Defence launched a local counselling scheme
> in partnership with Rochester City Council. Under that scheme, expert doctors pro-
> vide advice locally to former workers and their families. Since the scheme was launched,
> 210 enquiries have been made nationally for dosage records from the MOD, and 94 per
> cent of them have come from people who worked at Chatham. That demonstrates the
> success and importance of a local scheme rather than having to rely on a national one.
> On the same day, my hon. Friend announced that the MOD would invest £1 million
> on improving access to radiation dose records not currently held on computer.

Shaw further pointed out, that while he now represented the Chatham constituency,
there had been a previous Labour candidate, his friend and colleague, the ex-dockyard
worker, Tim Robson:

> He was selected at a time when we hoped that his health was improving, such was
> his determination to enter this House to represent the people of Chatham, a place
> where he had lived all his life and of which he was genuinely proud.[16]

The story, however, does not end at that point. It took a further year for the government to finally admit that workers at Chatham might have contracted cancer through contact with high levels of radiation.[17] Furthermore, it was also revealed that many of the health records formerly kept within the former Health Physic building had been lost or damaged, so making it difficult for those who might have a claim to actually make that claim.

Further claims against the Ministry of Defence have also been made by other groups of workers, demonstrating that there was a horrendous and hidden downside to life in the dockyard. An impossible to estimate number of those employed in the Factory, particularly those operating lathes, milling machines or when riveting plates were subject to a later hearing loss, with the Ministry of Defence having to accept liability due to the limited availability of ear defenders. One successful claimant, when working inside a ship or submarine, was quoted by his solicitor as saying, 'I was exposed to the noise created by the Chipper, who worked outside. For me, it felt like working inside an empty shell. The noise never went away.'[18] Others who suffered as a result of working in the dockyard were those who came into contact with asbestos. An insulation material used in the yard because of its corrosion- and heat-resistant properties, the resulting dust when breathed in can lead to asbestosis, a deadly disease that affects the lungs and for which there is no cure. In a typical refit during the 1960s, some 300 asbestos-containing materials were commonly used, most frequently in the insulation of hot steam pipes, hot water lines and fuel lines on pumps, turbines, compressors and condensers with boilers also given asbestos brick and asbestos linings. A radiological survey of 10 per cent of the whole population of the dockyard at Chatham showed that over 2 per cent had abnormalities attributable to the inhalation of asbestos.[19] In one well-publicised case, John Stepney recovered a substantial sum arising from his contraction of mesothelioma, a cancer caused by asbestos dust. Throughout his working life at the dockyard he was exposed to asbestos through the undertaking of his work on ships and from piles of rubble that also contained asbestos in the dockyard.

Despite the risk to health, combined with workplace accidents that varied in seriousness, the closure of the dockyard was not something to be reflected upon with any degree of pleasure. As Ben_10000, a contributor to the Kent History Forum blog site, recently noted in a discussion on some of the radiation dangers presented by the dockyard, 'it's odd to think that we used to live so close to a Nuclear facility (I could see it from my bedroom) and that we fought to keep it. But it was jobs I guess. My father worked in the yard for many, many years'.[20] And that was the point of fighting to keep the dockyard open: it was not just the jobs or the money that this work created for the local economy but it was also something more. The dockyard gave to the Medway Towns a feeling of pride and it gave the Towns a place in the world. For its work on naval warships, the Medway area could be justly proud. That changing technology had made it a more dangerous place in which to work was seemingly immaterial against this greater threat. For this reason, and despite the environment of the dockyard having become considerably noisier and less pleasant since the laying down of the first ironclads, any accompanying concerns were simply put to one side. The dockyard was threatened with closure and the future of the Medway Towns was looking as bleak as bleak could be.

11

THE RISE OF THE PHOENIX

Periscope, the Chatham naval base newspaper, carried a headline in its November 1980 edition that seemed to herald a bright future for the 16,000 workers of the dockyard. The accompanying lead story, in referring to a recent government publication, The Dockyard Study Report, indicated that a commitment had been made to the definite retention of Chatham as a naval dockyard. In assuring its readers that none might fear future redundancy, *Periscope* also paraphrased the words of Navy Minister Keith Speed who, in a written answer to a parliamentary question from Peggy Fenner, MP for Rochester and Chatham, had recently stated:

> The government accepts the recommendation in the report and confirms the need to retain the four home dockyards though the levels of employment in each dockyard will depend on the success of their management and workforce in improving efficiency.

The Historic Dockyard at Chatham has sometimes a strange and eclectic mixture of display items and none more so than this selection to be found under the roofing of the No.3 covered slip.

The parliamentary answer to this question also added a further piece of detail:

> The Government also accepts the report's conclusion that the introduction of private capital into the dockyards is not a practical solution at this time.[1]

The report, described in some circles as 'radical but realistic', had set out a means by which Chatham and the other home yards could achieve much higher levels of efficiency through a structural reform of the existing management process. Under the recommendations being made, those responsible for the dockyards would be given greater independence to manage resources while accountable for the performance of the yard against clearly laid down objectives. Harking back to the 1890s and the ship construction race between Portsmouth and Chatham, competition was also to be developed between yards. In a later account of his time as Navy Minister, Speed offered a further explanation of what was intended:

> In other words we should cut as many links as possible from the Civil Service attitude which was inappropriate for running a considerable industrial enterprise comparable in size to Vauxhall Motors or the Metal Box Company. There were many other proposals, most of which are standard practice in well-run profitable organisations but were greatly daring in a dockyard Civil Service context.[2]

Among these other proposals was that of a new pay scheme which, at that time, was being negotiated with the dockyard unions. This involved productivity payments based on measurable increases in performance and would result in a clear increase in take-home pay. In return and ultimately agreed by the unions, certain outdated work practices were to be removed, paving the way for better stop/start routines and more flexibility over demarcation of trades.

The optimism raised by the Dockyard Study Report was to be completely dashed one year later. Repeatedly, Conservative politicians had reaffirmed that under their watch the dockyard at Chatham would be completely safe. Many in the Medway area, prior to the closure announcement, freely stated that their vote was going to the Conservative party for this reason and no other. Irrespective of the rights and wrongs of

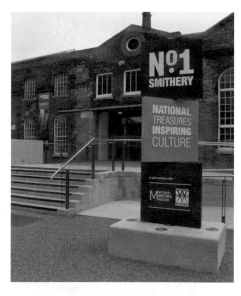

An exterior view of the No.1 Smithery following its opening in 2010 as a public gallery that focuses on works of maritime art.

One of the earliest public display exhibits within the area of the Historic Dockyard to get underway was that of 'Wooden Walls' which tells the story of how a seventy-four-gun warship of the eighteenth century was designed and built. It is located in a former mast house, with this part of the exhibition demonstrating how the lines of a warship were drawn onto the floor of the mould loft and from these templates were then cut.

actually closing the yard, the Conservatives on this occasion did a great disservice to the Medway Towns. It meant that large numbers of highly skilled and dedicated workers chose to enter dockyard service, believing that they had job security. In doing so, they rejected the higher pay rates to be found in the commercial sector while laying down their roots in the area. If political openness, combined with a more gradual running down of the dockyard had been allowed, the crisis that hit the Medway Towns from the summer of 1981 onwards could easily have been avoided.

As for the closure of Chatham, this was first disclosed in a statement given in parliament by John Nott, Secretary of State for Defence, on 25 June 1981 and resulting from a White Paper on defence entitled The Way Forward. A severe and devastating blow to the whole of the Medway area, it soon became clear that redundancies were to start almost immediately, that it also involved the additional closure of the naval barracks at HMS *Pembroke*, and that all was to be completed by March 1984.

Opposition within the Medway Towns to the closure of these two naval facilities was unanimous. A protest march was immediately organised, with 4,000 dockyard employees marching, on 3 July, from Pembroke Gate to a rally meeting on Jackson's Field, Rochester. Many of those who lined the streets, or leaned out of office and shop windows, offered their support by willingly signing a petition that was to be handed in to No. 10 Downing Street. Just over a week later, more than 1,000 dockyard workers from the area travelled to London in a fleet of coaches, joining with Portsmouth dockyard workers (a yard that was to be considerably reduced in status) at Clapham Common for a march to Westminster.

None of these efforts were to have any form of impact upon a government that was not intent upon a U-turn. In August, with a Manager of a Yard Closure Planning Department already appointed, the Chief Executive of Dockyards, Keith Thomas, made a fleeting visit to the yard, offering an explanation as to why the axe had fallen on Chatham. He began by referring to a series of financial constraints that had to be overcome by March 1984. Then, in turning specifically to Chatham, he affirmed that the dockyard had a good work record. However, the problem, as far as the Admiralty in London saw it, was that a home dockyard had to be closed for the purpose of economising and that Chatham was the only option. While the axe might have fallen on Devonport, Portsmouth or Rosyth, each of these had commitments outside of the immediate dockyard, something that was missing at Chatham. In providing further detail, Thomas referred to Portsmouth having many shore establishments and extensive berthing facilities for the fleet while both Devonport and Rosyth were operational naval bases, with the former having had considerable recent investment. Of course, what Thomas never chose to mention was that of the government's own hidden agenda, that of allowing private industry to acquire a bigger slice of the national revenue. It was something that Prime Minister Margaret Thatcher was determined to drive through, irrespective of the loyalty of those that were now to suffer the consequences of this one particular political philosophy.

Keith Speed, a somewhat less doctrinaire politician than that of his leader, recognised the potential folly of too much reliance upon the private sector, especially when it came to defence matters, and fought hard to keep the yard open. Of course, this made his position untenable within the government, and he was savaged by an angry premier and quickly returned to the backbenches.

As well as a series of permanent displays, the Historic Dockyard also holds a number of event days, with this a demonstration of the work of the wartime civil defence organisations. The building in the background is the former Officers' Offices while the railings are those that surround the former Commissioner's House.

Giving credibility to those who opposed the closing of the dockyard at Chatham was that of the Argentine invasion of the Falklands that took place in April 1982. In assembling a large task force of naval warships for the purpose of retaking the islands, the facilities and workforce at Chatham became a crucial factor. All redundancy notices were suspended, this to allow for a maximum effort that was to be directed to supporting the task force. Apart from structural alterations on a number of ships, those employed in the yard during this period were also involved in issuing urgently required fuel and stores for a number of those vessels destined for the South Atlantic. Furthermore, once the conflict was over, those soon to be redundant workers were engaged on the repair of battle-damaged ships and the returning of other vessels to service, namely *Berwick*, *Zulu* and *Falmouth*, these to replace ships lost in the Falklands. It was now deduced by many that the government had not only made a mistake, but that it would soon recognise its error and announce that the closure notice raised on the dockyard would be rescinded. While, in the event, this did not happen, with the redundancy notices soon reinstated, a clear conundrum has never really been solved. Should a British government, at any point in the future, wish to carry out any sort of similar operation, then where is it that the ship conversions, storing, fuelling, arming and structural alterations would be undertaken?

The retreat from Dunkirk, as re-enacted at Chatham Dockyard in September 2010.

Visitors should not fail to enter the ropery where rope-making demonstrations are often held. Alternatively, the guide, in full period costume and with an appropriate attitude that reflects the age he represents, makes an amusing addition to any tour of the yard.

Prior to the official closure of the dockyard and naval base on 31 March 1984, considerable attention had been given as to how the vacated land could be best used. From the outset, it became clear that a division of purpose was essential. To the south, and forming the site of the dockyard as established in the seventeenth century, there existed a magnificent collection of historic buildings that deserved preservation in their original historic setting. In total contrast to the historic enclave, was the area of the yard that had been developed during the nineteenth century. While there were several buildings certainly deemed to be of historic interest, this part of the yard was seen as much better suited to wholesale redevelopment.

'The Chatham Maritime stone' can be found alongside the No.2 Basin and was unveiled by Prime Minister John Major on 30 June 1995 to mark developments being made on the site.

A starting point, as regards to the preservation of buildings in the historic enclave was that of a Naval Base Joint Planning Team having suggested, six years prior to the closure announcement, that this area of Chatham yard could be released into the public domain. As a consequence, the Ancient Monuments Board, a government advisory body that was to be later subsumed into English Heritage, began to take an interest in how the site might be developed.

On the north side of the No.2 Basin a boardwalk has been installed that connects to various footpaths that pass through parts of St Mary's Island that is still verdant and undeveloped.

Boiler Shop No.1, one of the buildings removed from the dockyard at Woolwich and
re-erected at Chatham and which now survives as Dockside (an enclosed shopping centre),
is to be seen on the left. Just creeping into view on the right is the former Machine Shop
and also brought to the yard from Woolwich. Although this latter building was originally clad
in corrugated sheeting, it suffered substantial storm damage in October 1987 and had to be
removed with only the frame of the building retained. It is now a Grade II listed building.

Apart from ensuring that a number of buildings within the enclave were saved from
demolition (notably the No.1 Smithery and the eighteenth-century timber sheds) the
Board oversaw the production of a report that not only endorsed the historic value of
buildings within the enclave but also suggested that, in opening it out to the public, it
become 'an extension of the National Maritime Museum'.[3]

Within the dockyard there was a further important early development that pre-dated
the closure announcement. This was the formation of the Chatham Dockyard Historical
Society (CDHS) by a number of enthusiasts who were employed in the yard and keen to
ensure that its history should be properly researched and individual memories preserved.
With Admiralty permission, CDHS established a museum in the Lead and Paint Mill, an
important building that dated back to 1818, where historical artefacts from around the yard
were initially stored with a view to their preservation and eventual display. In February
1981 the first activity organised by the new society took place, members using their lunch
break and part of an afternoon working session to take into their newly acquired museum
a dozen old ships' figureheads that had been deteriorating while standing in the open outside Medway House. Numerous other artefacts soon followed, these collected from both
around the yard or presented to the society by fellow yard artisans who had also taken to
searching out their attics for tools and other yard memorabilia.

While preservation of the historic enclave might have been best served by it becoming
an extension of the National Maritime Museum, this was not to be viewed as a possibility
by the Conservative government that forced the closure of the yard. With the museum at
Greenwich a publicly funded body, any such attachment to this institution would have

The Ship and Trades public house which stands alongside the No.1 Basin is a former dockyard office and an engineering shop that dates to 1875.

imposed upon the government a long-term additional commitment. Instead, and in keeping with the government's overriding philosophy of seeking out market solutions, it was determined that a dedicated Trust should be established. Officially taking over the oldest part of the dockyard on 1 April 1984, the newly formed Chatham Dockyard Historic Trust (CDHT) began life with an £11.3 million government endowment, an amount that fell far short of actual need. In fact the Trust had originally bid for £18 million, its governing body aware that many of the buildings it had acquired were in considerable need of repair and renovation, with the ropery alone requiring £2 million for work on its conservation.[4]

The surprise announcement of the dockyard's closure created a much more extensive problem for the St Mary's Island end of the yard as it had always been assumed that this would be retained for warship repair and maintenance. An expansive area that was dominated by a number of ageing industrial buildings, it also contained a stretch of open land that had never witnessed any form of development other than that of an encircling river wall. In addition, and providing the area with a unique facility, was that of the three extensive basins (one of them replete with five dry docks) that ran the entire length of the former St Mary's Creek. Ensuring plenty of opportunity for imaginative planning, something that was not always present in the early stages of the project, it was to allow for a mixture of development that would eventually see a coalescing of industry, housing and leisure facilities.

First to take an interest in the St Mary's Island site was the Medway (Chatham) Dock Company, a body which had been established under the auspices of the Medway Ports Authority. Taking over the No.3 Basin some three months before the official departure of the Navy, Medway Dock Company at that time acquired responsibility for an area of land that amounted to 100 acres. Here were established eight separate commercial berths together with the subsequent development of a fully operational cargo terminal.

Another important player in the redevelopment of St Mary's Island was English Heritage, later English Partnerships, the government's urban regeneration agency. On 1 April 1984, upon the official departure of the Navy, they took over the area of the dockyard not already under the ownership of CDHT or the Medway Dock Company, an area comprising of 350 acres. In addition, the area of the former naval barracks, HMS *Pembroke*, fell into their remit, this allowing for a degree of integrated planning. Charged with the task of completely redeveloping the entire area, English Partnerships were the subject of much local criticism when they undertook a wholesale demolition of numerous former dockyard buildings that they considered to have no further use. They did, however, retain the No.8 Machine Shop, the Boiler Shed and the Machine Shed, all of which had begun life at Woolwich and had been brought to Chatham shortly after the closure of that particular yard in 1869. Another early move and seen as a simple marketing tool, was that of abandoning the word dockyard and redesignating the planned development as 'Chatham Maritime'.

Whilst there was some early use of existing buildings, mostly the barrack blocks and chapel that once belonged to HMS *Pembroke*; a major problem was that of limited road access into the site. This was alleviated by the construction of the Medway Tunnel and Northern Relief Road in the late 1990s. In addition, English Partnerships also carried out extensive work on flood defences, remediation, and the installation of services, in order to make it possible to attract new development to the Chatham Maritime project. In 1999 English Partnerships gave way to South East England Development

An important aspect of the redevelopment of St Mary's Island is that of housing; this an important asset to an area of north Kent desperately short of space for the construction of residential homes.

The Dockyard Engine House that once held the machinery, supplied by Messrs J. and G. Rennie of Blackfriars, used for the pumping out of the four original docks that were annexed to the No.1 Basin. The machinery was first trialled on 10 March 1874, running at 100 revolutions per minute. Within the building, a second, reserve engine was also in place, this formerly belonging to HMS *Forth*. On the occasion of the trial, 20,000 tons of water was pumped from one of the docks in 39 minutes, with a remaining 14,830 tons from the lower half, pumped in 66 minutes. The Engine House, itself, which has recently been restored, is a red-brick building of 77ft in length with an external arcade of brick piers. Immediately adjoining the Engine House was the Boiler House, having the same external appearance and which, itself, once housed nine separate boilers of the Cornish double flue style.

Agency (SEEDA), which continues to develop Chatham Maritime.

Overall, one must conclude that the redevelopment of the former dockyard has been a highly successful project. The three areas, into which the dockyard was divided, following its closure in 1984, have all recorded a significant number of successes and from this point of view it is worth viewing each in turn. Tucked away on the No.3 Basin, Medway Ports Ltd continue to develop the site. Now owned by Peel Docks, and simply known as Medway Ports, the port authority continues in its landlord role while directly operating one of the berths. According to the company's own latest figures, it now handles in excess of 1 million tonnes of cargo per year. As such, Medway Ports must be considered a definite success story bringing, as it does, a clear boost to the local economy while also providing a number of permanent jobs.[5]

CDHT, which was the second of the replacement products to the dockyard to get going, has slowly but surely pulled itself out of its early and rather disappointing beginnings. Most certainly it had a difficult hill to climb, being at that time perennially short of money and generally unable to pull in the number of visitors to which such a large-scale museum complex requires in order to ensure its survival. In its first decade of being open, it never really exceeded the 100,000 figure while the much less impressive and smaller historic enclave at Portsmouth dockyard was pulling in an annual 500,000 visitors. But then Portsmouth had then, and still has, HMS *Victory*, a Chatham-built ship, as its major attraction! What CDHT lacked in those early days was something 'sexier' than just buildings, even though forty-seven of them are now scheduled ancient monuments. Admittedly the ropery, itself an outstanding structure replete with machinery that dates back to the early part of the nineteenth century, was able to put on unique demonstrations of rope making that never failed to impress, but this was never going to be enough to excite the masses.

In those early years of redeveloping the historic enclave I was provided with the opportunity of photographing every aspect of this area. More than anything, it resembled a latter-day *Mary Celeste*, with workshops simply abandoned and trade tools seemingly awaiting the return of those who had most recently used them. This was particularly so in the colour loft, where row upon row of Singer sewing machines were simply gathering dust while in the No.1 Smithery an eclectic collection of heavy industrial machinery was beginning to rust itself out of existence. Poignant in its simplicity was a note that had been chalked onto the sail loft wall. Reflecting the family atmosphere that had once pervaded the yard it declared, 'this happy place was once the home of the painters C243. But thanks to Thatcher and Nott, it is now no more.' And further down the wall was added: 'Jobs they can axe; memories they cannot.'

Only with the permanent showcasing of a number of warships, these now occupying several of the dry docks, did visitor numbers begin to increase. In particular, the historic enclave, the most complete example in the world of an eighteenth-century dockyard, is now the home of three such vessels. While none date to the eighteenth century, they are the clear crowd pullers and include *Cavalier*, Britain's last Second World War destroyer, and *Ocelot*, a submarine that was also the last Royal Navy warship built at the yard. More recently, July 2010, with work on renovating the No.1 Smithery, which had lain derelict for a number of years, by then completed, this too was opened to the public. A joint venture with both the Imperial War Museum and the National Maritime Museum, and put together at a cost of £13 million, the building now houses more than 3,500 official Navy

A final component to the three-way redevelopment jigsaw is the use made of the No.3 Basin by Medway Ports. A commercial port complex, it handles in excess of 1 million tonnes of cargo per year. In looking into the No.3 Basin, the vessel to be seen is the *Sand Heron*, a Lloyd's-registered aggregates vessel.

ship models together with a number of important maritime paintings and a gallery to display international touring art. In addition there is the much longer established 'Wooden Walls Exhibition' and a sizeable museum that makes full use of artefacts collected by those early pioneer members of the Chatham Dockyard Historical Society. As a consequence of this much more all-encompassing visitor experience, further enhanced by a restaurant in the historic setting of a former wheelwrights' shop and a full educational programme, CDHS has now boosted its annual visitor numbers to that of 250,000.

Chatham Maritime has now also made considerable strides forward, with extensive housing having now been constructed on the north-west side of St Mary's Island. Of equal significance is that of the large-scale entertainment and shopping complexes, these to the south of the No.1 Basin. Here are to be found the Dockside Outlet Centre, an Odeon Cinema, the Dickens World visitor attraction, a Ramada Hotel, and the Ship and Trades public house. Helping to further preserve some of the dockyard's history is use that has been made of some of the former buildings of the yard, with the Dockside Outlet Centre housed in the former Boiler Shop No.1 (a former Woolwich dockyard building slip) while the Ship and Trades public house occupies former dockyard offices and an engineering shop that dates to 1875. A further building in this area, but one with no clear future, is Pump House No.5. A handsome red-brick building, it once contained the nine boilers that connected to the pumps that emptied the basin dry docks. A Grade II listed building, it has been refurbished by the South East England Development Agency but is currently unoccupied. As for the No.1 Basin itself, this serves purpose as a yachting marina, owned and operated by Marina Developments Limited.

While all of these developments might not have brought anything like the scale of jobs to the area that the dockyard was once able to boast, the various replacement schemes, projects and complexes have brought a degree of employment. Unfortunately, and when compared with the dockyard, the relative pay levels (when inflation is taken into account) are often much lower. This is an inevitable consequence of a changeover from the considerable skill levels required by the dockyard as compared with the service industries that now predominate within the former area of the yard. Furthermore, while the dockyard was a flagship industry with a long and proud history, it is difficult to suggest that any of its replacement products with the exception of CDHS (as a keeper of the yard's heritage) have anything approaching a similar prestige level. Nevertheless, in having gone through a good many years of suffering, the end of the tunnel has been reached and the dust created by the need to regenerate the Medway Towns in their virtual entirety has now begun to settle.

ENDNOTES

Chapter 1

1 Pipe Office accounts, 1547. The terms 'Jillingham' or 'Jillyngham' appear interchangeable at this time.

2 Among the earliest to make such a claim was the Revd Scammel, this made in a series of lectures that he had published at the beginning of the twentieth century and in which he staked a claim for the year 1514. Later, both Presnail (1952) and Baldwin (1998) suggested not dissimilar dates while the Chatham Maritime Trust website (2011), David E. Hughes (2009) and Roberts (1992) all lean towards the year 1547.

3 TNA AO1/2588. Pipe Office Declared Accounts quoted in Cull (1958), p76.

4 Acts of the Privy Council re-quoted from Cull (1972), p76.

5 Loades (1992), pp150–3.

6 *Ibid.*

7 Oakum was formed out from fibres picked from old rope.

8 Terms such as careening and breaming are also explained in the glossary.

9 TNA E351/2194, 28 June 1550 – 29 September 1552.

10 For further explanation of the careening process see the glossary.

11 B.L. Rawlinson Ms A.201, f.106.

12 Loades (1992), p187.

13 Pipe Office Accounts for 1569–70.

14 Cull (1958).

15 Pipe Office Accounts, 1572–79.

16 Oppenheim (1896), p150.

17 Oppenheim (1902).

18 See Chapter 5 of this book for a detailed discussion of this major problem and how it was ultimately solved.

19 SRO GD51/2/964/2. Extracts from Pepys Vol.10 f.463.

20 *Ibid.*

21 *Ibid.*

22 *Ibid.*

23 KAO U1311 O1. 'A booke of Lodging for the Midsomer Quarter', 1611.

24 *Ibid.*

25 McGowan (1971), *passim.*

26 Perrin (1918), p116.

27 Much more attention to the growth of Chatham as an urban conurbation can be found in an earlier book by the author; see MacDougall (1999).

28 Diary, August 1665.

29 Diary, 11 June 1667. Pepys later blamed Commissioner Pett for the loss of *Royal Charles*, a first rate warship captured by the Dutch. According to Pepys, Pett should have moved the vessel higher up river 'by our several orders, and deserves therefore to be hanged for not doing it'.

30 Diary, 14 June 1667.

31 Rogers (1970), p138.

32 *Ibid.*

Chapter 2

1 Wilson (2009), p54; Stenholm (undated), p2.

2 Unger (1978), p10.

3 Tsar Peter also made a brief visit to Portsmouth dockyard. Among those known to have worked under Peter the Great were Joseph Nye and Richard Cousins, both formerly of Portsmouth dockyard. At the time of Peter the Great's visit, Nye had established his own small shipbuilding yard on the Isle of Wight.

4 The report submitted to Maurepas is now readily available in translated form, see Roberts (1992). In addition to Ollivier's written submission, this chapter has been informed by several maps, including those of 1688 (BL Kings 43), 1698 (BL Kings 43), 1719 (C.R.E. Library, Chatham) and 1746 (BL Add Ms 31323).

5 BL Kings 43; BL Add Ms 31323; Roberts (1192), pp78–9.

6 Coad (1989), pp114–6.

7 Roberts (1992), p79; BL Add Ms 31323.

8 Roberts (1992), p80.

9 *Ibid.*, p114.

10 *Ibid.*, p161.

11 *Ibid.*, p117.

12 *Ibid.*, p115.

13 *Ibid.*, p116.

14 Fiennes (1901), *Through England on a Side Saddle in the Time of William and Mary*.

15 Roberts (1992), p100.

16 *Ibid.*, p102.

17 Wilkinson (1998).

18 Roberts (1992), p102.

19 BL Add Ms 31323.

20 *Ibid.*, p109.

21 *Ibid.*

22 *Ibid.*, p111.

23 BL Add Ms 31323.

24 Falconer (1780). William Falconer completed his highly regarded *Universal Dictionary of the Marine* while ensconced in the captain's cabin of *Glory*, a thirty-two-gun frigate laid up in the Chatham Ordinary. This was during the 1760s, with the then resident Commissioner at Chatham, Jonas Hanway, providing the necessary authority for this arrangement. Born in 1730, Falconer, who also served at sea, was additionally noted for his poems.

25 Defoe (1971 edition), pp123–4.

26 *Ibid.*, p109.

27 *Ibid.*, p109.

28 *Ibid.*, p109.

29 In 1774, there were exactly fifty-four river moorings. See BL Kings 44, map of river Medway.

30 *Ibid.*, p111.

Chapter 3

1 Mahan (1908), p7.
2 *Ibid.*, p10.
3 John Markham, re-quoted in Pope (1981), p252.
4 TNA ADM2/215, 10 November 1749.
5 TNA ADM3/61, 6 July 1749.
6 TNA ADM7/662, 1775.
7 TNA ADM7/659, 13 May 1771.
8 TNA ADM7/659, 13 May 1771.
9 Science Mus. neg 4254.
10 TNA ADM7/661, 25 June 1774.
11 TNA ADM7/660, 15 July 1773.
12 TNA ADM106/2508, 4 April 1771.
13 NMM CHA/L34, 27 December 1799.
14 TNA ADM106/2227, 30 June 1801.
15 NMM CHA L/29, 3 March 1791.
16 TNA ADM106/2227, 30 June 1801.
17 NMM CHA L/34, 18 July 1799.
18 Commission for Naval Revision, p9.
19 NMM ADM B/194, 7 May 1777.
20 Commissioners for Naval Revision, p29.
21 *Ibid.*, p29.
22 *Ibid.*, p54.
23 Wade (1832), p376.
24. Mahan (1908), p22.

Chapter 4

1 All references to numbers employed are taken from quarterly returns submitted to the Navy Board: see NMM ADM/B series.
2 Crawshaw (1955), p2.
3 PP Commissioners of Naval Revision. Second Report, p11.
4 TNA ADM106/2975. Description Book of Chatham Artificers, 1779.
5 TNA ADM106/2975; death certificate dated 24 January 1806.
6 NMM CHA/L/30, 22 November 1792.
7 NMM CHA/E/35, 18 April 1787; CHA/L/28, 18 March 1790.
8 NMM CHA/E/48, 31 January 1795.
9 NMM ADM/B/187. 25 November 1772.
10. *Ibid.*
11 TNA ADM106/2975.
12 Falconer, p59.
13 NMM CHA/E/33, 12 October 1778.
14 Haas (1969).
15 NMM ADM/BP/4, 1 October 1783.
16 A pension scheme was allowed to all dockyard workers who had fulfilled thirty years of service, this introduced in 1771. As for the permanency of workers, few skilled workers, upon taking up employment in the yard, were made redundant (other than as a form of retribution for theft or leadership of a strike), while no worker suffered a loss of day pay through poor weather.
17 NMM ADM/BP/4, 2 October 1783.
18 TNA ADM106/907, 30 August 1739.

19 TNA ADM106/2553, 30 August 1739.

20 *Ibid.*, 31 August 1739.

21 *Ibid.*

22 Jones, p81.

23 NMM CHA/L/32, 18 November 1795.

24 *Ibid.*

25 *Ibid.*

26 *Ibid.*, 19 November 1795.

27 *Ibid.*, 23 November 1795.

28 NMM ADM BP/21a, May 1801.

29 TNA ADM1/5126, f.252.

30 NMM ADM/BP/21a, 1 April 1801.

31 NMM ADM/B/201, 7 April 1801.

32 NMM ADM/BP/21a. May 1801.

33 TNA ADM3/306, 18 December 1823.

34 For a more complete discussion of the petitioning campaign see Chapter 6, while a more directed discussion appears in MacDougall (1997).

Chapter 5

1 BM Kings 44.

2 NMM/CHA/L/20, 29 September 1790.

3 TNA ADM7/660, 13 July 1773.

4 BL Kings 44.

5 *Ibid.*

6 The vessel concerned was *Chatham*, constructed for use as a dockyard hulk in 1694 and not to be finally broken up until 1813. She was not to be taken out of dry dock on this occasion until 18 December.

7 See Chapter 4 of this book for more detail on task work.

8 NMM CHA/E/32, 21 June 1776.

9 Chips (82), February 2011, pp16–17.

10 NMM CHA/E/36, 20 September 1785.

11 NMM CHA/E/35, 12 March 1785.

12 NMM ADM/BP/6b, 8 September 1786.

13 NMM CHA/E/36, 5 April 1787.

14 MacDougall (1982), pp112–22.

15 NMM CHA/ E/36, 18 April 1787.

16 Beamish (1862), p109.

17 Wildash, *The History and Antiquities of Rochester*, p73.

18 Coad (1989), p71.

19 NMM ADM/B/185, 21 August 1771.

20 TNA ADM7/660, 13 July 1773.

21 Rochester Bridge Trust Ms. 214.

22 For a full account of the projected Northfleet dockyard see MacDougall (2000). Consideration of the effect of shoaling on the royal dockyards can be found in MacDougall (2001).

Chapter 6

1 Rennie, *Treatise on Harbours*, pp46–8.

2 TNA, ADM106/3138, John Rennie to Navy Board: estimate for new dock.

3 TNA ADM140/32.

4 For a more detailed examination of the building of the first stone dry dock at Chatham, see MacDougall (1989).

5 TNA, ADM 106/1830, Commissioner Cunningham to Navy Board, 12 July 1825.

6 Rennie, Treatise on Harbours, p46.

7 *Ibid.*, pp46–8.

8 *Ibid.*

9 NMM ADM/BP/376. Navy Board to Admiralty: covering of docks and slips.

10 For a more complete account of the use of steam and the work of the ropery during the nineteenth century see MacDougall (2004).

11 Morriss notes that the use of the term 'leadingman' predates the 1822 reforms and was applied as an occasional and unofficial alternative designation for 'quartermen'. See Morriss, (1983), p139.

12 Observations on the Recent Abolition of Certain Situations, including Quartermen and the New Arrangement of the Clerks in his Majesty's Dockyards (Chatham, 1824), pp11–14.

13 NMM, CHA/H/1, 9 June 1832.

14 BL, Add Ms 41,400, 1 June 1818.

15 Tucker, *Memoirs of St Vincent II*, p425.

16 Commission to Inquire into the Civil Administration of the Army, 18 February 1836.

17 TNA ADM1/3404, 20 February 1837.

18 TNA ADM1/3394. 31 July 1833.

19 *Rochester Gazette*, 13 December 1836.

20 *Ibid.*

21 *Ibid.*, 2 June 1840.

22 *Ibid.*

23 *Ibid.*

24 NMM, CHA/H/37, 12 November 1840.

Chapter 7

1 NMM, CHA/E/126, 27 June 1816. Seppings, who held the post of Master Shipwright at Chatham from 1804 to 1813, was now a member of the Navy Board, holding the post of Surveyor.

2 TNA, ADM106/3233, Minutes: Navy Board visitation, 30 September 1819.

3 TNA, ADM106/2267, 28 June 1815.

4 John Fincham (1851), p331.

5 *Ibid.*

6 Brown (1990), pp114–5.

7 TNA, ADM85/7, Enclosure 2 Letter No.15. Report of Alex Lawrie. Chatham Yard, 23 November 1851.

8 *Illustrated London News*, 25 February 1854.

9 TNA ADM106/2234, 6 May 1805.

10 Goodwin (1998), pp39–40.

11 Hobbes (1895), pp143–8.

12 TNA, ADM85/7, 10 February 1852.

13 Previously, naval warfare had been dominated by muzzle-loading canons, the heaviest of which could propel a 32-pound shot a few thousand yards, whereas these new guns, as a result of having rifled barrels, could propel with greater accuracy an explosive shell for a distance in excess of five miles.

14 Barry (1863), xiv.

15 *Ibid.*, p133.

16 *Rochester Gazette*, 16 February 1862.

17 *Rochester Gazette*, 16 September 1862.

18 *Chatham News*, 13 May 1893. The writer incorrectly asserts the naval mutinies to have occurred in 1789 when, in reality, they took place in 1797. See Coats and MacDougall (2011), *passim*.

19 *Ibid*.

20 Dickens, *The Uncommercial Traveller* (1865).

21 Hobbes (1895), p308.

22 *The Times*, London, 6 August 1864.

Chapter 8

1 TNA ADM106/2273, 25 June 1817.

2 TNA ADM106/1841, 12 July 1831.

3 TNA ADM106/1836, 24 January 1828.

4 *Ibid*.

5 NMM, CHA/F/33, 7 December 1819.

6 RNM, Portsmouth Mss 286 (previously Da 0126), 8 January 1857.

7. *Ibid*.

8 Evans (2004), p182.

9 RNM, Portsmouth Mss 286 (previously Da 0126), 8 January 1857.

10 *Chatham News* and *North Kent Spectator*, 10 November 1860.

11 *Ibid*., 24 June 1871.

12 *Ibid*.

13 The cost of constructing the No.7 Slip cover at Chatham, undertaken during the mid-1850s, was in the region of £13,000. It is on this that I have based the estimated savings of reusing the existing Woolwich slip covers.

14 *The Naval and Military Record*, 8 February, 1894.

15 *Ibid*., 24 May 1894.

16 *Ibid*., 17 June 1894.

17 Re-quoted from Parkes (1990), p384. According to Parkes, it was generally held that 'should' would be a more truthful picture than 'might'.

18 *The Naval and Military Record*, 6 June 1895.

19 *The Naval and Military Record*, 3 October 1895.

20 Waters (1983), p169.

21 In 1906, as a result of the influence of the newly emergent Amalgamated Society of Shipwrights in Chatham, John Jenkins, an important ASS activist, was elected to represent the Chatham constituency.

Chapter 9

1 *Chatham News*, 20 August 1908.

2 *Ibid*., 17 September 1908. A further eight submarines were to be built at Chatham prior to the outbreak of war in August 1914 together with construction of several cruisers and the continuance of a great deal of maintenance and refit work. Among the cruisers was *Chatham*, name ship of her class, and launched in November 1911.

3 *Chatham News*, 19 December 1914. The General Labourers Union was one of several unions that represented those employed in the munitions factories or the dockyards.

4 Lockyer (1997). Mr Lockyer was employed in the dockyard from 1916 to 1919 and the essay was originally written for a Local Studies course taught at Chatham Technical High School.

5 *Ibid*.

Chapter 10

1 The cause of the collision was primarily the low silhouette of the submarine and so making her difficult to be seen but confusion over the lights being carried by *Divinia* on this dark night was a further factor.

2 Originally those employed in the joinery worked exclusively in wood. As furniture built from laminated plastics and metal became increasingly common, those in the joiners' shop adapted their skills to making furniture in these materials. The joiners also had a responsibility for the upholstery work on ships. The work of a draughtsman was to design ships or parts of ships and draw the plans, while the tracers were women who traced multiple copies of the original plans.

3 *Chatham Observer*, 17 June 1955.

4 *Chatham Observer*, 5 August 1955.

5 At this time, the school was probably located in one of the storehouses, with a permanent school constructed in 1847 and located in the sail field that adjoined the sail loft. Here it remained (although a separate Lower School building was established at the south end of the painters' shop) until September 1960 when the whole of what was then known as the Dockyard Technical College was relocated in the West and North Wing of the former Collingwood Barracks. See Crawshaw (1963), p10.

6 Crawshaw (1963), p59.

7 *Chatham Observer*, 14 January 1955.

8 *Ibid.*

9 *Chatham Observer*, 8 October 1965.

10 The last Navy Days, held in May 1981, attracted, despite bad weather, a total of 47,000 visitors.

11 TNA ADM1/19056, 17 August 1945.

12 *Chatham News*, 4 October 1959.

13 In the event only four were built, as the newly elected Labour government of 1964 chose to cancel the fifth vessel.

14 Whitley Committee, 12 June 1963, re-quoted from Haxhaj (2005), p563. In the event, *Onyx* was not the last submarine to be built, this for two reasons. First, *Onyx* was renamed *Ojibwa* shortly before her launch in February 1964 while two other 'Oberons', *Onondaga* and *Okanagan*, were also to be built at Chatham. All three vessels were commissioned into the Royal Canadian Navy.

15 HM Dockyard Chatham, Nuclear Submarine Refitting (no date, Rolls-Royce and Associates Ltd), p18.

16 Hansard, 27 October 1997 col. 667–9. Maiden speech of Jonathan Shaw, MP for Chatham and Aylesford.

17 BBC *Panorama*, 26 January 1998.

18 www.hearinglossadvice.co.uk/former-ministry-of-defence-employee-in-a-successful-claim-for-noise-induced-hearing-loss. Accessed 30 July 2011.

19 www.asbestosvictimadvice.com/asbestos-a-deadly-dockyard-secret.

20 www.kenthistoryforum.co.uk Accessed on 30 July 2011 with quoted comment added 17 May 2011.

Chapter 11

1 Hansard col. 148, 6 August 1980.

2 Speed (1982), p92.

3 Coad (2011), p326.

4 *Ibid.*, p329.

5 www.medwayports.com.

GLOSSARY

Admiralty, Board of	A body appointed directly by the government and with authority over all matters relating to the Navy, including dockyards.
Anchor	A large heavy iron instrument dropped from the side of a ship to hold her in position. Anchors, during the age of sail, came in various forms and were often manufactured in the dockyard smitheries. Falconer (1780) refers to the following: *Bower anchor* – carried on the bows of a ship. *Kedge anchor* – the smallest of all anchors, used while a ship rides in harbour or to move a ship from one part of a harbour to another. *Sheet anchor* – the largest and strongest anchor, used only under extreme conditions. *Stream anchor* – a relatively small anchor.
Ballast	Additional weight added to a vessel in order to achieve stability.
Basin	An enclosed area of water that can be used for fitting, supplying or preparing a ship for sea under safe and controlled conditions.
Black Yarn House	A building in the ropery used for storing tarred yarn.
Breaming	Clearing from the hull of a ship the various accretions (grass, ooze, seaweed and shells) that have become attached during a period at sea or in harbour. By heating the pitch that formerly covered the hull, the accretions are loosened and then scraped or brushed off. Grounding the ship on a suitable shore, introducing the vessel to a careening wharf or taking her into dry dock allowed the operation to be performed.
Caisson	A sealed floating chest that can be used to seal the entrance of a dry dock.
Captain Superintendent	Following extensive managerial reforms in June 1832, the post of Commissioner in the dockyards was replaced by a Superintendent who also possessed naval rank. In the case of Chatham, the appointed Superintendent held the rank of Captain and possessed greater powers over that of a Commissioner. As with the Commissioner, he was accommodated in the dockyard, with the house of the Commissioner becoming the Admiral Superintendent's House (now Medway House).
Careening	The operation of heaving a ship down on one side through the attachment of cables to her masts so as to allow one side of her hull to be suitably exposed for cleaning.
Cathead	Two beams of short timber that project over a ship's bow and used to suspend the anchor clear of the bow.

Caulker　　An artisan of the yard who carried out the specialised task of caulking.

Caulking　　Driving of quantities of oakum (old rope twisted and pulled apart) into the seams of planks in the ship's deck or side to prevent the entrance of water.

Classification　　A short-lived system introduced during the 1830s and used to divide the workforce into different classes for the purpose of determining levels of payment.

Dry Dock　　A broad and deep trench into which vessels can be floated and, with its entrance sealed, pumped free of water so that work can ensue on the underside of the ship's hull.

Establishment　　The agreed dimensions that governed the design of British warships during the age of sail. The first establishment, that of 1677, had standardised design and subsequent changes could only be made with difficulty.

Extraordinary　　The area of the dockyard administered by the Master Shipwright and devoted to the building, repairing and maintaining of warships.

Galley　　Shallow-drafted lightweight vessel propelled by oar and most frequently used in the Mediterranean.

Grappling Iron　　Small anchor-like device fitted with four or five flukes and used to secure one vessel to another. It was a product frequently manufactured in the dockyard smithery.

Graving　　The process of cleaning a ship's bottom when she is laid aground during the recess of the tide. In later years, with the development of dry docks, the process of graving was more normally carried out in dock.

Hatchelling　　The process of combing the tangled hemp fibres prior to their introduction to the spinning floor of the ropery.

Hatcheller　　A semi-skilled labourer in the ropery who was employed in hatchelling the hemp fibres.

Hogging　　The distortion of a ship's keel, with the two ends lying lower than the middle and resulting from the action of waves while at sea.

Job　　Payment by results when repair work was involved.

Keel　　The principal timber of any vessel, laid down prior to its construction. Used to hold the bottom of a ship together.

Knees　　A piece of knee-shaped timber used to connect the beams of a ship with her sides.

Mast Pond　　A pond of water specifically designed for the storage of masts fully immersed in water. Converted from fir trees grown in northern Europe, it was necessary that these timbers were kept underwater so as to ensure that they did not dry out and so become unusable when taken on board a ship.

Mast House　　A workshop used for the making of masts and their storage immediately prior to being stepped on board ship.

Mast Maker　　A skilled artisan of the dockyard who made and shaped the masts for warships.

Navy Board　　Appointed by the Board of Admiralty, those who composed this body directly oversaw, on behalf of the Admiralty, all matters relating to the civil affairs of the Navy including the dockyards. Abolished in June 1832, the Board was replaced by a

	number of individual principal officers who were not expected to confer but simply report directly to a designated member of the Board of Admiralty.
Oakum	Old hemp rope picked loose and used by caulkers to fill the seams of a ship's hull to make it watertight.
Oakum Boys	Responsible for picking old hemp rope into the oakum used by caulkers.
Ordinary	The moorings of a naval dockyard harbour set aside for ships laid up when out of commission and placed under the authority of the Master Attendant.
Ordnance Board	A British government body which, until its abolition in 1855, was responsible for the supply of armaments and munitions to the Royal Navy.
Ordnance Wharf	A wharf and working area operated by the Ordnance Board for the receiving and supply of guns and other ordnance to naval warships and also for the maintenance and repair of these items. An Ordnance Wharf was sited immediately to the south of the dockyard at Chatham.
Resident Commissioner	The senior officer in the dockyard and a member of the Navy Board. The office was abolished on 11 June 1832 and at Chatham replaced by a Captain Superintendent.
Rigger	A semi-skilled artisan who worked with the ropes for hoisting the sails and securing the masts. When employed in a naval dockyard, no training was offered as former seamen in the Navy frequently possessed the necessary skills.
Rigging	The ropes used to operate the sails of a ship (running rigging) or secure the masts (standing rigging).
Ropeyard	The area of dockyard that, at one time, was placed under the charge of the Clerk of the Ropeyard and which undertook all work connected with the manufacture and storage of rope.
Sawyer	A dockyard labourer skilled in cutting timbers.
Scavelman	A promoted labourer of the yard who was responsible for the cleaning of the yard, including the dry docks, and manning the pumping machinery and caissons that were also attached to the dry docks.
Shipwright	A skilled dockyard artisan who could undertake most tasks required for construction of a warship.
Smithery	A forge or workshop in a naval dockyard and primarily used for the manufacture of anchors.
Spinners	A skilled artisan of the ropery who performed the various tasks associated with the spinning and laying of yarn into rope.
Task	Payment by results when new work undertaken.
Treenail	Wooden nail used in shipbuilding during the age of fighting sail and timber hulls.
Treenail Mooter	A semi-skilled artisan employed in the treenail mooting house (which at Chatham was located in the central part of the yard), mooting or making treenails.
Wet Dock	An alternative name for a basin and the term favoured during the sixteenth and seventeenth centuries.
While Yarn House	Located in the ropery and reserved for the storage of white yarn (that is yarn that had yet to be tarred).

BIBLIOGRAPHY

Primary Sources

British Library (BL)

Add Ms 31323	A Plan and Prospect of HM Dockyard Chatham, 1746.
Kings 43	A Survey of HM Dockyards, 1688 and 1698.
Kings 44	A Survey of HM Dockyards, 1774.

The National Archive (TNA)

ADM1/3525-7	Bentham Papers.
ADM1/5125	Petitions.
ADM7/659, 660-2, 663	Report of Visitations to Chatham Dockyard.
ADM42/61-92	Chatham Dockyard books.
ADM106/1185-1300	Navy Board in-letters.
ADM106/2507-8	Navy Board Standing Orders.
ADM106/2975	Description Book of Chatham Artificers.
ADM106/3006	Dockyard Dismissal Book.
HO42/34-49; HO43/6	Home Office correspondence, 1795-6.

The National Maritime Museum (NMM)

ADM B/184-203	Letters from Navy Board to Admiralty.
ADM A/2627-2947	Admiralty Orders.
CHA E series	Chatham Dockyard: in-letters from Navy Board.
CHA G series	Chatham Dockyard: in-letters from the Admiralty.
CHA K series	Chatham Dockyard: Navy Board warrants.
Cha L series	Chatham Dockyard: out letters to Navy Board.

Parliamentary Papers (PP)

Report of the Commissioners appointed by an Act of Parliament to enquire into Fees, Gratuities, Perquisites and Emoluments, which are or have been lately received in the several public offices. Sixth Report, 1788.

The Report of the Commissioners for Revising and Digesting the Civil Affairs of His Majesty's Navy. First Report, 1805-6.

Corps of Royal Engineers, Library (CRE Library)

A Geometrical Plan and North West Elevation of His Majesty's Dockyard at Chatham, 1755
A Plan of His Majesty's Dockyard and Ordnance Wharf at Chatham, 1719

Books

Baldwin, Ronald A., *The Gillingham Chronicles* (Baggins Book Bazaar, 1998).
Barry, Patrick, *Dockyard Economy and Naval Power* (London, 1863).
Baugh, Daniel, *British Naval Administration in the Age of Walpole* (London, 1965).
Beamish, Richard, *Memoir of Sir Marc Isambard Brunel* (London, 1862).
Brown, D.K., *Before the Ironclad* (London, 1990).
Coad, Johnathan, *The Royal Dockyards 1690–1850* (Scolar Press, 1989).
Coats, Ann Veronica and MacDougall, Philip (eds), *The Naval Mutinies of 1797: Unity and Perseverance* (Boydell Press, 2011).
Defoe, Daniel, *A Tour Through the Whole Island of Great Britain 1724* (Penguin edition, 1971).
Evans, David, *Building the Steam Navy: Dockyards, Technology and the Creation of the Victorian Battle Fleet, 1830–1906* (London, 2004).
Dickens, Charles, *The Uncommercial Traveller* (London, 1865).
Falconer, William, *A Universal Dictionary of the Marine* (London, 1780).
Fincham, John, *A History of Naval Architecture* (London, 1851).
Hasted, Edward, *The History and Topographical Survey of the County of Kent Vol. IV* (Canterbury, 1798).
Hawkey, Arthur, *HMS Captain* (London, 1963).
Hobbes, R.G., *Reminiscences and Notes of Seventy Years Life, II* (London, 1895).
Hughes, David T., *Chatham Naval Dockyard and Barracks* (The History Press, 2009).
Lambarde, William, *Perambulation of Kent* (Adam & Dart, reprinted 1970).
Loades, David, *The Tudor Navy: An Administrative, Political and Military History* (Aldershot, 1992).
MacDougall, Philip (ed.), *Chatham Dockyard 1815–65* (Naval Records Society, 2009).
MacDougall, Philip, *The Chatham Dockyard Story* (Meresborough Books, 1987).
MacDougall, Philip, *Chatham Past* (Phillimore Books, 1999).
MacDougall, Philip, *Royal Dockyards* (David & Charles, 1982).
MacDougall, Philip, *Chatham Dockyard in Old Photographs* (Stroud, 1994).
MacDougall, Philip, *Sheerness Dockyard: a Brief History* (Ptarmigan Books, 2001).
McGowan, A.P. (ed.), *The Jacobean Commissions of Enquiry 1608 and 1618* (Naval Records Society, 1971).
Morris, C., (ed.), *The Journeys of Celia Fiennes* (London, 1949).
Oppenheim, Michael, *A History of the Administration of the Royal Navy, 1509–1660* (London, 1896).
Oppenheim, Michael, *The Naval Tracts of Sir William Monson Vols I and II* (Naval Records Society, 1902).
Parkes, Oscar, *British Battleships* (London, 1990).
Perrin, W.G., (ed.), *The Autobiography of Phineas Pett* (Naval Records Society, 1918).
Presnail, James, *The Story of Chatham* (Chatham Borough Council, 1952).
Roberts, David H., (ed.), *Eighteenth Century Shipbuilding: Remarks on the Navies of the English and Dutch by Blaise Ollivier* (Jean Boudriot Publications, 1992).
Rogers, P.G., *The Dutch in the Medway* (OUP, 1970).
Scammell, Revd S.D., *Chatham Long Ago and Now* (London, 1903).
Speed, Keith, *Sea Change* (Bath, 1992).
Stenholm, Leif, *The Naval Town of Karlsrona* (unpublished, undated).
Unger, R.W., *Dutch Shipbuilding Before 1800* (Assen, van Gorcum, 1978).
Wilson, Derek, *Peter the Great* (London, 2009).

Journals

Bellamy, Martin, 'Financing the Preservation of Historic Ships: Should the UK tax payer pay?' in *Mariner's Mirror* (February 2011), 97:1.

Coad, Jonathan, 'Indifference, Destruction, Appreciation, Conservation: A century of changing attitudes to historic buildings in British naval bases' in *Mariner's Mirror* (February 2011), 97:1.

Cull, Frederick, 'Chatham Dockyard Early Leases and Conveyances' in *Arcaeologia Cantiana* (1958), Vol. 73, pp75–95.

Goodwin, Peter, 'The Influence of Iron in Ship Construction' in *Mariner's Mirror* (February 1998), 84:1.

MacDougall, Philip, 'A Demand Fulfilled: Analysis of an industrial dispute between the Admiralty and the civilian work force employed in the naval dockyards of southern England, 1833-41' in *Southern History 19* (1997), pp112–134.

MacDougall, Philip, 'Ropemaking at Chatham during the Early Nineteenth Century' in *Archaeologia Cantiana CXXIV* (2004), pp1–24.

Waters, Mavis, 'Changes in the Chatham Dockyard Workforce, 1860–90' in *Mariner's Mirror* (May 1983), 69:1 and 69:2.

Wilkinson, Clive, 'The Earl Egmont and the Navy, 1763–6' in *Mariner's Mirror* (May 1998), 84:5, pp418–33.

Unpublished Works

Atkinson, Dan, 'Shipbuilding and Timber Management in the Royal Dockyards, 1750–1850: An Archaeological Investigation of Timber Marks' (Ph.D. thesis, St Andrews University, 2007).

Crawshaw, J.D., *A History of Chatham Dockyard School* (1955).

MacDougall, Philip, 'A Social History of Chatham Dockyard, 1770–1801' (M.Phil thesis, Open University, 1983).

INDEX